MAZDA RX-7
PERFORMANCE HANDBOOK

MIKE ANCAS

MBI Publishing Company

First published in 2000 by MBI Publishing Company, PO Box 1, 729 Prospect Avenue, Osceola, WI 54020-0001 USA

The information in this book is true and complete to the best of our knowledge. All recommendations are made without any guarantee on the part of the author or Publisher, who also disclaim any liability incurred in connection with the use of this data or specific details.

We recognize that some words, model names and designations, for example, mentioned herein are the property of the trademark holder. We use them for identification purposes only. This is not an official publication.

MBI Publishing Company books are also available at discounts in bulk quantity for industrial or sales-promotional use. For details write to Special Sales Manager at Motorbooks International Wholesalers & Distributors, 729 Prospect Avenue, PO Box 1, Osceola, WI 54020-0001 USA.

Library of Congress Cataloging-in-Publication Data Available

ISBN 0-7603-0802-0

On the front cover: The third generation RX-7, built from 1993-1995, was a radical step up from the previous generation. With new turbo technology, the engine was able to consistently build boost from low rpms, thus dramatically reducing turbo lag. The meager 1.3 liter rotary turbo engine produced a whopping 255 horsepower with 217 ft/lbs. of torque. The new RX-7 sped from 0 to 60 in 4.9 seconds and attained a top speed of 163 miles per hour.

On the back cover: top: Tokico Illumina shocks/struts have five damping adjustments that can easily be changed in a matter of seconds. These externally adjustable shocks allow you to dial-in a stiff rate for competition and a softer rate for the street. *Racing Beat*

bottom: When it comes to making the RX-7 a fast race car, these special race rotors are an essential part of the package. These rotors are available for all 1979–1992 RX-7s, and housings featuring peripheral intakes are also available for those same cars. *Racing Beat*

Designed by Katie Sonmor

Printed in the United States of America

Contents

Dedication4

Introduction5

1 RX-7 History10

2 The High-Performance RX-7 Transformation26

3 Chassis and Suspension34

4 Brakes46

5 Wheels and Tires52

6 Intake Systems61

7 Exhaust Systems66

8 Engines and Engine Transplants73

9 Ignition and Timing92

10 Fuel-Injection and Carburetion Systems98

11 Turbocharging, Supercharging and Nitrous-Oxide Systems112

12 Transmissions124

13 Street Tuning on a Budget129

14 A Brief Guide to Racing Your RX-7139

Appendix RX-7 Tuning Shops148

Index159

Dedication

This book is dedicated to the memory of Bobby Eakin, a friend and fellow racer who is still missed by all who knew him.

I would like to thank my family, Brenda Ancas and Zac Tolan, and my parents, Ed and Millie Ancas. I also want to recognize two people who assisted me with this book and contributed pieces that are credited in the text: Dale Black is a third-generation enthusiast and president and founder of the West Penn RX-7 Club (www.rx7.org). He is extremely knowledgeable regarding all three generations of the car, and deserves co-author status for this performance book. Dennis Witt is a long-time friend who has more useless car information stored in his head than could ever be put into any one book. He extracted some of the useful stuff for this project and put it to good use. I would also like to thank my friends and RX-7 advisers. Ted (spin to win) Weidner provided me with my first opportunity to race an RX-7 in the late 1980s. Norm

Chute also shared his (and my former) RX-7 several times for major SCCA events. And the Lipperini boys (Dan, Dan Jr., and Joel) were always available to answer questions regarding rotary performance. I'll never forget watching Joel and company swap 1G RX-7 engines in the paddock (cow pasture) at an SCCA Hillclimb in less than an hour, without missing a run.

This book would also not have been possible without the support and friendship of my friends at *Grassroots Motorsports* magazine: Tim and Margie Suddard, David Wallens, J.G. Pasterjack, Gabe Barrett, and fellow author Per Schroeder.

Finally, over the past 10 years I have received a great deal of support

and advice from the following experts and companies: Jim Langer, Jim Mederer, and James Tanner of Racing Beat; Cameron Worth of Pettit Racing; Dave Lemon of Mazdatrix; Peter Farrell Supercars (PFS); Michael Caldwell at Mustang Dynamometer; Dave at KD Rotary; Javier Gutierrez of JG Engine Dynamics; Tim Marren of Marren Motorsports; Russ Collins of RC Engineering; as well as the helpful staff of The Mazda Motor Company, Inc. And I can't forget all of the RX-7 fans who have contributed photos of their cars for this project. It is people like you who continue to give life to the Import Performance Movement.

Your comments and questions are welcomed at: Speednation, 228 Route 980, McDonald, PA 15057; Fax: 724-926-0215, or visit the RX-7 Performance Handbook Web page at www.speednation.com, where you can e-mail the authors. The Speednation site will be updated constantly with the latest information and articles about RX-7 performance.

Introduction

The Mazda RX-7 was first imported into the United States in 1978 (model year 1979), and would eventually become one of the most respected and enduring sports cars in American history. With a taut chassis and a powerful Wankel rotary engine, the RX-7 provided a unique driving experience that struck a chord with American sports car aficionados. Since its introduction, it has been the flagship of Mazda's technical brilliance. Against a backdrop of America's relatively dull, uninspired, and underpowered cars of the late 1970s, the RX-7 was fresh, innovative, and exciting.

The foundation for the RX-7 was laid in the U.S. market years earlier. Toyota began importing its Corolla back in 1965. Datsun brought the 240Z over in 1970, and Honda followed in 1972 with its 600 coupe. These models' ability to grasp a share of the market showed that the American public was receptive to Japanese cars. The 240Z was especially significant, as it proved American drivers would go for a sports car with a six-cylinder, rather than a V8, engine. The Wankel rotary, of course, was an even more radical departure.

Form and function came together in the third-generation (1993–1996) Mazda RX-7. But there is room for improvement in any car. The key to a successful performance improvement project is to first decide what you want to do with your car. Then, set your priorities, come up with a plan, and stick to it. *Courtesy of Charlie Martin Photography*

Mazda had been developing the rotary engine for many years before bringing the RX-7 across the Pacific. It introduced the power plant in the relatively anonymous 1970 R100 and 1971 RX-2. The latter was designed specifically for export. American auto manufacturers and the public barely noticed the development work

Mazda had performed on this revolutionary engine. Not until the sleek RX-7 hit U.S. shores in 1978, as a 1979 model, did the public notice its unusual source of power. Sure, it looked like a sports car, but the rotary engine was completely different from previous engines. It was barely larger than a standard size differential. Right

The three generations of Mazda RX-7 in the United States: 1993-1995 (left), 1986-1992 (right), and 1979-1985 (center). The fourth-generation RX-7 is currently made only for the Japanese domestic market.

from the start, the RX-7's mission was to gain the respect of skeptical U.S. sports car enthusiasts.

The car's looks and nimble handling won over most critics. With each new model year, Mazda made slight improvements in the body style, frame, and engine. Then, when the company introduced a newly designed six-port 13B for the 1984 GSL-SE, the RX-7 high-performance enthusiast market really took off. Now RX-7 owners could upgrade their older 12A-powered cars by transplanting this new, more powerful engine into their 1979–1983 RX-7s. The new 13B was more refined and more powerful than the old four-port 13B design that originally came in the RX-4 and Cosmo. It was a significant steppingstone that showcased advances in fuel injection and engine development, and it would eventually lead to the development of the high-tech, third-generation cars. This also got the attention of Mazda tuning innovators, such as Dave Lemon (Mazdatrix) and Jim Mederer (Racing Beat), who developed new technologies to make the older RX-7s match the performance of the new 1984 GSL-SE.

The import performance movement reached new heights in the late 1990s. This was probably due to a readily accessible supply of aftermarket performance parts, the growth of motorsports in general, plus a wealth of information and support that became available on the Internet. Peter Farrell, Cameron Worth, and Sylvain Trembly kept inventing ways to make more and more reliable horsepower from the two- and three-rotor Wankel, and it didn't take long

before the third-generation (3G) RX-7 began to establish itself as a true supercar. Now, with hundreds of RX-7 clubs in the United States and throughout the world, the RX-7's popularity has reached new heights, despite the fact that the car was no longer imported into the United States after 1995. It remains as one of the most beloved and enduring sports cars in history.

Form Versus Function

The first thing the car owner needs to address when it comes to improving an RX-7's performance is form versus function. In the past, form was often diametrically opposed to function, and the car owner had to choose one over the other based on desired performance goals and intended use. Racing Beat and Mazdatrix were two of the first companies to provide performance parts for form as well as function, but

If you want to spot a few first-generation (1G) RX-7s, the best place to go is to your local SCCA racing event. Whether at an autocross, hillclimb, or road race, the 1G RX-7 is one of the most reliable, fun-to-drive, and easy-to-build race cars money can buy. Pictured is the *Grassroots Motorsports* magazine project RX-7, which is a 240-horsepower, Haltech-injected, street-ported 13B rocket. Norm Chute is behind the wheel waiting his turn to attack Giant's Despair, a hill climb in eastern Pennsylvania. Mazda RX-7 tuning wizard Dan Lipperini, Jr., is holding the wheel chock that prevents the car from moving off the starting line so that Chute doesn't have to worry about keeping his foot on the brake.

SCCA's ITA class is dominated by 1G RX-7s. You would be hard-pressed to pick a better car to campaign on a regional road racing circuit. That's precisely why Colin Mason and his wife, Suzie, chose this 1G as their race car. They are both part of the Houston Region SCCA and the Houston RX-7 Club. *Colin Mason*

Probably one of the best sports car bargains on the planet is the second-generation (2G) RX-7. Often, you can get a 1986–1989 model in good condition for under $3,500. They lend themselves perfectly to a performance project. There are hundreds of aftermarket hop-up parts available, from turbos and superchargers to struts and springs. The only thing holding you back could be the limit on your credit card. This unique 2G belongs to George Dodworth. It has an aftermarket turbo, Electromotive TEC-II injection with a couple of extra injectors, and the highest-tech stereo and on-board computer system we have ever seen.

for a particular application. Stiff, gas-guzzling race cars don't make good street cars. Comfortable, good-looking street cars don't make good race cars because they lack a competition-calibrated chassis, suspension, and engine, and all the necessary racing equipment. In addition, street cars are often too heavy.

The first and most important axiom of high-performance tuning and modification is that all improvements come with a trade-off—and that trade-off is often a loss of streetability. In order for your car to produce more horsepower or handle better, you need to make some sort of compromise. You may sacrifice a comfortable ride to get precise handling, or a quiet exhaust note for an increase in horsepower.

Sometimes even with the best intentions, many of us go too far trying to build a faster street car, and end up turning our daily drivers into race-only vehicles. But by our exercising some margin of restraint, we can build an RX-7 to serve both purposes well. Learning from others' mistakes and successes that are recounted in this book, you should be able to build an awesome high-performance street car that has both a humane ride quality and the capability of blowing the doors off most other road cars.

But let's return to the fundamental dilemma: before undertaking any type of performance improvement project, a car owner must decide to build his or her car for either form or function. Once a decision is made, this book will provide some guidance to help you realize your goals. Most chapters cover form as well as function. Street racers will be able to take advantage of the latest good-looking "go fast" and handling modifications, while pure racers will be able to access practical

initially, the products were more expensive than many RX-7 enthusiasts could afford. As interest in the cars ramped up in the 1990s, so did parts availability and the level of competition among aftermarket

manufacturers. Today, RX-7 owners can choose from many affordable performance parts that possess both function and form.

For any RX-7 to perform at its best, it must be tuned and modified

The third-generation (3G) RX-7 was a great car right out of the box. There were no performance weaknesses. The car did suffer from reliability problems, however, partially because it was so hi-tech that the Mazda dealerships couldn't support it properly. Gordon Monsen's car has almost all the best go-fast goodies on board, but the Peter Farrell-built car in the background has gone as far as you can go: 20B triple rotor transplant, aftermarket turbo and intercooler with two extra injectors, and too many other things to list.

Mazda promoted the new monocoque chassis as "light and strong," and it lived up to the billing. The new car had a full 20 percent more torsional rigidity than the 2G cars it replaced.

information to help their cars become more competitive.

This book assumes that anyone planning performance improvements to his or her car will use a workshop manual. This book is in no way intended to replace or supersede any information provided by an RX-7 workshop or owner's manual. For that reason, it is devoid of the boring charts and schematics—the exploded views of your car's suspension or engine—that typically abound in aftermarket performance handbooks or workshop manuals.

In addition, this book doesn't provide technical component analysis, or in-depth demonstrations of any internal engine modification procedures. It doesn't cover procedures like bridge porting a rotary engine because this goes beyond the average enthusiast mechanic's skills and tools. This type of work should be left to the experts, and there are many competent RX-7 specialists out there. In any event, 99.9 percent of the people who buy this book don't have the equipment to do this type of job properly, and if you are the 0.1 percent of those who do, you don't need this book to tell you how to do it.

Also, many of the changes that race car drivers make to their RX-7s will result in failed emissions tests. From engine porting to the addition of a header or downpipe, be aware that you could make expensive changes to your street vehicle that could result in your not being able to drive it legally on the street.

Check with your state and local ordinances before you make any of these changes.

This book concentrates more on what average weekend mechanics can do to improve the performance of their cars. It discusses countless aftermarket parts, and reviews many do-it-yourself projects. The first step in any project, however, is setting priorities—such as form versus function. Chapter 2 will help you make some preliminary decisions and get you started on your way to a great experience in the realm of Mazda performance. The modifications discussed in this book won't help anyone with his or her journey to achieve meaning in the new millennium, but they should allow some high-speed fun along the way.

CHAPTER ONE

RX-7 History

Today, it's hard to picture a world without the rotary engine, given the legion of dedicated fans that it has attracted. After all, rotary engines power one of the most beloved sports cars of all time: the RX-7. Can you imagine an RX-7 with a piston engine? Sure the styling is great, but it's the rotary engine that has made this car unique for the past 20-plus years. Despite the engine's success today, though, Wankel's vision for the rotary engine nearly died back in the 1970s. If not for the Toyo Kogyo Company in Japan, the rotary engine may have only been a footnote in a book of automotive technologies.

The rotary engine got its start in the early 1950s with a German company whose primary focus was manufacturing motorcycles—an interesting coincidence, given that many of Japan's largest auto companies, such as Honda, got their start designing and building motorcycles. Honda even used a motorcycle engine to power its first U.S.-spec automobile—the 1972 Honda 600.

But the company that started the rotary movement, and was once the leading motorcycle manufacturer in the world, no longer even exists today.

NSU (Neckarsulmer Strick-machinen Union), was the first company to enter into an agreement with engineer and designer Felix Wankel to help develop his dream of a rotary power plant. His first task at NSU, however, was to develop a "super-charger" for a 500cc engine that NSU would use to set a new speed record for motorcycles. His resulting creation was a belt-driven rotary compressor that, when added to the 500cc engine, boosted its performance eightfold. He went on to improve on that basic design, and by 1954, a crude version of a rotary internal combustion engine was born.

Although Wankel was the inventive visionary behind this unique engine, it was NSU engineer Dr. Walter Froede who, in 1958, actually took Wankel's design and built a

The third-generation (1993–1995) RX-7's life in the United States was short-lived, but the car sure made an impact on car enthusiasts. Many Porsche and BMW owners quickly became converts, and never looked back. *Courtesy of Excellent Performance/Pettit Racing*

much simpler and more practical model. He mounted a single rotor inside a stationary housing (a drastic departure from Wankel's design). This inner rotor was mounted on an eccentric shaft that also acted as an output shaft. Froede also designed improvements for the rotor seals, which eventually led to a two-rotor engine very similar in basic design to today's power plants. This new motor went on to power the first rotary-engined automobile: NSU's Prinz. The Prinz chassis closely resembled an Alfa Romeo Spyder and was driven by a 498cc single rotor engine.

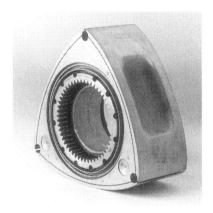

Inside the heart of every RX-7 beats the simple and powerful design of Felix Wankel's rotary engine.

After World War II, the Japanese economy began to change from a local to a more regional one, gradually requiring a change of lifestyle. There was an increasing interdependence between communities, creating the need for better transportation. Walking and bicycling weren't cutting it. Even motorcycles—very popular at that time—were not able to meet these needs since they weren't efficient in moving goods from one place to another. To keep up with the increasing demand for four-wheeled transportation in the Japanese marketplace, NSU needed to turn up the production of its automobile division. The

company decided that it could not perform this task without help, so it looked for ways to increase revenue as well as to form a network of cooperative partnerships. One way to do this was to sell licenses to other companies, giving them the right to use NSU's exclusive design of the rotary engine. Taking the bait first was an American company, Curtiss-Wright (C-W), which entered into a multi-million dollar deal with NSU.

Known for aircraft engine production, C-W first purchased the U.S. licensing rights to develop the rotary engine from NSU in 1958. Even though Curtiss-Wright never produced a rotary engine that would go on to power a four-wheeled production vehicle, many automobile companies began to show interest in this new and very different technology. The Wankel engine seemed to be only a novelty at first, but after some major auto companies began to explore the potential of the power plant, novelty quickly turned into serious interest. The engine's main attractions were that it had fewer moving parts than a piston engine and didn't rely on valves or pistons to produce power. As more and more companies began to take notice, interest grew, and soon the rotary engine was being dubbed "the engine of the future."

Nearly all of the automobile companies became interested in obtaining rotary technology, but they all went about it in different ways. By the 1960s, NSU had fallen on hard times financially, so it began to sell licenses to allow the development and production of rotary engines. Initially, only a few companies seemed interested, but soon there was a flurry of activity, resulting in the issue of more than 20 licenses. Everyone wanted to get in on the act: Ford, GM, Rolls-Royce, Suzuki, Yamaha, Daimler-Benz, Porsche,

AMC, Toyota, Nissan, Alfa Romeo, Citroen, John Deere, and Volkswagen (who eventually bought NSU).

None of these companies' efforts to successfully mass-produce a rotary-powered vehicle produced a notable car. Ford even went so far as to put a Curtiss-Wright designed engine into a 1965 Mustang. GM ended up making one of the biggest plays, establishing the GMRE (General Motors Rotary Engine) division. The company planned on equipping 80 percent of its Chevy Monzas with a GMRE power plant. The ever popular Vega, as well as the Buick Starfire, were also on the list. Or how about a four-rotor 1973 Corvette?

And remember the Pacer (brought back into the ranks of "coolness" thanks to the movie *Wayne's World*)? AMC had big plans for the Pacer, and dubbed it the "car of the future." What would be better for the "car of the future" than to be powered by a rotary engine? You could listen to Queen's "Bohemian Rhapsody" on the eight-track while being soothed by that high-pitched rotary whine.

Daimler-Benz planned a three-rotor (320 horsepower) and four-rotor (420 horsepower) Mercedes. Each rotor displaced 600cc (wow), but the car was never produced. Toyota and Nissan also gave it a good shot, but their projects never really got off the ground. These three companies and Ford, Rolls-Royce, Suzuki, and GM spent billions of dollars in license fees and research and development, but when the Organization of Petroleum Exporting Countries (OPEC) oil crisis hit in 1973, it seemed to all go down the drain. When gasoline cost $.30 per gallon, no one could have anticipated that the rotary engine's thirst for fuel would be its downfall. One by one, Ford, Rolls, Suzuki, and eventually GM would give up the ghost. With GMRE power plants no longer available to AMC, the Pacer was denied its place in history, and quickly went from becoming the "car of the future" to being the punch line to a com-edian's joke. Who would have thought that one of the world's coolest and most innovative inventions would end up nearly killing the automotive industry? But that's what happened. It took the automotive community years to recover from its unfortunately timed rotary speculations.

There was one company, however, that never gave up on Wankel's dream. In 1961, the Toyo Kogyo Company bought license No. 4 from NSU, and the rest, as they say, is history. Toyo Kogyo had just started manufacturing automobiles a year earlier. The company relied on the Wankel-designed rotary engine to power its cars. Over the next few years it continued to develop this power plant, improving on the NSU design, and by the late 1960s it was successfully manufacturing a line of cars powered by rotary engines. These newer engines utilized carbon-aluminum apex seals, dual spark plugs, a side port intake design, and twin rotors.

By 1970, many of the Japanese companies were looking to export their cars to the United States. It was a huge market, but a difficult nut to crack because of the size and influence of the "Big Three" automakers. The Americans wanted large cruisers—"The bigger, the better," seemed to be their mantra. Even the horns on these cars sounded like a ship coming in from the fog to dock. Competing with sounds of this volume and pitch, thought the Japanese manufacturers, a little Japanese "beep" would barely be heard. But despite the odds, Toyo Kogyo decided to take its little dog-and-pony show on the road. The company chose Seattle, Washington, as its entry port—possibly because it had previously established a connection with nearby Vancouver, British Columbia.

What's in a Name?

Toyo Kogyo (meaning "Orient Industry" in Japanese) set out to conquer the United States. But first the company thought it prudent to slightly Americanize its name, and set up a separate import company. The

name the executives chose for this company was once used by General Electric on its light bulbs—Mazda. This even sounds like the name of TK's founder, Juriro Matsuda. In the Persian culture, "Mazda" refers to the "god of light."

In contrast, the company that provided electrical systems to British imports MG and Triumph—Lucas—came to be known as the "prince of darkness" due to frequent short circuits at inopportune times. With Mazda, TK seemed to have chosen an opportune name.

Getting Down To Business

The newly formed Mazda Motors of America started with a small team of engineers and several cars that were targeted for the U.S. market. Between the years of 1970–1971, the first vehicles to see U.S. shores were the R100, Familia (the Japanese 1200cc-piston-powered R100), 1800, RX-2, and 616 (piston-powered RX-2).

It would make a great story to tell how Mazda struggled for the first few years before it finally experienced

The name "Mazda" was first used by an Westinghouse to name the company's automobile lamps. Mazda translated into the "god of light" and later graced the hoods of our favorite sports cars.

The first rotary-powered car brought into the United States was the Mazda R100. Sharing its chassis with the piston-engined 1200 Familia, the R100 helped establish the first Mazda dealership on American soil in Seattle, Washington. This fine example of an original 1971 R100 is driven by John McBeth, of Sparks, Nevada. *John McBeth*

success, but that would not be true. The American consumer loved these new Japanese cars, especially the rotary-powered ones. But as quickly as Mazda grew, it would fall. During the so-called oil shortage of 1973, the rotary-powered Mazdas were unfairly labeled as gas-guzzlers. But little Mazda Motors kept right on plugging away.

Over the next few years, things got a little better for Mazda. Even though the RX-2 and RX-3 weren't exactly hits, the RX-4 was a slightly different story. It was plagued with reputations of unreliability and poor gas mileage (which was not true, compared to the American V-8s), but it was blessed with Mazda's most powerful engine to date: the 13B. The next few years saw little change.

A very effective original ad for the Mazda RX-3SP. I can't imagine why Mazda didn't sell more of these with ads like this. It was just bad timing for a rotary car to be introduced to the U.S. market in the early 1970s. Now, they wouldn't be able to keep enough of these in the showroom. *Photo courtesy of Mazda and John McBeth*

Mazda seemed to be still looking for what Americans wanted, and came up empty. The 1976 Cosmo was a perfect example of trying to predict what would succeed in the U.S. market. It was specifically designed to capture the interest of the U.S. sports car enthusiast, but failed. They loved it in Japan, however.

That same year, hints of a redesigned sports coupe to be introduced in 1978 began to surface. But Mazda nearly didn't make it to 1978. All RX-7 lovers need to give

thanks and due respect to the car that saved Mazda Motors. It was not the RX-7. But if not for this car, the RX-7 may never have been produced. The piston-powered Miser, introduced a year earlier was a minor hit, but it wasn't until the GLC hatchback was brought to the United States in 1977 that Mazda gained the confidence and financial boost to bring the RX-7 project across the finish line. It was the piston-engined GLC that saved Mazda Motors of America. They didn't call it "Great Little Car" for nothing.

It's hard to imagine a world without Mazdas, but initially, nearly everyone believed that Mazda's efforts would never amount to much more than building novelty vehicles. But riding the wave created by the GLC, Mazda changed the face of sports car history in 1978 with the introduction of the RX-7. This one-two punch finally seemed to put Mazda on the map.

The Japanese Philosophy

When the first Mazda automobile hit U.S. shores in 1970, the American manufacturers didn't feel that the smaller Japanese cars would ever be a

threat to their U.S. market. In the meantime, however, Mazda began to listen, learn, and quickly respond to what the American car buyer wanted in a vehicle. In fact, it seemed to know what we wanted before *we* knew. As the quality began to improve, auto magazines began to take notice. The U.S. auto consumer had never been exposed to the high quality, reliability, and fuel economy that Mazda and other Japanese manufacturers were offering.

By the time U.S. manufacturers began to notice that people were buying Mazdas, it was too late. The Ford Pinto, Chevy Vega, and AMC Gremlin could not measure up to the superior engineered Japanese imports.

Still, the biggest difference between Mazda and the U.S. manufacturers was not in what they produced, but in how it was produced. The United States began to hear strange stories about Japanese auto workers who loved their jobs, and how management loved them. Workers and managers would do morning exercises in a large group before starting their day's work. Assembly plant workers were included in management meetings, and managers empowered them to make suggestions as to how to improve operations and design. And management would listen. It appeared as though Mazda was treating its workers better than their American counterparts, and this caused some dissension in the "Big Three's" rank and file.

The Mazda Motor Company, along with many other Japanese corporations, approached business in a way that was philosophically different from companies in the West. Long-standing Eastern cultural and religious traditions formed the basis for the Japanese business philosophy. This philosophy taught, among other things, that all people and creatures should be respected. Japanese companies,

like Mazda, treated their workers with respect, allowing them to feel more involved. The result was increased productivity.

The final component that allowed Mazda to adapt so well to the U.S. market was that it listened to the American consumer. Often, the company made changes to its automobiles midyear, reflecting the opinions of both the U.S. buyer as well as the Japanese assembly worker. Conversely, the American automotive bureaucracy was so big and unresponsive, it traditionally took years for a simple idea to filter up through the many levels of management.

(Now the Daimler-Chrysler corporation has become known for getting a car from the drawing board to the assembly line in record time, and with little change made to the initial fresh design. But in the 1970s, it was a different story.)

In the past, a good-looking prototype—picture a Ferrari—would go through so many changes as it passed from one conservative committee to another, and the end result (after years of scrutiny) would look something like a Yugo. Mazda's management philosophy, on the other hand, was quick to respond to change, and it both rewarded and encouraged new ideas.

Still, in the late 1970s, Mazda was not yet a big threat to the industry, except when it came to the overseas market. Europe began to embrace the little Mazdas, and U.S. exports began to slow. Then, Mazda delivered the blow that would forever change the face of the auto industry. The RX-7 was introduced in the United States in 1978. Immediately, demand far exceeded supply. RX-7's were being sold at the docks much as the R100s were nearly 10 years earlier. Americans who wanted to buy an RX-7 were often faced with waiting lists. The reasons are as obvious today as they were then. The

RX-7s were good looking, economical, and faster than many of the U.S. cars.

Soon, the Japanese business philosophy would sweep across the Pacific and reach American shores. Now, the cars that Ford, Daimler-Chrysler, and GM produce reflect a high degree of quality, and are designed to last. But the credit for these changes, which came to fruition in the late 1980s, rests squarely on the management model that was created by companies like Mazda during the 1970s. Honda, Toyota, Nissan, and Mazda set the standards by which all other cars would be judged, and "Made in Japan" no longer meant "cheap imitation."

The First Mazda Motorcars

Rotary engines have powered everything from lawn mowers, chain saws, outboard motors, and snowmobiles, to full-sized and radio-controlled airplanes, motorcycles, and generators. Most of us would pay big bucks to have a working model of one of these applications in our rotary collection. But here are some better examples of rotary history that are more affordable, practical, and more fun to own.

Following World War I, Toyo Kogyo's first production vehicles were bizarre-looking three-wheeled trucks built mostly for commercial use. But following World War II, the economy and culture had shifted, and the demand for automobiles among the Japanese public increased greatly. Mazda produced its first car in 1960, which started one of the most interesting and varied enterprises in automotive history.

R360

Powered by a 356cc V-twin motorcycle engine, this was an instant hit with Japanese citizens. Back then, before you were allowed to buy a car, you had to demonstrate proof of a parking place. A complete industry resulted from this strange but practical ordinance. A series of kei (light) cars were produced by most manufacturers at that time as a way around the ordinance. At one time, Mazda dominated kei-car sales in Japan, and continued to design and manufacture these small creations well into the 1970s. The P-360 Carol was introduced in 1962, and included a four-door coupe. These are no 0–60 times recorded for the Carol Sedan, since the car couldn't reach 60 miles per hour unless dropped from an airplane.

110S Cosmo Sport (1964–1972)

Mazda's first rotary-powered car was also the most unusual—a two-seater car. Not to be confused with the Cosmo of the mid 1970s, this was essentially a prototype vehicle created to showcase the Toyo Kogyo's new Wankel rotary engine. Two-seaters were frowned upon in Japan because they were not consistent with the doctrine of practicality, but production of this car did proceed. Like it or not, the Cosmo Sport was exactly what Mazda needed to showcase its new technology. The two prototype vehicles that were introduced at the Tokyo Motor show in 1964 had 798cc engines, designated as the L8A (8 referring to 800cc). Test production began the following year, except that the smaller engine was replaced with a 982cc power plant (designation: L10A). These cars were never offered to the public. It wasn't until 1967 that the Cosmo Sport actually went into limited production. The 110S name came from the L10A engine that put out approximately 110 horsepower. A dual ignition (twin distributors) and a four-barrel carb helped give this twin rotor engine life. Over the years, the chassis, body, and engine were slightly tweaked until production ceased in 1972. Made one at a time, only 1,500 Cosmo Sports emerged over that six-year period. During its final year, the L10B engine produced 130 horsepower. Couple that with a top speed of 124 miles per hour and a 16 second quarter-mile time, and the Cosmo Sport clearly brought notoriety to Mazda, while at the same time acting as a showcase for the new rotary engine. It was a financial loss, but a promotional success.

The 1200 Familia

Sparsely imported to the United States, a few actually did make it into the country in 1970–1971 as part of the initial delivery to Mazda Motors of America in Seattle, where the invasion first took root. Powered by a 1200cc piston engine, these cars were a hit in Japan, along with their big brother, the 1800. The line included a coupe, sedan, and station wagon.

R100 (1970–1972)

Also part of the initial offering to the United States, the R100 was the first true production rotary-powered automobile. The chassis was the same as the 1200 Familia, but it's what was under the hood that was most significant. Using the same engine as the Cosmo Sport, this Mazda may have looked Familia, but it was a completely different creature. The R100 also was significant in that it was the beginning of Toyo Kogyo's venture into the U.S. market, and it helped launch the Mazda name.

From this point on, there was no turning back for Mazda and its commitment to mass-producing rotary-powered vehicles. Of course, the 10A Wankel was detuned slightly, hence the designation R100. An anemic carburetor could only manage 100 horsepower out of a 982cc engine that was capable of nearly 120. But it was a start.

RX-2 (1971–1974)

Possibly to avoid confusion with the R100 or R-130 (a front-wheel-drive rotary only available in Japan), Mazda skipped right over the "RX-1" designation and named its new rotary "RX-2." This car also had a piston-powered counterpart: the Mazda 616. But this new rotary sedan was a vast departure from the R100. First and foremost was the engine. By slightly

The RX-2 can still be found in decent numbers if you know where to look. It was heavier than an RX-3, but with more horsepower. The RX-2s that do survive don't just sit around in a garage. This one is being raced by Nicole Cooper in SCCA's Solo I ITA class, where it competes with 1G RX-7s.

enlarging the rotors of the 10A, this 2-door 2+2 coupe was capable of producing 120 horsepower. Coupled with its low curb weight, that was enough to make it one of the fastest small cars in the United States at the time. This new 12A engine made its debut in the RX-2 chassis, and would live on for many years, going through several design changes in the process, not all of which served to increase horsepower. With the onset of the gas crisis, the 12A was detuned to the point of losing 25 horsepower! Without that move, Mazda executives felt that the fuel-thirsty RX-2 would be in less demand, and they were right. The RX-2 did well in 1972, but sales plummeted over the next two years until the model was discontinued in 1974.

Mazda kept working to improve reliability of its power plants, which is one of the reasons the 12A stayed around for another decade. Although the 12A of this generation did not have as long a life as the nearly bulletproof 12As that graced the first-generation (1G) RX-7, its short life was an exciting one in terms of horsepower and torque. Due to growing emission concerns, this engine (in stock trim) would never hit the 120 horsepower mark again.

RX-3 (1972–1978)

You would think that the RX-3 would have been bigger and more powerful than its predecessor, but that was not the case. It was faster, but only due to the fact that it was lighter and smaller than the RX-2. In fact, its wheelbase was a full 6 inches shorter overall. It used the new 12A motor, but due to emission regulations, the 1973 RX-3 produced only 90 horsepower. Oddly, that was the year that Mazda sold the most cars. But if you are in the market for an RX-3, the model to look for is the RX-3SP.

In 1976, Mazda pulled out all the stops and went after the U.S. performance enthusiast market. While the "SP" had several cosmetic "go fast" upgrades, there was some thought put into actual performance. One nominal item was a competition-type intake fitted to the standard 12A RX-3 power plant. While called a competition intake, this part provided no boost in either horsepower or torque. A more genuine enhancement was a different gearbox that yielded quicker 0–60 times. This new five-speed certainly made the car feel faster. And a huge front spoiler made it look like it meant business. Mazda also threw on a few other goodies, like a larger radiator and oil cooler.

The RX-3SP was a good sign for the sports car lover, as it showed that Mazda was interested in the high-performance market. By taking a previous generation car, then making it leaner and meaner, the company gave an indication of what was to come.

RX-4 (1974–1978)

It's not like Mazda was taking the United States by storm, but the

It didn't take long for the RX-3 to make an impact on the racing scene. Chuck Ulinski is seen here pulling away from a Renault on his way to another win in early SCCA road racing. *Courtesy of Mazda*

company was holding its own. In 1974, between the RX-2 and RX-3, Mazda sold nearly 40,000 cars, taking fourth place in the import market behind VW, Datsun, and Toyota. That year was also unusual in that all three cars (RX-2, -3, and -4) were being produced and could be bought new at a Mazda dealership. The RX-2 was seen as the economy car (it carried the lowest price), the RX-3 was the "sporty" car, and the new RX-4 was designed to appeal to the luxury market. It was longer, heavier, and more powerful than the other two sedans.

But the reason the RX-4 deserves its place in RX-7 history is that this was the vehicle that Mazda chose to introduce its new engine, the 13B, into the American market. An early version of the engine, called the 13A, appeared in the R-130, a car available only in Japan. The unique thing about the R-130 was that it was Mazda's only front-wheel-drive rotary-powered car.

The RX-4's 13B actually didn't produce much more horsepower than the current 12A, mainly due to a restrictive carb and exhaust system. But the new RX-4 was fast, completing a 0–60 trial in nearly 9 seconds. Too bad it was so heavy—more than 500 pounds fatter than the RX-3!

With the RX-4, Mazda was clearly focused on the V-8 buyer. This car came equipped with a much nicer interior than previous models had had, and was marketed as Mazda's top-of-the-line automobile. But overall, the RX-4 did not hit its target. Why would Mazda release the gas-guzzler 13B right in the middle of the oil crisis? The company tried to get the EPA to reevaluate how it rated cars, but success at this came too late to save the RX-4 from poor sales. Due to

its extensive lobbying, however, Mazda claims responsibility for there now being two different miles-per-gallon ratings for autos: city and highway. The RX-4 fared rather well compared to the V-8s in highway fuel economy, but Americans still weren't abandoning their big blocks.

The Rotary Pickup (1974–1976)

Who can forget Mazda's infamous rotary-powered truck? Powered by the RX-4's 13B, this was not your father's pickup. If introduced today, it would probably be a big hit, given the truck-buying frenzy of the late 1990s and first part of 2000. But 25 years ago, it was a different story. After only three years and a limited production run, Mazda pulled its truck from the assembly line.

RX-5 The Cosmo (1976–1978)

Mazda Motors back in 1976 had a few decent engines to work with: the

12A from the RX-2, which cranked out 120 horsepower, and the new 13B from the RX-4, which was capable of 125. The body of the RX-3 was nearly 300 pounds leaner than the RX-2, and more than 500 pounds less than

The Mazda Cosmo, or RX-5, was designed as a luxury sports coupe targeted for the U.S. market. The Cosmo looked nothing like its namesake, the Cosmo Sport, and was a flop here, but sold well in Japan. Collectors have been grabbing them up lately since they came with the 13B (from the RX-4), and because they were the last rotary car produced before the introduction of the RX-7. *Courtesy of Mazda*

The rotary Mazda pickup truck was one of the most unlikely and rarest rotary-powered vehicles imported into the United States. It was sold in the American market in limited quantities from 1974–1976. *Courtesy of Mazda*

the RX-4. If you wanted to make a faster car from existing stock, the choice was clear. Putting the 13B engine into the RX-3 chassis should create a new coupe that could do 0–60 in the 7-second range. Too bad Mazda didn't do it.

Instead of going for speed, Mazda went for size with the bloated RX-5 Cosmo. Weighing in at 2,800 pounds, the car was huge. Using the RX-4 engine, the Cosmo was 1.5 seconds slower to 60 miles per hour, and it failed to lure the American V-8 buyer into a Mazda dealership. For RX-7 fans, that may have been a lucky break, since this car's failure probably added even more fuel to the RX-7 project. Japanese buyers loved the car, but the market Mazda had targeted was on the other side of the world, and sales in the United States were slow.

When I was towing a rust-free 1976 Cosmo back from Florida recently, I would have sworn the car was filled with sand. The RX-5 is a rare bird indeed. Resembling a cross between a Chevy Vega and a 1970s Cougar, the Cosmo is unique. And unlike most of the cars from that era, its lines are more pleasing now than ever before. One of my favorite things to do is to drive it to a sports car meeting, or put race tires on it and take it to an autocross. Nowhere on the car does it actually say "Mazda." You should hear some of the guesses that come from the younger participants.

By the time that the first RX-7 hit our shores, Mazda sales from 1970–1977 (including the rotary-powered cars above, plus the Miser and GLC) totaled well over 400,000 units. Obviously, the majority of these numbers belong to the piston-driven autos that Mazda achieved success with during the gas crisis.

It didn't take long before this new rotary rocket was being raced. Rod Millen modified his 1980 RX-7 for SCCA Pro Rally competition. Soon, having to deal with John Buffum driving an Audi Quattro, Millen further modified the RX-7 to be four-wheel drive. *Courtesy of Mazda*

X605 Project Car

Toyo Kogyo had been planning a two-seater sports car since the late 1960s, but the OPEC oil crisis and resulting Mazda U.S.A. woes buried the project in 1973. Project RS-X, which included the planned X020A and X020G prototypes, never really got past the drawing board phase. But were it not for that, the RX-7 as we know it may never have been made.

Mazda needed a solution for its falling sales in the United States After a trip to the states in 1975, Mazda management became convinced that the way to save the rotary engine (and possibly the company) was to produce an affordable and competent sports car. Plans to build the new car on a slightly modified RX-5 chassis were scrapped. Instead, the company would create an extremely rigid unibody construction as the foundation for the new two-seater.

This car would be engineered from scratch, solely with a rotary power plant in mind. Unfortunately, with the U.S. emission and gas crisis in full bloom, the 13B engine from the RX-4 and Cosmo would not find a place in this new chas-

sis until 1984, when the gas crisis had subsided. Instead, a reworked 12A was designed to power this new pocket rocket. The new car was designed to compete with the Fiat X1/9, Porsche 924, and Datsun 280Z. In both speed and initial cost, it blew these cars away.

Although Mazda had decided early on not to compromise in the production of the X605, a few concessions were made. Four-wheel disc brakes were scrapped in favor of front discs and rear drums. An even weaker link was the steering. Instead of rack and pinion, project X605 came equipped with a slightly modified version of the recirculating ball system found on the earlier RX-3. It must have looked good on the drawing board—or the balance sheet—but it laid a foundation for imprecise steering in the production car to follow.

The First-Generation RX-7 (1979–1985)

X605

Project X605, as it was known in Japan, didn't take too long to get from the drawing board to production. It was introduced to the United States in mid-1978 as a 1979 model, and was an instant hit. In just the RX-7's first two years, U.S. sales exceeded all Mazda rotary-powered cars to date. Looking back, RX-7 fans may see this as no big surprise, but the extent to which the RX-7 took the U.S. market by storm was not quite expected by either the U.S. dealerships, or even Mazda executives themselves.

In the late 1970s, Japanese cars were in high demand. Just as potential buyers of the 1977 Honda Accord would have to wait up to a year just for the right to purchase one, so was the case with the 1978–1979 RX-7. Waiting lists were commonplace, and dealerships were often asking—and getting—$2,000 or more over the sticker price. Part of the reason for this was the RX-7's low price compared to the competition. Even if you paid that extra cash, you would still be saving money over a Porsche 924 or a Datsun 280Z. You would also be able to blow their doors off if you chose to challenge them at a red light.

The initial offering sold for less than $7,000, and that included both the base model and the GS. You could select a four-speed, a five-speed, or three-speed automatic transmission.

Not many changes took place the first few years of production. One change was to replace the contact point distributor with electronic ignition. There were two special edition RX-7s offered in 1980: the Tenth anniversary edition, celebrating Mazda's tenth year in the United States, and a Leather Sport edition that featured leather seats, gear shift knob, and steering wheel.

Due to the RX-7's great power-to-weight ratio, coupled with the extraordinary durability of the 12A engine, it wasn't long before some began to appear at the racetrack.

RX-2 and RX-3 owners had already laid the foundation. Back in the mid-1970s, Mazdatrix founder, Dave Lemon, started his racing career behind the wheel of a British car. But while he was in the pits under the car with a wrench in his hand (an all-too-frequent occurrence), he was taunted by that high-pitched, unmuffled tone that sounds like giant bees swarming on the track. It seemed that the only time the noise stopped was when the RX-2s and RX-3s came in for fuel. Finally, he walked over to an RX-2's pit, spoke to the crew, and discovered another advantage of the rotary. One engine lasted a dozen races before it had to be rebuilt. At that time, Lemon was rebuilding his engine every one to two races. Struck by an unavoidable dose of logic, he switched to an RX-3 soon afterwards, and the rest is history.

The RX-7's first major change came in 1981, when a dual catalytic converter system replaced the heavy and outdated thermal reactor assembly. This upgrade saved nearly 100 pounds, a meaningful sum at the track. This was also the first year for the GSL trim option, featuring leather seats, alloy wheels, and a sunroof. The real advantage of this "top-of-the-line" RX-7 was the rear axle, which included disc brakes and a limited-slip differential. Racers flocked to the showrooms to put in their order. The GSL's only drawback was a bit of extra weight from the power windows.

Other notable changes in 1981 included a larger gas tank and improved gas mileage (due to leaner carb settings) that extended the cruising range by nearly 100 miles! All these improvements came at a price, however: $2,000–$3,000 to be exact, depending on the model. That was the price tag increase over the

1978/1979 model year. To a trained eye, there were other subtle differences. The rear tail lights were redesigned, and the recessed license plate area was filled in and smoothed over to form a bridge between tail lights. The front bumpers were also more recessed into the body, further reducing the drag coefficient. And finally, the four-speed transmission was dropped from the line, leaving only a three-speed auto and a five-speed manual box.

There were no major changes over the final three years other than a Limited Edition model released in 1983 that came with wider alloys and tires. In Japan, lucky buyers were treated to a turbocharged car with nearly 60 more horsepower than the U.S. version. This model, the GT-X, never made it across the Pacific, but the following year, we did get a consolation prize.

1984–1985 GSL-SE

Major changes took place for Mazda in 1984. The base model, GS and GSL, remained the same, but members of the enthusiast community finally were offered an RX-7 they could really sink their teeth into.

Instead of a supercharged or turbocharged car for 1984, Mazda instead chose to further refine the normally aspirated rotary for the U.S. market. Engineers enlarged the combustion chambers and widened the block by 10 millimeters. This resulted in 1308cc worth of total displacement and an increase of 14 percent. Although nearly identical in appearance to the previous RX-4 and RX-5 power plant, which was also called the 13B, this was a much more reliable and sophisticated creature.

Subtle and effective changes gave the new 13B a great deal more torque and horsepower than the

The 1984–1985 GSL-SE was a hint of things to come for the RX-7. With fuel injection, a bigger 13B engine, a limited-slip differential, and rear disc brakes, this is the most sought-after 1G RX-7 among enthusiasts. *David Lane*

12A and the old 13B. The RX-4 13B had four intake ports, but the GSL-SE had six. Both secondary ports were enlarged and split in two, resulting in the six-port 13B. A complex intake system was used to take advantage of the twin secondary ports. When the tach would wind up beyond 5K, the two new ports were opened by a pair of rotary valves, allowing more air and fuel into the engine. With these new ports doing the work when the motor was at high rpm, fuel mix and ignition timing for the primary ports could be designed to optimize low- to mid-range performance.

The new intake was also engineered to accelerate the air entering the chambers. Couple that with an excellent electronic fuel-injection system, and you get 35 more horsepower and nearly 20 ft-lbs of torque over the 12A. These sorts of improvements are discussed in detail later in the book. Chapter 8 discusses the advantages of porting, which, in a way, is what Mazda did to the new 13B. And chapter 10 discusses the merits of a good fuel-

injection system. With appropriate modifications to the air, fuel, and exhaust systems, an old four-port 13B can be cranked up to around 200 horsepower!

The GSL-SE models had a limited-slip differential and disc brakes. In fact, the brakes and calipers were also bigger. A different five-speed tranny and heavier-duty clutch rounded out this car's ability to get the power to the road. There were also suspension improvements that made the car handle substantially better than its predecessors. The lower rear trailing arms were dropped nearly an inch, which reduced oversteer (losing traction in the rear during a turn). To top it off, the GSL-SE finally got some rubber to play with. Bigger 14x5.5-inch alloys with 205/60/14 tires further enhanced cornering. The GSL-SE helped boost RX-7 sales through the roof in 1984, and they remained strong the following year despite the news that a new model would be introduced in 1986. From 1978–1985, Mazda sold more than 370,000 RX-7s.

The Second-Generation RX-7 (1986–1991)

P747

In 1986, sports car enthusiasts were finally treated to a new RX-7. Although the first-generation car was changed considerably during its final two years of production (GSL-SE), major car magazines were referring to the old look as being stale. Mazda had been working on a new body since 1981.

The next generation of RX-7 was more civilized, and had more power. Nearly a completely different car from the 1G, the 1986–1992 RX-7 was designed to compete with the Porsche 924 for a share of the U.S. sports car market. *Chad Weber*

Three different prototypes were developed in 1982, and the project was given a name: P747. The goals were to improve aerodynamics, suspension, steering (yes!), overall refinement, engine performance and reliability, wheels/tires, and the EFI system.

The shape of this new RX-7 tells you that this car spent some time in the wind tunnel. The suspension was completely redesigned, and included a pseudo four-wheel steering system built into the rear suspension. The DTSS (Dynamic Tracking Suspension System) maintained negative camber in the rear, even during hard cornering. A special front bushing design induced toe in when g-force was applied. As you will find out later in the book, toe in coupled with negative camber in the rear is the goal for many rear-wheel-drive racers. Mazda was clearly on the right track.

The reciprocating ball steering was finally replaced by rack and pinion, giving the second-generation (2G) drivers a much better feel of the road. The engine was also updated. Newly designed three-piece apex seals replaced the older two-piece item. These new seals were also only 2 millimeters wide, while on the 1985 and earlier engines they were 3 millimeters wide. An additional injector was added to the intake to help the new engine produce more power, while at the same time getting better gas mileage. The oil-injection system was also redesigned. Now it would be squirted directly into the primary intake manifold and the trochoidal chamber.

The American public responded to the 1986 car, making it the best sales year in RX-7 history, with more than 56,000 units sold in the United States alone.

Although the RX-7 community is a close-knit group of dedicated fans, there remains a split between

One of the big changes that took place in 1986 for the redesigned 13B power plant was lighter rotors. Racing Beat offers rotors that are even lighter, for those who want even quicker acceleration. *Racing Beat*

1G and 2G owners. Many 1G lovers felt that Mazda was too conservative with the design of the 1986 model. They also felt that the "seat of the pants" experience was compromised. For most early 1G fanatics, however, this was a blessing in disguise, as the older body style, especially the GSL-SE, was now more affordable than ever. In the late 1980s, a used 1984–1985 GSL was a bargain, and many 1978–1981 owners traded up to this more technologically advanced model.

Those who plunked down for the new version were treated to a sports car that continued to keep pace with the world's best without compromising the car's roots: rotary power. Although the world had all but given up on rotary-powered vehicles by the late 1980s, Mazda continued to carry the torch, making steady refinements along the way. There were a few special models that were released during the second-generation run, most of which turned up the heat a little on Porsche and BMW drivers who liked to think *they* had fast cars.

In fact, as the years passed, Mazda may have offered too many versions. These included the basic RX-7 (no designation number), a

2+2 option (back seat), all the way up to a turbocharged model. In 1986 there was just the basic RX-7 and the GXL. In 1988, however, there was the SE (the new name of the base model), GTU, and GXL, which was an attempt to lure the luxury sports car buyer to the rotary lifestyle. Anti-lock brake systems (ABS) were available as an option on both the GXL and Turbo II in 1987. And in 1988, there was a 10th anniversary edition produced celebrating the RX-7's 10th year in the United States. It was a cross between the GXL and the Turbo II, compromising a little performance in favor of luxury and special features.

The GTU, which made its debut in 1988, was a celebration all of the IMSA wins that the RX-7 had accumulated over the years. It was a serious sports car. Wider and bigger wheels and tires, stiffer springs and struts, and a limited-slip differential were just part of the package that sold for about $2,000 more than the base SE. It offered most of the performance goodies that could be found on the turbo, without the actual turbo. To date, it is the model to look for since it offers a great deal of bang for the buck.

RX-7 Turbo (1987–1991)

How about some power, finally? The Turbo was the car that RX-7 fans had been waiting for. The engine that powered this energetic car was designated the Turbo II. No one really knows where "II" came from, but Mazda historians believe it designated that this was the second generation RX-7. With over 180 horsepower on tap, this car could really fly. It was, however, extremely thirsty. But fans were willing to put up with 17 miles per gallon (or less, depending on how excited you were) to get this level of performance.

The GXL had more options than the base model, called the SE, in 1986–1987. The GTU made its debut in 1988, and came with a slightly stiffer suspension, bigger wheels and tires, and a limited-slip differential. Ryan Andreas owns this 1987 GXL, and has installed an HKS stainless steel exhaust and a K&N intake system. *Ryan Andreas*

Here is the car that we in the United States never got the chance to buy. Sascha Horstkotte owns this beautiful 1989 convertible turbo (yes, turbo). With 200-plus horsepower on tap, Sascha drives around Germany with a factory turbo under the hood and the wind in his face. Aftermarket goodies include 17-inch wheels, Koni struts with Eibach springs, and a stainless steel exhaust manufactured by Rotary Engineering Germany, Ltd. He designed the Web pages for the RX-7 club, Europe. *Sascha Horstkotte*

Even without the turbo, this was a true sports car. The suspension was stiffer, the wheels and tires were bigger, and just like on the GTU, a limited-slip differential was standard to help get all 180 horsepower to the pavement. Actually, take away the turbo, and you pretty much have a GTU. But it's rather easy to tell a GTU from a Turbo. Just look for the ram-air hood scoop.

Convertible (1988–1992)

Mazda fans had a great year in 1988. And it only got better when the Cabriolet that was introduced a year earlier in Japan made its way across the ocean. This was a true factory convertible as well—not a hardtop shipped to an aftermarket specialist for conversion. The only downside of the convertible was that (as usual) Japan kept the best power plant for itself. To avoid a "gas guzzler" tax in the United States, we could only buy the SE engine mated to a five-speed tranny. In Japan, the Cabriolet came with the Turbo II engine, with a choice of five-speed or automatic transmission.

Infini IV (1991–1992)

Japan had another domestic-only model that has become a legend here in the United States—mainly because 99.9 percent of us have never seen one in person. Right before the third generation (3G) was introduced, Mazda decided to go all out and make a Turbo II that had more power and was lightened. This was indeed the design of things to come. Since it was a Japan-only vehicle, the designation "RX-7" never appeared anywhere on the car. There were cool ground effects, suspension updates, and too many other things to list. Even though it looked like a 2G, it had much more in common with a 3G. It seemed as if Mazda executives had designed a concept car—which would eventually turn into the 3G—but decided to run off a few copies just for themselves.

When first introduced to the public, the third-gen RX-7 quickly went on most sports car enthusiasts' wish list. It was designed with light weight and lots of power in order to compete with the other supercars on the market at that time. Gordon Monsen knew he wanted one, despite being a Ferrari-type guy. But he wanted it to be the quickest car in his garage, so he bought this one sight unseen, brand-new out of the showroom and had it sent to Peter Farrell Supercars for some tweaking. With a Farrell intercooler, single-stage sport turbo, extra injectors and controller, an EFI Systems ECU unit, and Farrell-modified computer, etc., this car flies.

Conclusions About Second-Generation RX-7s

The second-generation car was more refined and better to drive than its predecessor. What it no longer had, however, was the low price tag that had helped to lure so many buyers away from competitors in the beginning. The basic second-generation car sold for $11,995 in 1986. By 1991, that price had risen to $19,335—a $7,000 increase over six years. And there was only a 14 horsepower gain to show for all that extra money. The 1991 model was much more refined than the 1986 car, but sticker shock, and a changing marketplace, drove buyers elsewhere. The record 56,000 sales chalked up in 1986 had plummeted to only 6,000 cars by the time the second generation was retired in 1992. You would think Mazda would be discouraged by this trend and as a result scale back its sports car development efforts. If that's what people thought, they were wrong. Mazda's answer to sagging RX-7 sales in the United States came in the form of one of the most beautiful, technologically advanced, serious production sports cars the world had ever seen.

The Third-Generation RX-7 (U.S. 1993–1995)

Series VI

Media and auto enthusiast alike were speechless when Mazda introduced the dynamic third-generation car in 1993, representing the high point for RX-7 design and development. The body was a work of art, and the 13B power plant had been nearly completely redesigned. Although still a 13B at heart, the new engine boasted twin Hitachi turbochargers. Called the 13B REW engine, it included a large turbo intercooler and, in the "R" version, dual oil coolers located at each front corner of the car.

The turbos were powered by exhaust gases that were initially sent to the primary turbo for quicker off-the-line performance. Even at low rpm, however, Mazda designed it so that some exhaust gases would be diverted to the secondary turbo, keeping it "spooled-up" so that it was ready to kick in when needed. This minimized the dreaded "turbo lag" condition from which many high-horsepower turbocharged cars suffer. The result was 255 horsepower and 217 ft-lbs of torque out of just 1.3 liters! Weighing in at just under 2,800 pounds, that translated into one of the best power-to-weight ratios of any affordable production car.

Three different versions of the RX-7 were offered the first year of production: the base model (if you can call it that), a touring package (creature comforts: massive Bose stereo system, leather, etc.), and the R1 (stiffer suspension—more of a pure sports car). Either way, 0–60 times were in the range of 6 seconds, and the top speed was clocked at 163 miles per hour! And the car was more than happy to tackle roads with a few twists and turns. Even with the softer ride of the touring package, the car handled the autocross course with competence and ease.

Due to some quality control problems, however, there are many uniquely different 1993 RX-7s on the road, depending on what recalls and other quirky problems were addressed—or ignored—by their respective owners. The list of redesigned items on the 1993 model year alone was impressive: wheel center caps, front door glass guide, upper A-arm bushings, engine mounts, steering rack boots, rear hatch hinges, black interior pieces, stronger intercooler hose, shift select spindle, etc. There are a few other major changes worth noting, including added sub frame connectors to aid in preventing the power plant frame from cracking, and to help reduce wheel hop. The electronic control units (ECUs) for both the five-speed and automatic tranny models were also redesigned. When buying a used 3G, always bring a checklist of the things just listed to ask the previous owner about.

With the 1994 model came additional variations. That year's list

More of Pettit's handiwork is showcased in this RX-7. As soon as the third gen was introduced, Pettit and PFS were offering performance packages that could boost power up to 650 horses. *Courtesy of Excellent Performance/Pettit Racing*

Here's a look at a unique RX-7. This 1995 "R" came with a factory sunroof. *Dale Black*

includes redesigned turbocharger housings, clutch facing material (for longer life), water pump seal, water level sensor, upper radiator hose, radiator cap (lower pressure), filler cap and body, thermostat gasket, throttle body coolant sensor, air separator tank coolant hose, high-temp fuel hoses, fan relay control module (allowing cooling fans to run for 10 minutes after shutting down the engine), and a smaller ABS control unit. Additional modifications were made to the rear sub frame.

For those who wanted even more performance, Mazda offered

the R1 in the first year of production. You can usually spot one by its rear wing—however, many 3G owners buy aftermarket kits to duplicate the R1's look and performance. With a strut tower brace (a very popular add-on) and dual oil coolers, the R1 is designed for serious motoring. The seats are even devoid of leather since, as most racers know, under high Gs, a leather seat won't hold you in place as securely as a cloth one. The suspension was also tuned to be stiffer. The following year, the R2 was Mazda's higher performance model. It's

nearly the same as the R1, but the springs and struts were not as stiff.

As hot as the third-generation car was, the year of its introduction, 1993, was the beginning of the end for the RX-7 in the United States. Despite giving Mazda cognoscenti all they could ask for in a sports car, the car just didn't attract a wider public following. There were other problems that hurt sales, too, including the fact that Mazda dealerships were not prepared to support this highly complex and technologically advanced automobile—even today, many 3G owners believe you are better off going to Peter Farrell or Cameron Worth to doctor your ailing 1993–1995 RX-7 than to a dealer. The car also displayed initial problems in many areas, from the glove box light remaining on and the paint chipping to more serious problems such as fuel and coolant leaks. More complex issues included ECU malfunctions and sticking solenoids. The majority of dealers were stumped when trying to track down the cause for a car's hesitation, or why the secondary turbo wasn't kicking in properly. With miles of wires, countless relays, and solenoids tucked away in nearly every nook and cranny of the engine bay, the car was often one big frustration to Mazda technicians.

In a way, the 3G is the opposite of the earlier cars. This time performance was awesome, but reliability was lacking. And because of poor sales, the refinements that time would bring to the 3G in Japan would not make it to our shores. U.S. imports ceased after the 1995 model year.

That same year, Australia got a special version of the RX-7 called the SP (reminiscent of the RX-3SP). The SP had more horsepower. From 1996–1998, the Series VII RX-7 made its debut in the Japanese market. Some continued to be sent to our friends Down Under (lucky blokes). The Series VII underwent a few improvements over the 3G that produced, among other things, yet more horsepower. Reports from Japan indicate that in 1999, the new 3G (Series VIII) was more popular than ever.

Aftermarket rear wings are a popular choice for RX-7s, especially the 3G cars. You need to go over 100 miles per hour in order to get any real aerodynamic benefit. Sounds like something we should do testing on for the next book. *Dale Black*

As part of the American/Japanese Bonneville Salt Flats Challenge, Racing Beat put together this 3G and captured the record for its class. *Racing Beat*

CHAPTER TWO

The High-Performance RX-7 Transformation

Creating a hot rotary sports car can be a rather simple process, as long as you proceed with a specific, logical, step-by-step plan. And often, the end result is so rewarding that you will form a bond with your finished project that will rival that blind dedication you see in European car owners. There will be two big differences, however: your

hopped-up RX-7 will be able to blow the doors off most of those British, German, and Italian cars, and it will also start more faithfully when you turn the key.

Even some classic supercars (as nice as they are to look at) can't make that claim. Some of them seem to spend more time in the shop than

they do on the road. Their parts cost a fortune, and so does auto insurance (not to mention the initial purchase price). But with a slightly modified RX-7, that is not the case. You can enhance the performance of your rotary rocket to the point where it will rival those supercars, while still getting remarkable reliability—all at an affordable price.

LESSON 1: Save Yourself Headaches and Cash by Buying an RX-7 Someone Else Has Built

There are few things in life as rewarding as turning the key and driving down the road in your newly completed RX-7 project car. After all, it was your sweat, blood, time, and money. The only thing we have found to be more rewarding is to buy someone else's completed project!

No, you didn't build it yourself. Yes, it's probably not in perfect shape and may need some minor work, but you couldn't build one for less money. So what about that wonderful feeling of accomplishment you won't get to experience by having done it yourself? If your main goal is a fast car, chances are you'll get over

Before you decide what modifications to make, you really need an overall performance strategy. This can save you a lot of money in the end by keeping you from buying a part that you may need to upgrade later, or that will render your car ineligible for competition in certain racing classes. If your goal is autocross, then depending on the class in which you want to run, you should stay away from certain projects, such as porting or supercharging. Read the SCCA rule book first before you open your wallet. Co-author Dale Black's plan was to have the fastest RX-7 in the area. At the time of this photo, he was competing in the Solo II Street Prepared class. *Dale Black*

If what you want is a faster and better-handling street car, then your priorities will be much different than for someone who wants to go racing. Certain modifications, such as stiffer springs, polyurethane suspension bushings, and engine porting could render your RX-7 a pain in the @$$ to drive on the street.

We have a guy in our town and club named Mike Healy, who is an excellent RX-7 mechanic. Whether it is a 1G, 2G, 3G, or whatever, Mike can fix it. This is just the kind of guy from whom you need to buy an RX-7. Keep an eye open for your local RX-7 guru to put one of his cars up for sale, and then jump at it. Let him work all the bugs out so you can concentrate on doing the fun, bolt-on modifications.

it. Add a few customizing touches, and you will soon forget that someone else did all the work (and spent all the money). After you own the car for a few months, it will feel like it's part of the family. And the best part is that if you get tired of it in the future, you can always sell it without taking a big loss.

You've seen the ads: "1979 RX-7. Custom paint, no rust. Excellent condition. Lowered, header, rebuilt limited-slip, Centerforce clutch, custom exhaust, Carbeau seats, Pettit-built 13B with Haltech fuel injection dynoed at 240 horsepower, Revolutions plus racing wheels and tires, over $15,000 worth of parts and labor. Sacrifice for $6,000." The author purchased this actual car from a friend, raced and drove it on the street for two years, then sold it for the same price to another friend. If you take the time to read the classified ads from enthusiast magazines, you could end up saving yourself a lot of money in the long run.

On the other hand, another friend recently purchased a 3G RX-7 for less than $9,000 that had once been a full-blown, gutted race car, and soon regretted his decision. If his goal had been to get it back on the racetrack, there would have been no problem. In trying to fix it up for the street, however, he ran into so many obstacles that, by the time the project was finished, he had spent countless hours and shelled out an additional $6,000. He would have been wiser to pursue a car that better matched his performance goals.

If you're careful and know what you want, you can find a very reliable and well sorted second- or third-generation RX-7 on which a previous owner has spent thousands to make performance upgrades. With a car like this, the price you pay will always be less than what the current owner paid for those upgrades, saving you a significant amount of money. That brings us to Lesson 2.

LESSON 2: Be Prepared to Spend Money on Your Car That You'll Never Get Back

If you insist on hopping-up your RX-7, then you must be willing to accept that you will spend

If you truly love your RX-7, and money is no object, then by all means, go for it. But remember that even F1 racing teams have budgets, and you should have one, too. Also, be prepared to put more money into the car than you will ever get out of it if you sell it. David Lane obviously loves his 1G and plans on keeping it forever—and why not? But with the addition of a turbo, trick suspension, custom gauges, ignition, etc., he is one of many people (including us) who has gone past the point of diminishing returns. The upside is, you might be able to purchase someone else's beautiful rust-free 240-horsepower, Haltech-injected 13B, all-tricked-out 1G for much less than what you ever could have built the car for—that's what I did. The best way to get into road racing is to follow this philosophy. Even if you already own an RX-7, it is much cheaper to buy someone else's race car than to build one from scratch. *David Lane*

money you'll never recoup. Now don't get us wrong—the process is often worth the price you pay, even if you can't recover the investment in cash. Even with all of the free parts my fellow journalist friends and I manage to scam as part of being authors, some of us have still put lots of our own money (not to mention time) into projects that end up being worth only about half what we invested. At least that's the excuse we give our wives for never selling any of our project cars.

But most of you know what we're talking about. This process forms a union between the car and owner that non-enthusiasts can't understand. So if you choose to take this path, then hold onto this book, and we can help you get the most for the money you spend on performance improvements.

LESSON 3: Start with the Right Car

Try not to take this next statement too personally, but the RX-7 you own right now (as much as you love it) may not be the best choice to meet the performance goals you have in mind. You may be better off selling it and buying a different RX-7 model that will be easier to transform into the car of your dreams. Otherwise, you may end up spending more money than necessary to get the performance you seek.

The first step is to decide what you want your car to do, and how you want to use it (street, dual duty, autocross, road racing, drag). Only then can you decide on which RX-7 would be best. Maybe it's the one in your garage. But if it isn't, you may be able to save money by switching to a model that has certain options or characteristics to better meet your needs.

Starting with the wrong car is a big mistake. Modifying the wrong RX-7, whether it's intended for the street or the strip, will add a lot of unnecessary labor, hassle, and money to your project. Certain RX-7s are good candidates for upgraded engine transplants or turbo kits, while others aren't. For example, if you want to go road racing on a budget and already own a 3G car, you will likely exceed your budget very quickly unless you choose to run in a stock class that restricts the number of changes you

The key to planning out a good project is to start with the right car. Just because you already have a perfectly good-running 1980 RX-7 in your garage doesn't mean you should use it. Keep in mind your final goal for the car. If it involves adding fuel injection, then sell the 1980 and buy a 1984–1985 GSL-SE or a 2G RX-7. And don't start with a GTU if you plan on adding a turbo unit later on. Go buy a 2G turbo and sell the GTU. There are so many things you can do to a Turbo II engine (even with a small budget) that in the end, will more than make up for the extra cost you paid for a better car. Chad Weber from Salem, Oregon, has followed this philosophy and is getting excellent power out of his 2G without spending all his money and time. *Chad Weber*

are allowed to make. If your goal is to run in the more highly modified classes, you will need to spend a great deal more time and money to be competitive. If you are restricted by a budget and road racing is your goal, then it makes more sense to start with a cheaper car (first- or second-generation non-turbo). The main reason for this is because the performance parts for the 1G and 2G are cheaper, and the cars are easier to modify. Just remember this: The faster your RX-7 is in stock trim, the higher the class in which it will be placed. In other words, a 1G 12A-powered car is usually put in the same class as a Honda CRX, but a 3G RX-7 is classed with Ferraris, new Corvettes, and Dodge Vipers.

Starting with the right car can give you an edge—an edge that you would otherwise be penalized for if you started with a slower model and then tried to upgrade performance and handling. A 1984 RX-7 GSL-SE, for example, had a limited-slip differential and bigger wheels/tires as standard equipment. The limited-slip differential helps to keep the inside wheel from spinning as you exit a turn, and coupled with bigger wheels/tires, gives much better traction than other 1G models. But all non-turbo RX-7s are placed in the same class. For SCCA (Sports Car Club of America) autocross, however, if you tried to add a limited-slip differential and bigger wheels, you will be bumped into the Street Prepared Class, where you would have to run against lighter-bodied RX-7s (like the 1981) with transplanted 13Bs, aftermarket EFI, and 15x10-inch wheels. That could get very expensive very fast.

It's best to avoid 2G convertibles, automatics, and GXLs for stock competition due to higher weight. Because convertibles don't have the structural support of a roof, they experience much more chassis flex than a hardtop and the handling is diminished. The earlier cars (1986–1988) are also substantially lighter, but the 1988 GTU combines the lightest body with a limited-slip differential. In 1991, the GTU received 14 more horsepower, but also added 160 pounds. I always go for the lighter-weight car in an instance like this because your race tires will last longer, and I find it easier to get a lighter car to handle better.

Good candidates for stock competition are RX-7s with the best power-to-weight ratios. Any 3G is nearly a perfect car right out of the box, but if you are serious about racing, the R1 or R2 versions would be the best choice. A touring model is heavier by 60 pounds, and an automatic tranny adds less control and a lot more weight. The main reason not to run a 3G car in a highly modified class is the fact that you would be gutting a car that is worth too much money in stock trim. Since 1G cars are already inexpensive, you would not depreciate your investment by nearly as much as you would if you had started with a 1993–1995 RX-7.

Be careful, too, not to make changes before you learn the rules of the competition class you have in mind. One of the most common mistakes is to buy bigger and wider wheels before you go racing. Many stock classes restrict wheel size to the factory diameter and width. Wider wheels will often bump you out of a "stock" class, which is where most beginners will have the best chance of winning. Adding a turbo where once there was none could force you to compete in the modified classes. Boost is also restricted in many autocross classes, and turbos are often not permitted at all in SCCA IT or SCCA road racing. You don't want to have to choose between undoing an expensive modi-fication you're proud of and competing in the class in which you have the best chance to win.

Set your goals first, then decide whether your present car is up to the task. And don't overlook people who have traveled this road before. Although we've tried to give you all the helpful information possible, you can always learn something from experienced competitors. They will likely have useful feedback on your ideas, or may know of a car that would be perfect for your purposes.

LESSON 4: Establish a Budget for Your Money and Time

Anyone who has ever gotten into a car modification or restoration project knows that hours and costs pile up quickly. When starting out to build the project car of your dreams, establish a budget. Even if money is no object, a budget can still be extremely helpful. The reason for this is that budgets set limits, and limits will help you to prioritize how your money is to be spent based on what aspects of the project are most important to you. That's why even large multi-billion dollar corporations have budgets. Those budgets serve to keep the companies focused on their goals.

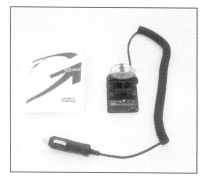

If you can't get your car to a chassis dynamometer, a tool such as this G-Tech may be helpful. It is by no means a substitute for the new state of the art dynos.

Dynamometer testing is the key to successfully fine tuning your RX-7. As authors, we rely on the chassis dyno to tell us which parts work and which ones don't. Dynos, like this one owned and operated by Steve Pillic of Dynotec Motorsports, are invaluable in determining how a car will run with more boost, a different fuel program, a bigger intercooler, etc. Your local RX-7 club may want to consider having a Dyno Day to help tweak the maximum horsepower out of your car.

For the project car builder, there are two types of budgets to consider. Clearly, a financial budget is important, even for those people with plenty to spend. Just as it is for the billion-dollar company, a financial budget is a good way to help you prioritize how your money will be spent. And in order to do that, you will be forced to decide exactly what phases of the project are the most important to help you meet your goals. All of us are dealing with a limited amount of time and money; therefore, building a project car often involves compromise.

Money

Many auto enthusiasts make the mistake of buying their car, then immediately purchasing a cool set of rims and a slick-looking rear wing, or installing a killer stereo. A few months later, however, their project car starts to come together, and they decide to do some amateur racing. That cool wing may then have become a wasted expense, and will likely result in exclusion from the stock or entry-level classes. Then there are those wheels, which could offer the same restrictions as the wing, plus pose some additional problems. For instance, did those aftermarket wheels/tires change your final drive ratio so that you are not as quick off the line as your competitors? Do the best racing tires come in sizes that will fit on your new wheels? How often do you see nearly brand-new parts being

sacrificed by people who did not take the time to plan out their project? The parts that they initially purchased no longer meet their needs because their goals have changed, so they sell them for a fraction of the original purchase price. If you plan your project well, then their loss can be your gain. Remember, even the top racing teams have budgets.

Your budget should take every basic system of your car into consideration. To get started, first look at the chapters in this book and decide your RX-7's needs, based on what exactly you want to do with it. List suspension, engine, intake, exhaust, ignition, and appearance as categories, then add subsections based on the book chapter. For example, under "suspension," you should have springs, shocks, sway bars, wheels, tires, etc. Even if you already have a nice set of wheels, put a $0 on the line next to "wheels." Under "shocks and struts," however, you may want to upgrade to an adjustable Koni system, and should therefore budget about $600. Use parts catalogs, the Internet, and any other available source to get fair prices for all the items on your list.

This itemization will also serve another purpose. If you are using a computer program that can calculate your expenditures, you will have a running total of what you've spent on your car. This will help keep your head out of the clouds and your feet on the ground, protecting you from spending too much more on the car than what it's worth. It will also help you to keep track of exactly what you have done, essentially giving you a readout of your car's modifications.

Finally, the budget could help with your insurance claim in the event that your car is stolen. Receipts for both aftermarket parts and labor should be kept in a folder accompanying the hard copy of your budget. You may as well put a "before" photo of your car in the folder. If you take the time to compile this information, you will be glad you did. When your project is completed, as it will serve as a tribute to the time, effort, and money that went into your RX-7. And if the day ever comes that you decide to sell your baby, prospective buyers will recognize that you are a detail-oriented person who likely took good care of the car. It will prove, for example, that there actually is a rebuilt limited-slip installed in the transaxle, or that the engine really was rebuilt a year ago.

You've got a vision of a great car in your mind. Don't let it end with a half-finished project and a pile of threatening letters from your credit card company. If you build in a thorough list of parts and costs up front, and then space these items out over time, your project will come together smoothly and stay within your financial means.

Time

Besides budgeting finances, you need to budget your time. In a perfect world, you could wake up in the morning, go out to the garage, and work on your car all day. But, unfortunately, most people have to go to work. Then there are friends and family responsibilities, and all of the other time constraints that come with life in the twenty-first century.

Don't underestimate the importance of setting a time budget. Your relationship with your partner can often be put into some degree of jeopardy due to an automotive project. Your significant other may think the car has become the most important thing in your life. But there are ways to avoid this potential problem.

First, limit the time you work on your car when your spouse is home. If you have children, try to involve them in your project so that there is a family element to what you are doing. And most important, empower your significant other. Give her (or, for the women competitors—more power to you!—give him) the power to decide, for instance, how long you will work on your car for a given day.

Let your significant other know that she is more important to you than your car. Tell her what aspect of the project you will be working on today, and give her an estimate of the time you think this will take. And tell her that if she begins to feel neglected, all she needs to do is to come to the garage and tell you. Usually you will be able to come to an appropriate stopping point and get cleaned up in about 30 minutes from the time she

Before you decide what you want to do to your project car, get to the nearest chassis dynamometer. Our Speednation dyno can guide you as you adjust ignition timing, air and fuel mixture (EFI systems or carbs), turbo boost, and more so that your car will deliver maximum horsepower. It will also record extremely accurate 1/4 mile times, and help determine exactly at what rpm you should shift in order to get more efficiently from point A to point B. Call 724-926-3735 or go to www.speednation.com to find the dyno nearest you.

asks you to come back into the house. If this seems "unmanly," then you may want to reexamine your priorities in life. Machines should never be given more importance than people. If you compromise your relationships for the sake of building your car, in the end there will be no one around to help you enjoy it.

From a completely different point of view, time management is important when it comes to deciding the amount of time you want to spend on specific phases of your project. Spending five hours wrestling with the installation of an exhaust system, for example, may cost a lot more than the $100 you could spend to have it installed at a muffler shop in 45 minutes. We recently completed an aftermarket fuel-injection project that took over two years, and the car is still not functioning at its potential. Did it save money to do it ourselves? Possibly, but shops like Pettit or Peter Farrell Supercars could have done it in a few days, and we could have been racing the car these past two years. Heck, we could have blown two engines in that time.

Some people actually tow their vehicles 1,000 miles to expert performance shops just to get them tuned properly. Much of the time, it appears that this is money well spent. That's because hours and hours on a dyno will do no good unless you know what to do with the information you are receiving. That's the mistake we made with our project car, and if we could do it over again, that puppy would be on Pettit's doorstep tomorrow. But wouldn't you be sacrificing all of the valuable knowledge you will gain by doing a project by yourself? Absolutely, and if this is one of your priorities, then go for it. If not, you need to decide which aspects of your project you want to do yourself, and which you

should give to an expert. We gained some valuable knowledge by doing the fuel-injection project by ourselves: we learned that next time we'll leave it up to the professionals.

LESSON 5: Read the Whole Book

One more thing to keep in mind: although the performance parts and modifications outlined in this book have been proved to work, your results may vary. Your particular car, depending on its age, condition, engine size and efficiency, gearbox, and other variables, may respond differently to performance modifications. Often, the addition of a single performance component may not yield the targeted performance improvement. There can be many reasons for this, but often the primary one is that all the components in a system (intake, exhaust, combustion) need to be properly matched. In other words, horsepower gains often only take place when the individual performance parts in a system complement each other.

Since RX-7s are such great sports cars, sometimes your modifications can do more harm than good—especially when dealing with 3G cars. Mazda engineers have already designed the engine components to be both efficient and powerful. Adding off-the-shelf performance parts may lend more power to 1G and 2G models, but you need to be more careful making modifications to 3G cars.

Another good example of the need for balance is the intake system. It is a sound decision to add an air velocity intake system to a fuel-injected engine; however, if a monster throttle body is added to this equation, without upgrading to bigger injectors, a decrease in horsepower may actually result.

And a final thought: if a particular type of performance part is not covered in this book, it may not perform as promised—or at all. Don't listen to the claims made by some companies and advertising-driven magazine articles that boast of horsepower increases that seem too good to be true. They probably are. Even

Mike Seymour is a member in good standing of "Rotary Rockets Canada." His 1994 Touring Edition is an excellent choice for an improved street car project. If you plan on lowering your car and stiffening the suspension, however, you probably should look for a 1993 R1 or 1994 R2. *Mike Seymour*

"dyno tested" claims can't always be trusted. Under the right conditions, using an engine dyno, someone could probably show that adding dirt to your engine will increase power. The real test is putting the engine in a car and driving it over a period of time. Then a chassis dyno plus some serious track time will tell you if the product passes muster. We own one of the best dynos ever made: a Mustang Chassis Dynamometer. And we have countless years of racing experience. The best advice we can offer is to read this entire book before you get on the phone to start ordering parts.

LESSON 6: Keep Up with Current Product Information

This book provides information based on current technology as of the year 2000. Traditionally, a book like this has no mechanism to report on new developments in performance technology. But due to the wonderful world of the Internet, RX-7 owners who buy this handbook will have access to our constantly updated Web page (http://www.speednation.com). This Web site offers the latest in tech news and articles providing ongoing advice for all RX-7 owners. In addition, for all of the latest information on new performance products, as well as ongoing tricks of the trade regarding RX-7 tuning, there are three magazines that are essential to any Mazda nut's library.

Grassroots Motorsports magazine has been covering RX-7s since the mid-1980s. From the latest project cars to tech tips, *GRM* provides loads of information that any RX-7 fan should enjoy.

If pure speed is your goal, *Turbo Magazine* will take your breath away with some of the coolest Japanese cars on the planet. Along with helpful how-to tips, *Turbo* gives no-nonsense advice on how to improve RX-7 performance (if you can get past all of that Honda crap).

Finally, *Sport and Compact Car* is an import lover's fantasy come true. Although many of the project cars the magazine features are way beyond the budget of many RX-7 fans (same with those in *Turbo Magazine*), the magazine presents a great deal of useful information that can help you with your more practical performance projects. And the editors seem to be particularly fond of RX-7s, evidenced by the series of articles (over 10 parts) that they ran in 1999–2000 devoted to their third-gen project car. You gotta love that.

Finally, www.speednation.com is the Web page devoted to providing "the truth in automotive performance." There is no advertising-driven hype here, just common-sense, dyno-tested results. We at Speednation own a Mustang dyno, and we let that do all of our talking. Neither this book nor the Web site contain advertising, so we don't have to worry about offending a manufacturer/advertiser by exposing that its product really doesn't work as claimed. Stay tuned to Speednation for updates and additional information pertaining to this RX-7 Performance Handbook.

CHAPTER THREE

Chassis and Suspension

A properly calibrated suspension and chassis are vital to realize the maximum potential of the RX-7. A chassis and suspension must be tuned and built for a mode of use—road racing, autocross, high-performance street. Even drag racers need to pay attention to their suspension, or else all that newfound power will never find its way to the pavement. Since most fuel-injected Mazdas are already fast, light, competent beasts right off the showroom floor, all other applications require just a few simple suspension tweaks to help you make better use of that power.

The RX-7's factory suspension setup is too soft for competition. Mazda knew the car appealed to enthusiasts but didn't want to deal with complaints about overly stiff ride quality.

Handling characteristics actually varied from one generation to another, since there was such a drastic

Mazda RX-7s are great-handling cars right out of the box. For competitive purposes, however, even drivers that compete in "stock" classes must do some suspension tweaking. Most rules will allow only limited modifications, such as the addition of aftermarket struts. Pictured is SCCA national-caliber driver Lindsay Lowe, threading his 1993 RX-7 through the finish gate.

change in weight, balance, and power among the three models. Essentially, when it comes to handling, they are three different cars, and we will treat them as such.

First, a word of caution: a stiffer spring setup is not for everyone. It takes a good driver to take advantage of a properly balanced suspension. The best way to sort out which suspension setup may be right for you is to take your car out to a local autocross. If the understeer you experience causes you to yearn for a more balanced car in the turns, you may be ready to change your stock spring setup. If you have fun sliding the car around a turn, then you may want to leave well enough alone. If you are not planning on doing serious racing, you should match the suspension you want to the way you drive. Of all the cars I have raced, RX-7s handle pretty well right out of the box. Serious racers should set the car up properly, then learn how to best drive the optimum setup. Many would argue that the driver should set the car up based on his or her driving style, and not the other way around. Should racers pursue one, optimum setup and then alter their driving to suit it? They should if they want to win. Put your ego aside here, and set your car up the way the guy who wins the national championship sets his up.

The best-handling RX-7s have less understeer (push), and they will oversteer (rear-end rotation) when driven with some degree of skill. The biggest problem with understeer is that, when entering a turn carrying too much speed, there is little chance to stay on the desired line. The front tires will screech and lose traction, and the car will tend to go straight. This could put you into the weeds (or worse), because when you lock up the front tires, you won't be able to steer the car.

If, on the other hand, you lose traction with the rear tires, steering is still possible. That's why with a little oversteer a good driver can go around turns carrying more speed, with more g-force, and under better control. The best way to reduce understeer is to create a balanced suspension.

This chapter can help you transform your daily driver into a weekend racer, as well as give you better control on the street. The latter element can help you better avoid obstacles in the road and get out of dangerous situations. If you want to drive fast, of course, don't do it on the road. Instead, get involved in racing (see chapter 15).

One last thing about buying a suspension setup. A good parts distributor should be able to quote you the spring rates for the suspension package you want to order. If the distributor doesn't know the spring rates, the quality of springs may be suspect. In addition, the dealer probably will not be able to give you the information and advice, so you can obtain the desired handling and suspension characteristics.

Handling Characteristics

In order to understand what contributes to your car's handling, you must be familiar with certain technical terms. One of the most important concepts is camber. Put simply, camber is the angle of your car's wheel tilt (outward or inward) from the vertical. Imagine what your car's wheels would look like if Godzilla stepped on top of your car. The bottom of the wheels (where they meet the road) would be squashed outward while the top of the wheels (nearest the top of the fender well) would be pushed inward. That condition is referred to as negative camber, and tends to counteract the effects of body roll

on your RX-7's suspension geometry. Without negative camber, only the outside portion of the outside tire will have significant contact with the pavement in a hard turn. In effect, the car "leans" over the outside of the tire as it corners, lightening the pressure on the inside contact patch—the portion of the tire touching the road. Negative camber will counteract this effect, causing the "lean" that occurs in cornering to put the whole width of the tire on the road. If your RX-7 has negative camber in the front end, the tires will appear slightly tilted while you are moving in a straight line, but as soon as you turn the wheel, the angle of the outside tire (which has to bear the force of the turn) will appear to "dig in" as you make the turn, maximizing the tire's contact patch. Positive camber, on the other hand, will allow for some wheel slippage under hard cornering, and is not typically used in any RX-7 application.

"Toe" describes the alignment of the wheels compared to the car's centerline, when viewed from above. If the fronts of the tires (toward the front of the car) are closer together than the backs of the tires, that condition is called "toe in"—as if your car were a little pigeon-toed. If the front portion of the tires is farther apart than the back, you have "toe out." A little toe in of the front tires can improve straight-line stability, but it hurts cornering ability. Toe out, by contrast, improves cornering by counteracting the inward force generated in a turn. Toe out, however, will make the car wander a bit in a straight line. Many racers prefer a little toe out to improve cornering. Too much, though, and you'll get excessive tire wear and poor straight-line handling. See the following "Alignment" section for more on toe.

Stiffness is a condition induced by stiffer sway bars, shocks, and struts. The stiffer your car's front or back end is, the more likely that end will rotate. Since most RX-7s tend to oversteer in a turn (rear end wants to come out), some racers actually remove their rear sway bars completely to decrease stiffness. Most front-wheel-drive cars, by contrast, have a tendency to plow (understeer), as the car pushes to the outside of a hard turn. These racers will stiffen the rear and loosen the front struts and sway bar to induce some oversteer.

Shocks and Struts

The first thing to try when you want to improve the handling of any generation RX-7 is to install a new set of shocks/struts. The main difference between the two is that a strut contains a cartridge insert that can be replaced if it fails, and different valving can be installed to provide specific ride and handling characteristics. Also, the top of

a strut serves as a mounting point for the top of your suspension. Ride quality should be a little stiffer, but there will be a big difference when you take the car to a track or autocross. Struts/shocks are also legal for all "stock" racing classes; springs, however, are not. Unless you intend to do a lot of racing, the struts may be all you will need. Obviously, if your car will be used primarily for racing, you may want to do the strut/spring conversion at the same time to save money. We have received e-mails from many people who were disappointed with the decrease in "streetability" after they added stiffer springs.

A strut will dampen the effects of weight transfer to a particular corner of your RX-7, both in compression and rebound. A strut will compress under braking and will rebound under acceleration. Many per-formance struts can be adjusted to control one or the other, or both.

Initially, cars from all three generations will have a few choices when it

comes to adjustable aftermarket performance struts/shocks. It is hard to recommend one over another, but the two with the best racing tradition are Tokico and Koni. In the past, Tokico had the advantage over Koni of external adjustability, whereas you had to remove the Konis in order to change their damping characteristics. On the other hand, Konis are slightly better quality. So there was a trade-off.

In the late 1990s, however, Koni also began to offer an externally adjustable strut. Make sure the strut you are interested in has this feature before you place an order. The Konis have a "non-click" damping adjuster knob on top of the strut, and this makes Konis technically "infinitely" adjustable. They also offer the option of lowering your car an additional 20 millimeters by removing an insert prior to installation. Another thing to keep in mind: Konis don't allow you to easily keep track of your settings because they have no indicator component. If you shop for Konis, compare prices with Overseas Distributing (800-665-5031), which has been a Koni dealer for 40 years.

KYB struts/shocks are also strong players in the market. Mazdatrix recommends KYB over both Tokico and Koni. The main difference is that the KYBs are adjusted from under the car, while the Tokicos, for example, adjust from the top. Depending on how your RX-7 is configured, you may have to remove your rear speakers to adjust the Tokicos.

Installation is rather simple, but the older your car is, the harder it may be to remove its current shocks/struts. We would simply recommend taking cars that grew up in the Rust Belt to a professional mechanic. Removing rusty suspension parts can be a hassle and often requires a torch.

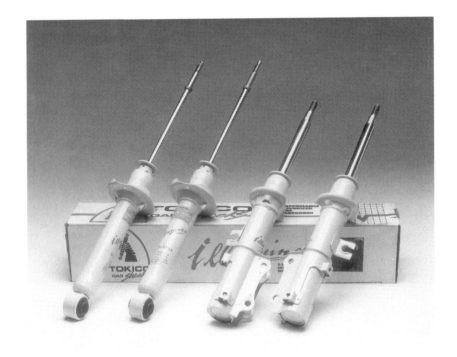

Illumina Tokico shocks/struts have five damping adjustments that can easily be changed in a matter of seconds. The fifth position provides a stiff damping rate, first position provides a soft damping rate, and the third position falls in the middle. *Racing Beat*

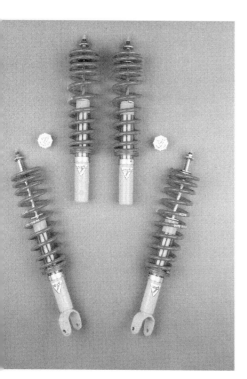

A quality Koni coil-over kit is an asset in many ways. You can fine-tune handling with a twist of a knob, which will help you feel comfortable on the street, at an autocross, or even at a driver school track event. *Courtesy Overseas Auto*

Stiffer springs are not for everybody, as they compromise streetability. The stiffer the spring, the harsher the ride. But if you want a tighter-handling car and live where the roads are smooth, the trade-off will be worth it. *Courtesy Mazda Competition Parts Department.*

Springs

As RX-7 weights changed over the years, Mazda compensated with different spring rates depending on the car, or whether it was, for example, a 1989 GTU or SE. The sport versions usually had stiffer springs and struts with improved dampening. One way to convert your 1988 SE to GTU performance is to take a trip to the boneyard, but that is probably more trouble than it's worth. Brand-new aftermarket springs are readily available to help transform your RX-7 into a flatter-cornering beast.

Keep in mind that if your car body tilts, it doesn't necessarily mean it isn't handling well. Most cars flex to some degree. At times, a twisting body, like a 1G, can add traction when driven correctly. Too much body roll is not desired and could mean that your shocks or springs are worn. The older your car, the more likely this is true.

Performance springs will also lower your car anywhere between 3/4 of an inch to an inch or 1-1/2 inches (or more). To save money, some people will cut the stock spring to lower the car, but we do not recommend this procedure. This may cause the shock to compress too far, resulting in restricted piston travel. If the springs are cut down too far, the shock can be rendered useless. In addition, the spring rate will change if you cut it, and the spring rate and travel must match a set of performance goals. It takes a great degree of mechanical acumen to successfully cut a spring for a specific performance application. For the hobbyist mechanic, it is safer and simpler to buy a shorter aftermarket spring. Although we *have* successfully cut springs, this procedure should only be attempted by a professional mechanic. There are

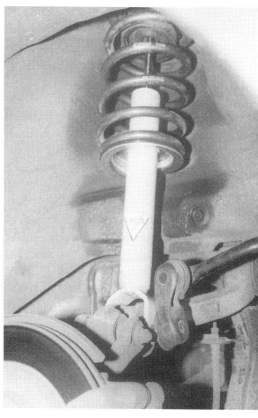

New Koni struts with Eibach springs in place on co-author Dale Black's 1993 RX-7. The procedure is not very complicated, and the end result is a drop in ride height of between 1/2 and 3/4 of an inch in front and approximately 1 inch in the rear. The Eibach springs are stiffer than stock springs, but only by 5–10 percent. Koni struts without the springs are pictured below. *Dale Black*

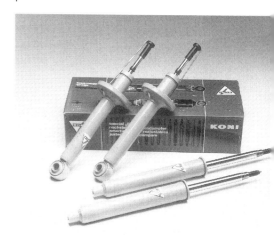

consequences to lowering your car that we will discuss later. For now, let's review each generation car and its spring rate recommendations.

First Generation RX-7

The lightest RX-7 didn't necessarily come with the lowest spring rates. The stock specs were (front/rear) 100/85. Installing aftermarket springs will increase both front and rear rates by a small percentage, depending on the brand you choose. The Big Three are Eibach, Suspension Techniques, and Racing Beat. There is a considerable difference in philosophy among these companies, although the differences will not be very noticeable off the track. Some lighter race cars use spring rates two to three times the stiffness of these RX-7 performance springs. You will notice a difference when you double a spring rate. The Suspension Techniques (ST) springs are the most streetworthy of the three. There is a dual-rate spring rate up front. This means that the spring is designed to compress more easily at first, but the more weight you add, the harder it becomes to compress. This makes for a decent compromise for a dual-duty car. The variable rate, however, will probably not perform as well on an autocross or road race course as the other two selections. Rates for the ST springs are 85/120 front and 80 for the rear. As you can see, the aftermarket rear spring is not as stiff as a stock spring. This is common for the inexpensive brands. If lowering your car is your main priority, then STs are for you, as you will see a ride-height change of 1 inch. Famous discount house J.C. Whitney Co. carries springs by Suspension Techniques. You can get a pair (front or rear) for any

RX-7 for only $80. We wouldn't recommend these springs for racing, however.

The two remaining springs for a 1G incorporate a similar philosophy, as the numbers speak for themselves. Eibachs are (f/r) 171/100 and Racing Beat (RB) offers 145/110. Both yield increased stiffness front and rear over the stock setup. The spring that makes the most sense, however, is the one from RB. Despite the reputation that 1Gs have for being tail happy (which is true, compared to many cars), in reality they still have a touch of factory understeer. The RB springs address this problem more effectively than the Eibachs. Granted, there is not a major difference. As we stated earlier, some racers use 400–500-pound springs. The difference between these two is more a matter of finesse and balance, and given that, the RB springs come out on top.

Second Generation RX-7

The concepts here are the same as in the previous section on the 1G, so let's get right down to the numbers. Stock spring specs for a 2G RX-7 are 95 front, 90 rear. This time, the variable rate springs are offered by Eibach. With 70/185 front and 85/165 for the rear, the range is impressive. Useful, probably not, but impressive. Suspension Techniques have 120s all the way around, while Racing Beat's solution is (f/r) 140/132. Who do you think has really done their homework here? Again, the nod goes to Racing Beat.

Third Generation RX-7

When it comes to spring rates, there are no absolutes on how to set up a car's suspension properly. Sometimes, a particular modification that is considered to be ridiculous will work better than the traditional solutions. Some manufacturers were not

willing to share their aftermarket spring rates with us for the 3G car, but Racing Beat was happy to share its information. Overall, increasing spring rates by 20 percent over stock (and that means for the front and rear) is a good starting point. From there, it's just a matter of continued research, development, and refinement. RB quotes (f/r) 284/212 for its aftermarket performance springs. Proven solutions for the 3G are also offered by Pettit, Farrell, and many others.

Actually, one of the top tuners in the country told me that he sees no reason to change anything on the suspension of a 3G car, despite the fact that his company sells a good deal of suspension performance parts for that car.

Adjustable Spring Perches

For street applications, an adjustable spring perch system may be overkill, as it could render your 3G uncomfortable to drive. Any of the aftermarket springs available through reputable RX-7 performance shops will likely serve your street project well. But if you are serious about improving lap times, you may benefit from a completely adjustable suspension.

These systems are available for all three generations, and there are several advantages that they can offer. First is the ability to pick the exact spring rates you want for your car. That is definitely the case with first- and second-generation cars. Since the adjustable perch uses a Carrera-type universal racing spring, you can choose 150 pound, 250 pound, or even higher. It's also very nice to be able to dial in the desired ride height. Some guys keep their cars at a stock ride height for the street, and when they go to the track, they lower it. Marking these points on the perch makes it easier to make the change, and offers more consistency when you are trying to get used to how your new springs/struts handle.

For third-gen cars, we recently installed a system marketed by Koni that can be adjusted through a range of 4 inches. The springs the system uses are Eibachs, and not even Koni has been told exactly what the rates are. In practice, the setup works very well and is available through Overseas Distributing.

Another advantage of a threaded perch setup is that you can change the cornerweights of your car. More on this below.

Anti-roll Bars

The installation of an anti-roll bar is the final component (in other words, the last step to perform) in a superior-performing rear suspension, and it is is also the simplest to install. A sway bar is one of the best ways to keep the rear of your car under control while reducing its tendency to push or understeer in the turns. Some models, such as the base model 1979–1980 RX-7, did not

come equipped with a factory rear bar. Since the base model and the GS from that year share the same chassis, a sway bar from the rear of the GS (18 millimeters) will work just fine. Beginning in 1981, first-generation cars came with a 15-millimeter bar, including the GSL-SE. Second-gen cars have a range of factory bars. The SE and Convertible had a small, 12-millimeter bar, but the Turbo, GTU, and GXL used a 14-millimeter bar. Determining which bar is right for you depends on your application and performance goals. Usually, a stiffer rear bar needs to be offset by a stiffer front bar. For the street, you can stick with the bar that is already on your car. For the track, a rear bar alone will tend to unsettle the rear. The key is to balance the suspension. If you are serious about making your car ready for the track, and have already replaced your stock struts and springs with competition parts, then an adjustable rear bar is the best choice, so you can fine-tune your handling.

There were three different-size bars used on the third generation: a 19-millimeter tubular (the one to look for) from the 1993 base and R1, a 17-millimeter bar for the 1994 base model, and a smaller, 15.9 bar for the 1994 Touring and R2 versions. Again, base your choice on what else you are planning to do to your suspension (as above). If you plan on doing nothing else, then upgrading to the 19-millimeter tubular bar is the best choice.

There are many aftermarket rear sway bars from which to choose. Most import performance shops have them in stock. You can also call your local junkyard. Addco bars are another inexpensive alternative, and in the past they have been distributed by the J.C. Whitney Co. for less than $100. We wouldn't recommend these, however, for the 3G RX-7.

Whether your goal is to drive an excellent-handling street machine or a full-blown race car, the quest for neutral steering is often realized only with the installation of a fully adjustable rear sway bar. Be aware, however, that besides the higher price ($200-plus), welding and/or hole drilling may be required to install the new bar. But then the fun begins.

Front and rear anti-roll bars (sway bars) are a great finishing touch to your suspension system. In other instances, this may be all you need to do to improve the handling of your car. Sway bars offer a great value when it comes to decreasing body roll. This set, which includes front and rear bars, can be found through Peter Farrell Supercars.

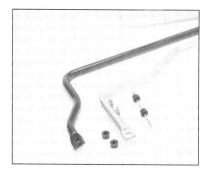

These Racing Beat sway bars come with polyurethane bushings, for a stiffer feel. The rear bar is fully adjustable—a must if you are about to enter the world of racing and haven't yet sorted out your car. *Racing Beat*

If the rear bar completes your suspension package, then a trip to the local autocross should be next on the priority list. Start with the bar in a loose setting, then tighten it up until you begin to feel the rear end bite. If the car becomes too unstable or spins, simply loosen the bar a notch until there is a compromise between understeer and oversteer. In the event that you are someday faced with having to perform a high-speed emergency maneuver on the street, you'll be glad you first sorted the car out autocrossing.

For pure race vehicles, many drivers prefer having predictable oversteer as opposed to neutral handling. With some practice left-foot braking, you can learn to make the rear of the car slide out on command while simultaneously keeping the throttle pegged. Done properly, there are few thrills in life that compare to this experience.

Finally, many RX-7s are raced successfully even with the rear bar removed. The balance of these cars is a delicate thing. Through one turn, your car could be understeering; through the next turn it could be oversteering. A sway bar should therefore be the last thing you do on the suspension.

Another consideration for 1G or 2G cars is a front strut tower brace. These were standard on 3Gs and are also found on most of today's sports cars. It's also cool to do, but a waste of time and money if you are not planning to run your car hard on a racetrack. The "flex" of an RX-7 is not necessarily a bad thing when it comes to handling, unless you're going to race.

Polyurethane Suspension Bushings

Rear stiffness can be increased by replacing the sway bar bushings with

polyurethane. The 1987–1988 cars had rubber bushings, and the 1989–1992 cars had plastic pieces. Either way, you could have a problem. The rubber bushings age, crack, and even when new have a great deal of play. The plastic bushings also crack with age. An aftermarket polyurethane kit, fortunately, will solve both problems. Sway bar mounts are relatively simple to replace, but changing the rest can be a weekend project. The old bushings (especially the ones in the control arms) usually need to be cut off. Remember to grease the new bushings when installing them, or they will squeak (great—another irritating noise) and could wear out prematurely.

Stiffer bushing material will resist excessive suspension movement that causes camber and toe changes during hard cornering. If you're racing, check the rules before you do anything, as some stock classes do not allow the substitution

A front strut tower brace is a suspension modification that is gaining popularity with the import racing crowd. For many cars, this is more of an image thing, but most 1G (left) and 2G (above) RX-7s have a degree of front-end chassis flex that can be decreased by adding this type of brace. Even 3G cars, like the one on the right, with their factory-tuned suspensions, are good candidates for a strut tower brace. After all, the R1 and R2 models came equipped with them.

of a harder compound bushing. In some cases, solid (metal) bushings are allowed. This will make your RX-7 feel like it is bolted directly to the chassis and is something only pure racers will do.

The trade-off with polyurethane bushings is that every vibration formerly absorbed by the spongy rubber bushings will be transferred along the suspension system right to the steering wheel and chassis. You will keenly be able to feel the road—every little nook and cranny, bump and pothole.

Alignment

Lowering your car can have a marked effect on both camber and toe. But don't go for an alignment until you are finished making suspension changes, and you are satisfied with ride height, wheel/tire selection, etc. Once this has been finalized, go to a local alignment shop that will tolerate your asking that minute adjustments be made with you inside the car.

That's right, sit in the car during this process, as it will ensure true settings. If you don't believe that, after the car is up in the air and the initial settings are on the screen, shift your weight a little to the right and watch those numbers change. Also make sure that your car is wearing the wheels and tires you will be using at the track. If you have installed an adjustable camber kit (recommended for pure racing, including autocross), then you're really in business.

With the alignment apparatus still attached to the wheels, have the technician slide the camber plates inward as far as they will go. You can also use aftermarket end links that can be substituted for your stock links, which will also allow for adjustability. The goal is to dial in some negative camber to the front

Camber plates are a must for serious race cars, whether autocross, Solo I, IT, or SCCA road racing. Some stock classes do not allow this modification, but as you progress to the more highly prepared classes, the ability to dial in high degrees of negative camber becomes increasingly important. This "homemade" camber plate is a work of art and incorporates an offset mount for the strut tower brace to keep it out of the way of the intake manifold.

end. Start with a degree or two, and then test your car at an autocross. You will likely need to return to try different settings until you get the feel you want. Remember, after you have finished the rest of your suspension project, alignment is the last thing to do.

The 2G cars are a little more complicated. You will still need a camber kit for the front, but the rear can be adjusted. The 2G car was engineered with active toe adjustment that automatically adjusts the rear toe as you corner. Although O.K. for the street, it does not lend itself to racing applications because you want your toe to remain as constant as possible once you set it. A rigid bar called a "toe eliminator" is available for the rear, and that will eliminate this "rear steering" design on the 2G RX-7s.

Your goal is to find a setting for the way you are going to drive your car, whether on the street or track. As

we said earlier, lowering a car will change its suspension geometry and result in both negative camber and toe out. To get your RX-7 to corner better, you may need a healthy amount of negative camber. Too much is not recommended for the street. Autocrossers like at least 1.5 degrees of negative in the front, and if possible, a degree in the rear—1Gs don't have a rear camber adjustment. This is just a starting point, and much depends on what you have done to your car. The best thing to do before you schedule an alignment appointment is to check with the guys who are racing your generation RX-7 and find out what settings they use. You may discover that the specs are all over the board. Hopefully your discussions will suggest a decent initial setup, from which you can then make subtle changes once you figure out how the car behaves.

If you want your car to do dual duty, you could always try marking

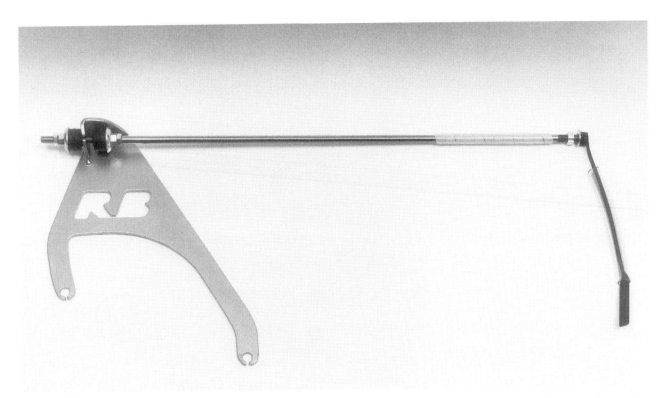

Racing Beat offers this engine torque brace that reduces, and often eliminates, that nasty "shuddering" you sometimes experience when engaging the clutch in either first gear or reverse. The braces are available for all 1979–1992 RX-7s.

the "street" and "race" location right on the camber plates. After a few races, however, you will probably get lazy (like we did) and keep the camber adjusted for racing. Your street tires will wear out faster, but you can weigh that against the value of your time spent switching the camber back and forth.

Toe is another adjustment to consider at the alignment shop. Most race cars run between 1/32- to 1/4-inch total toe out in the front. The alignment technician may fight you over this. If so, just show him this book. The more toe out you have, the quicker your car will turn in—but you don't want to go too far because that will produce excessive tire wear and straight-line wander. Experiment in small increments. Remember, do not change anything other than toe or camber in between align-

ments in order to get a true indication of what works best for your car and your driving style.

Third-gen RX-7s require a little more finesse in order to get maximum performance out of an alignment. Depending on how much power you have at your rear wheels, and whether or not your car has the upgraded/reinforced sub frame, you will need to go through some trial and error. The important question is this: How much negative camber and tow out can you get away with in the front before the rear end gets too loose? Usually, even with the front set at zero, you will experience torque steer when shifting (unstable rear end, jerking of steering wheel) due to the power you command. For racing, to keep the rear planted, you may need to dial in up to 2 degrees of negative camber and 1/4 inch of total toe in on the rear

wheels. That should induce a small amount of understeer. Start with just a little camber and toe in at the rear and then move to the front. Up front, add some negative camber and toe out (helps car turn in better) and see how far you can push it before the rear gets unstable again. If you go too far, back off the front. If you can't get the car to drift anymore (which is unlikely), you may need to back off the rear settings a little. This can be a real exercise of trial and error, as each RX-7 out there is unique. You may need to make several trips to your local alignment shop before you are satisfied. And remember, make only one change at a time, so you can keep track of the effects of each adjustment. Remember that toe out for the front and/or rear corrects for understeer, and toe in helps control oversteer.

Final Suspension Adjustment (all models)

If you've got externally adjustable struts, such as Tokico Illuminas, start with a setting of No. 3 (middle) in both the front and rear. Konis use similar arbitrary settings, so just start with a setting in between "full soft" and "full stiff." You should never crank a Koni up to full stiff, as it will overrestrict both compression and rebound. Always find the stiffest setting, and then back off a few turns. Tokicos are much easier to adjust, and you can use the No. 5 for the stiffest setting, and No. 1 for the softest. You can set a Tokico on full stiff without rendering the strut useless.

Here's another way that a trip to your local autocross can be invaluable. After each run, analyze your car's handling characteristics. Was it understeering or oversteering? If it's pushing (understeering), then make the front struts a little softer and the rear stiffer. Do the opposite to compensate for oversteer. If you have the struts adjusted all the way—front fully loose and the rear stiff—and your car is still understeering, then try some tire pressure adjustments (see next chapter). If there is still too much understeer, you will need to add a stiffer rear sway bar.

A shock tower brace is another inexpensive performance part that many rear-wheel-drive Mazda owners feel compelled to buy, unless they have a 3G, R1, or R2 model, on which they were standard. This will cut down a little on front-end flex, and add some extra stiffness. Cost is around $150–$200.

A final touch for the serious competitor is to relocate the battery for better weight distribution. Drag racers especially like to move it to the back for improved traction, but road racers and autocrossers often put the battery on the deck behind the passenger seat. The best way to determine the right location for your battery is to get the car on a set of scales and look at how the cornerweights change when you move it from place to place. Just be sure to locate it somewhere where safety is not compromised—you don't want it flying at the occupants in an accident—and isolate the positive lead so that it cannot ground itself to any adjacent metal parts.

Balancing Act

In racing, a poorly balanced car could shave some time off your life, especially in Solo I or road racing. Downshifting and hard braking at more than 100 miles per hour will exaggerate any weight imbalance your car may have, even though you may not have noticed it at slower speeds. A properly balanced car will react in a much more predictable fashion, allowing the driver to push the limits of tire adhesion without excessive twitch and roll.

So what does it take to set up a well-balanced machine? For many vehicles, all it takes is access to accurate scales and a little help from a friend. A fully adjustable suspension (threaded spring perch) doesn't hurt either. You really need to be able to raise and lower your car at will in order to take full advantage of a set of scales. So with pen and paper at hand (to record changes from inside the cockpit while your buddy reads the weights), push the car onto the scales. The heaviest weight you will ever add to your car is you, so get in and set the driver's seat to the desired driving position.

Take baseline readings, and then prepare your plan of attack. If you want to move your battery, do that first before you proceed further. Next, determine which is the heaviest corner of your car (usually the driver's side front) and lower the suspension slightly (1/2 inch) in that corner. You will be shocked by what happens. That corner gets lighter! How can that be? The car is lower to the ground. Doesn't that make that corner heavier? Actually, it's just the opposite. Repeat after me: "lower is lighter." If you're scratching your head, think of it this way: when you raise a corner, what the suspension is actually doing is pushing down harder on the scale in that corner. Thus, when you lower the corner, the suspension pushes down less in that spot. If you get that in your head, the rest of this exercise will be a piece of cake.

So where did the weight go when you lowered the driver's front corner? It went diagonally across to the passenger side rear. With some practice and a lot of trial and error, you will soon have a well-balanced car. We recommend that you don't drive yourself crazy trying to reach a "zero" or 50/50 differential. As long as you get an improvement over your baseline numbers, the task should be called a success.

Corner weighting can be a relatively simple procedure if you have an easily adjustable suspension. But if you can't take advantage of the aftermarket suspension systems or are not permitted to alter ride height, don't be too discouraged. There are still some options available.

For example, experimenting with different spring rates can also change the balance of a vehicle. This would involve much more time, since the springs would have to be removed and replaced, then the car reweighed with each combi-

A great way to improve handling is by corner weighting your car. You will need a set of scales, and a friend to record the weights of each corner while you sit in the car. Even moving the passenger seat backward or forward, removing/retaining the spare tire, and keeping the gas tank full or near empty can make a difference in balance. You can get the most out of a set of scales if you have a fully adjustable suspension, unlike this 3G. Under SCCA ProSolo restrictions for the stock class competition, the driver will have to settle for very minimal control of his car's corner weights.

nation you attempt. In principle, the stiffer the spring, the less it will be able to compress, resulting in more weight being transferred to that corner. But is it a good idea to have different spring rates on each corner of the car? Wouldn't that create instability? It depends on the course you're driving.

Circle track drivers have been doing this for years, as have road racers. Even in stock classes, some car builders shop for natural variations that can occur in stock spring rates, and bias the car based on these variations. Another trick is to use older, worn "stock" springs in some corners, and fresh new springs in others to create the desired effect. Although spring rates don't tend to change with age, spring length can, through sagging—shorten the spring over time. The reason to put a slightly shorter, or sagging, spring in one corner would be to increase corner-weight. You would have to be really serious to do that, however.

So will all this exercise actually make your car handle better? If the car is poorly balanced (like most 1G and some 2G cars), the answer is yes. But if the weight is already within 2 percent from the left to right side (that's about 60 pounds in a 3,000-pound car), be prepared to accept a trade-off if any further changes are made.

Remember the cardinal rule of fine-tuning: Changing one thing usually affects something else. So if your car understeers a little when turning right (caused by your weight in the driver's seat), you can improve this situation if you are willing to sacrifice some of the good handling you are experiencing when turning left. Here are a few lessons to keep in mind when approaching this project: 1) have a definite plan in mind before you begin, and 2) don't make too many changes at one time. There's more to corner weighting than meets the eye.

CHAPTER FOUR

Brakes

A number of high-performance brake upgrades are available for every generation of the RX-7. This does not mean that the original system is inadequate. If you drive an RX-7 primarily on the street, a substantial upgrade is not necessary. The RX-7's stock brake system provides competent performance on the street.

The main thing to keep in mind when upgrading your brakes is balance. The various components of a braking system—calipers, pads, rotors, fluid—are designed to work as an integrated system. If you enhance the performance of one component, another part of the system may be overwhelmed. Therefore, if you choose to upgrade your brakes, be sure that all the parts of the system you end up with are compatible.

Your brakes must be able to handle the demands you put on them. The first step in helping them meet that requirement is regular maintenance. Check the fluid level often, and flush your entire system every two to three years to avoid moisture buildup. Moisture in the brake lines can decrease stopping power and corrode brake components and lines from the inside. Calipers and pads should be checked annually, and rotors should be cut whenever new pads are installed, or replaced if they are too worn or warped. With routine maintenance, your original braking system is fine for street duty, especially in 2G and 3G cars. There are a few situations, however, where brake upgrades are either recommended or required.

Increase Horsepower, Increase Brake Power

Any time you boost horsepower, you are likely to put more of a strain on your brakes. Additional strain is especially significant with the first-generation cars, as their pads and rotors are small for the weight of the car.

Performance brake pads may alleviate the problem, but these pads can be a pain to live with on a day-to-day basis. Yes, they'll stop your car faster than stock pads, but they make a squeal that sounds like you have a pebble caught between the pad and rotor. And there is one other drawback: they can warp your stock—or even aftermarket—rotors. More on this later. Often, it's easier in the long run to buy larger and more efficient calipers, along with a bigger rotor. Make sure before you install them that

Cross-drilled rotors are a favorite among hop-up enthusiasts, but they are not for everyone. If you are getting them just to make your car look cooler, then go for it. But most RX-7 drivers will never have the need to go to this extreme. This modification should be low on the priority list unless you are a road racer or have substantially increased horsepower and need that extra stopping power. Keep in mind that this modification often chews up brake pads faster than the stock setup. *Stillen*

Bigger rotors and competition calipers/pads are a necessity for road racers.

they'll fit within your rims. Oversize brake components may create clearance problems for stock wheels.

You should also consider upgrading your brakes if you add a turbocharger to your car. Given the fact that you will likely be going faster, it follows that you'll be asking more of your brakes. Probably the soundest approach to a brake upgrade in this situation is to acquire the braking system (calipers/rotors) from the RX-7 turbo car or sport version that corresponds to your model. Following are some examples.

Upgrading the 1981–1985 1G's brakes is relatively simple, at least to start. All you need to do is to find the entire rear axle from a 1984–1985 GSL-SE, and while you're at it, buy the front rotor and calipers, too. The SE was built for both speed and stopping power, and its vented discs are nearly 1 inch bigger in the front and over 3 inches bigger in the rear. The 1979–1980 1Gs didn't even have disc brakes in the rear, so the axle swap is a major improvement for these cars. And as a bonus, you get the SE's limited-slip dif-

ferential! Transplanting an axle is not an easy task, but most weekend mechanics can figure it out with the help of a good shop manual. Be advised that Mazda changed the brake-line threads in 1981, so you'll have to replace or retap the threaded connections when doing any brake swap using the newer systems.

For 2G cars, the GTU, Turbo, and GLX all had bigger brakes than the 1986 base model and its sisters, the 1987–1990 SE models. In 1991, there were bigger brakes all around, so look for these in the boneyard. Or you can just buy brand-new aftermarket calipers and rotors.

For the 1993–1995 RX-7, the best choice is to go with aftermarket pads. As described above, the "competition" pads may be so hard and make so much noise that you will want to take them off and throw them away. An intermediate pad will probably meet your needs and be more civilized. Ask your favorite Mazda performance dealer about your choices.

Road Racing

If you push your braking system beyond normal limits, such as in road racing, track events, or driver schools, an upgrade is required. The heat generated from constant high-speed racing has been known to melt a wheel's center cap, warp a rotor, boil brake fluid, or even turn a brake pad into dust. Late-model 2G and all 3G RX-7s have decent stock braking systems, so all that may be needed is to change to a performance brake pad.

Autocrossers usually do not need, or want, a harder pad. The reason is that the performance pads are designed to disperse heat better than stock pads, so they do not heat up as easily. In Solo II, you want pads that will heat up fast so that you can drive deeper even into the first turn without fear.

For road racing, a stock pad will heat up and stay hot, causing the brake fluid to boil and making it impossible to stop. Road racers often come into the pits with their rotors

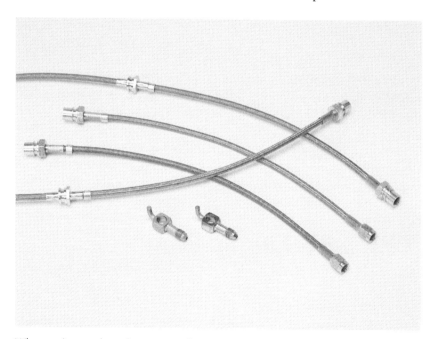

When racing, pads and rotors can become red hot. Under those harsh conditions, stainless steel brake lines will contain brake fluid that could blow out stock rubber lines. Brake cooling ducts will help cool your pads and rotors when you are heading down the straightaway, increasing the chances that you will have some braking power by the time you reach the next sharp turn. *Courtesy of Mazda Competition Parts*

glowing bright red. Recently we observed a 3G RX-7 come upon a part of course where the driver needed to do some hard and sustained braking in order to make the approaching turn. It was easy to see both sparks and flames light up the calipers in a circular pattern as the performance pads attempted to combat inertia. Stock rotors, pads, and fluid were not designed to withstand this degree of heat, and will sometimes fail.

A solution that is gaining popularity among racers and "track time" junkies is to convert to multiple piston calipers. This can improve the way the pad contacts the rotor, resulting in more even distribution of caliper force along the rotor surface. Some of the newer aftermarket braking systems use two or more pads per side, further increasing contact patch and overall grip. But be careful not to go overboard. Discuss your plan with your favorite performance shop before you buy. It is important not to stray too far from the original design as you will find (as we continue to stress) that you may create another

Here's a brake conversion that is gaining popularity with the RX-7 crowd. This 3G sports some cool Volk TE37 wheels, but if you look a little closer, you can see Porsche brakes. Say what you want about that German automaker, but they do make great braking systems.

weak link in the system, such as your brake fluid not being able to provide adequate force to compress the calipers.

So what are the popular choices for brake upgrades? Road racers seem to agree that there are two good choices. Although the Porsche 911 big brake conversion will stop your car in record time, these brakes weigh considerably more than the brakes offered by Pettit Racing and Peter Farrell Supercars.

Aftermarket Brake Pads and Rotors

What harm could possibly be done by investing in a trick set of brake pads? You would expect these high-quality, expensive pads to stop your car quicker and with less brake fade. This is often the case, but there is a hidden price to pay.

Everyone knows that friction is required to make brakes operate properly. Friction, however, causes wear. A stock RX-7 braking system is designed to wear the stock pads, but if you upgrade to performance pads, you may be wearing your rotors. That's a devil's bargain, since pads are cheaper and easier to replace than rotors.

Another common problem with using competition brake pads on the street is that your rotors may warp. One solution to this problem is to buy performance rotors, then send them off for cryogenic treatment. This process uses liquid nitrogen, followed by heat, to harden the rotor, and this allows the rotor to resist warping.

Another solution is to simply stick with the stock pads and replace them more often. Performance pads and rotors will lower your 60–0 mile-per-hour times, but your needs may not justify the cost—unless you're a racer. If you race, you have no choice. You must have the best brake system possible. In your list of priorities, a better set of tires will give you more for your

money, so long as your current braking system is up to the task at hand.

There are many different brake pads on the market, composed of everything from asbestos (old type) to Kevlar, the new compound in town. Kevlar pads won't wear the rotors as much as a high-performance metallic pad, but will provide increased stopping power once they get warm. But they are expensive, and when cold, will not stop the car faster than the stock OEM pads. As a general rule, the cheaper the cost of the pad, the more the pad tends to wear and the less it wears the rotors.

We are often asked about the advantages of cross-drilled rotors. Why do small holes drilled in the rotors improve performance? Cross-drilled rotors pick up pockets of air, which cool the pads as well as the rotor itself. A cooler pad and rotor combination should then be expected to stop the car better. That's not always the case, however. The reason is that every hole, while it moves cooling air, represents brake surface area that no longer makes contact with the pads. Therefore, as long as your stock pad is not overheating and causing brake fade (vapor lock), you should be able to stop quicker than the guy with drilled rotors. If heat is an issue, then cross-drilled rotors may be the way to go. Keep in mind that cross-drilled rotors can eat up brake pads. And don't forget about your ABS system. As with most other items in the engine bay, the ABS unit should be protected from the heat. Excessive heat could cause the ABS to malfunction or fail.

And speaking of heat, the fastest way to ruin your new system is to drag race from light to light. If you bring your car to a screeching halt, and then sit at the next light with your foot on the brake waiting for it to turn green, you may as well just throw money out the window. Your pads and rotors will be red hot, and

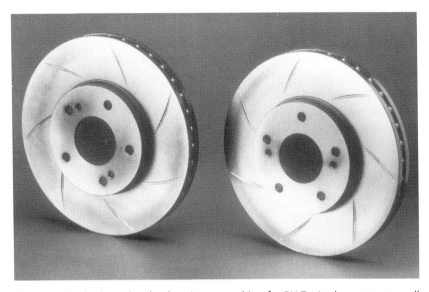

Carbon-kevlar brake-pad technology is a great thing for RX-7s. In the recent past, all that was available for improved stopping power was the carbon-metallic pad, which could easily warp rotors under heavy braking—especially for drivers who race from one traffic light to the next and leave their foot on the brake in between times. That leaves a hot spot on the rotor while the rest of the rotor is allowed to cool. The result is warpage. Slotted rotors help cool the pads as you brake, and are a good compromise over drilled rotors, which can sometimes hurt braking since there is less rotor surface to contact the pads.

as you sit, most of the rotor will cool except for the part that is being pinched by the pads. There is no faster way to warp a rotor.

Possibly the best and cheapest way to control brake fade and avoid rotor warpage on the track or the street is to use an air-ducting system to cool your pads and rotors. The more air you can blow across your system, the better. Don't underestimate this simple solution. For street applications, it may be all you really need. You can cut a hole in the car's front air dam, install a small metallic

flex hose, and aim the other end at your calipers. Road racers should use a larger diameter hose, if rules allow. Most aftermarket front spoilers have slots near the brakes that help direct air to the pads to help with cooling.

Steel-Braided Lines

A lot of the "mushy" feel of your brakes could be due to the expansion of your rubber brake hoses under hard braking. The fluid could also be trashed, but the likely suspect is the flex of your stock rubber lines. Replacing them

with braided stainless steel lines will eliminate a great deal of that flex, and give your brake pedal a much better feel. If you do a lot of high-speed braking (road racing, track time events), this project should be on your priority list. Older RX-7s that have cracks in the car's visible rubber components probably have some cracking in the brake lines as well. When was the last time you checked them? In addition to greater strength, steel hoses also look great and will still be shiny when your infant son or daughter grows up and asks for the keys. If you are uncomfortable with doing the installation yourself, don't fear, a good speed shop or brake shop is experienced in swapping brake lines. Of course, if you replace a line, you should bleed the entire system and replace the fluid.

Large Caliper and Pad Upgrades

In theory, the bigger the pad and caliper, the more surface will contact the rotor, and the quicker you will stop. For this reason alone, the conversion to aftermarket "big brake" systems is gaining popularity, especially with third-generation owners. Why? Mostly just because it's possible. As we stated before, the 3G braking system is excellent, but if you increase power and tend to drive like you are on a race track, your brakes could become the weak link in your project car. Road racers do seem to want the biggest and hardest surface they can find to help them stop quicker. But does this theory hold water for the street? Yes and no. Yes, it will decrease stopping distance if your current brake system is not able to lock up the brakes at high speed. And if you *are* able to lock 'em up, that doesn't mean your brakes are the problem.

The weak link could be your tires. The stickier the tires, the harder it is to lock the brakes, which is why racers upgrade. Set your brake/tire priorities based on what you are planning to do with your car. The best bet is to get tires suited to your purposes after checking applicable competition rules. Then, if you experience braking problems, look into upgrading that system (again in accordance with the rules).

Another important thing to consider is that the large rotors used by most of the aftermarket big brake kits increase the unsprung and inertial weight of each corner. For that reason, this type of conversion is not recommended for autocrossing purposes. Rotating weight affects performance and should be minimized whenever possible. The stock rotors for third-generation RX-7s have been engineered to keep mass low while maximizing stopping power. For the street or Solo II applications, we don't recommend changing them.

Finally, some of the aftermarket big brake conversion systems may require you to change to 17-inch wheels for caliper clearance. That will be an additional expense that should be figured into the cost of the conversion. But check with the manufacturer first, as we have heard of many instances where there have been clearance problems.

Brake System Conversions

The Lipperini family out of Wilkes-Barre, Pennsylvania, has engineered one of the coolest brake conversions we have seen. A major road racing and hill-climbing family, Dan Sr., Dan Jr., and Joel Lipperini became RX-7 enthusiasts during the 1990s. Racing seems to breed experimentation and ingenious low-buck ways to make your cars work better. One week, with some minor fabrication, the Lipperinis converted their first generation GT-3 car's braking system to one that was originally fitted to a Nissan 300 ZX. The results were so impressive that the current owner of the car still uses the system.

Another popular conversion is to use Porsche 911 calipers. As mentioned earlier, this conversion is effective, but the Porsche parts are heavier than the stock calipers and rotors. Add weight to your car only if you feel the trade-off is worth the gain. In this case, you would be forcing your car to overcome more initial resting inertia on acceleration.

Brake Fluids

There are definite advantages to replacing your stock brake fluid with a synthetic or high-performance product. Brake fluids are graded based on their boiling point. Regular fluids are fine for regular driving, but when you add either more weight or power to your car, you increase the stress on your brakes. If you live in a part of the country that is particularly hilly, such as San Francisco or Pittsburgh, you could also benefit from a fluid that resists boiling.

Regular brake fluid will barely make it to 300 degrees Fahrenheit before boiling, but the popular hi-performance brands, such as Castrol, will go to about 440 degrees Fahrenheit. The best fluid we tested was Motul synthetic, which resists boiling up to 570 degrees Fahrenheit. Compare the boiling

You should select your brake fluid based on what type of driving you do. Harder and sustained braking, such as in road racing, will tend to boil standard brake fluid. Synthetic fluids, like those pictured, have different boiling points. Read the labels carefully before you choose.

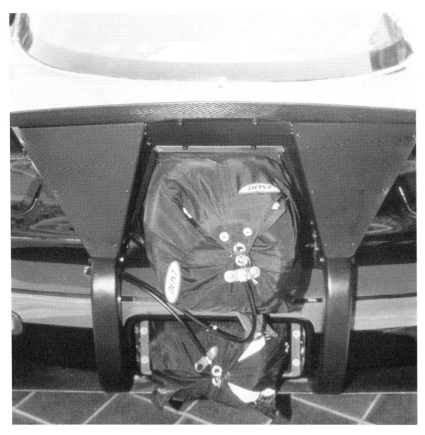

Slowing down from 240 miles per hour can be tough on brakes. Actually, they would probably catch fire, melt, then completely disintegrate—and you would still be going 100 miles per hour. This was Jim Mederer's solution to slow down his triple rotor, triple turbo 3G at the Bonneville Salt Flats. *Racing Beat*

point of the synthetic fluids in your local parts store to see which is best for your application.

When brake fluid boils, it produces vapor lock because the boiling fluid gives off a gas, and that gas becomes trapped in pockets within your brake lines. When you then push on the brake pedal, the gas pockets compress, rather than sending the force you exerted along the fluid to your calipers. Thus, less fluid compresses the piston in the caliper and braking force is reduced.

All brake fluids are rated by the Department of Transportation (DOT), and have been assigned grades based on performance standards. As time has passed, performance and grade numbers have increased. DOT 5 brake fluid meets all the latest standards set by the U.S. Department of Transportation. Never use a standard lower than is recommended for your car. Once you've established a baseline, choose your fluid based on the boiling point and whether or not you want synthetic or standard fluid.

Conclusions

If you decide you need to upgrade your system, make sure you maintain a balance among the components. Check with your favorite rotary tuner (Pettit, PFS, Racing Beat, etc.) to get a system designed to match your purposes (street, track, autocross, drag). If you are planning to do most of your driving on the street, don't use race pads, calipers, and rotors. If you plan to do some road racing or track events, on the other hand, your stock system will likely be inadequate. In short, the harder your stress your brakes, the more likely you will need an upgraded system. Whether it's better to retrieve one from a boneyard or order something new will depend on your purposes, and how much time and money you have to spend.

CHAPTER FIVE

Wheels and Tires

Choosing the right wheels is a little more complicated than selecting parts that don't play an aesthetic role on your car. There are a lot of attractive aftermarket wheels that can personalize your RX-7, and there is also a selection of wheels that perform well in competition. The overlap between these two categories is more limited. The soundest approach with respect to wheels is to make performance your primary concern, and appearance secondary. In other words, follow your head first, and then your heart.

If you're going to compete, you need a wheel that's strong and light enough to go the distance without undue risk of failure. Determine how you're going to use your wheels first. Then, once you've established what you need in a wheel, choose the style you like best among those that meet your specifications. And don't forget to consider tires before you purchase wheels. The width and profile you want in a tire will determine the best wheel size to buy, and vice versa.

Wheels for the Street

For general street use, the aftermarket wheel choices available for the RX-7 seem limitless, almost overwhelming. Wheels cost between $200 to upwards of $4,000 for a set of four. But how do you decide what wheel and tire combination is best for your car?

If you do not have a set budget for your project, then looks can be your priority. The particular design of the wheel selected should be one that enhances the overall look that you have planned for your vehicle. Then shop around, as prices can vary as much as $100 per set for the more expensive brands.

But if you have taken the advice in chapter 2 and created a budget, then this budget will help dictate what wheels will best meet your needs. After buying the stereo, spoiler kit, Farrell intercooler, and Racing Beat exhaust, you may find that you won't have enough money left over to get expensive wheels. Then again, wheels may be more important than that stereo. A budget is all about compromise—remember, you need to have enough money (or credit) to go have fun with your car after the project is finished.

One of the big decisions that will come into play when planning a wheel purchase is the diameter of the rim. A large diameter wheel, without a small profile tire, will change the final drive ratio of your transmission—the larger the wheel, the fewer revolutions it will make to maintain a certain speed.

Wheel and tire choices are numerous. The solution for a given car is often as unique as its driver. Combinations can range from expensive aftermarket 3G rims with low-profile, high-performance tires to the classic look of stock 1G alloys with basic street rubber.

3G owners often decide to change from 16-inch to 17-inch wheels. From what we have seen, there is no performance benefit from such a switch, but they do fill up the fender more than the stock rims.

your car can grab. The wider the tire, the greater the contact patch. And in turn, the better it should hold the road. For street use, however, wide tires are unnecessary. They may look cool, but they're more expensive. Wide tires also do poorly on snow, if you live in a part of the country where that's an issue.

Wheels for the Third Generation

Since the 3G is a totally different creature than the other two body styles, we need to review some specifics based on our experience in RX-7 racers and high-performance street cars. The stock wheel is a 16x8-inch alloy with a 50-millimeter offset, and although there are few options for aftermarket wheels, you have to be careful with the offset (backspace). As you increase the width of the wheel, that extra inch or two needs to go somewhere. It is either tucked inward toward the suspension, or extends outward beyond the fender well (wider track). Obviously, there is a limit before

A tire with a greater circumference will throw off many of your vehicle's systems, including the speedometer and odometer. It will give a reading that is too low because your car is traveling farther with each tire revolution than the system acknowledges. You'll put more stress on your transmission because it will have to work harder

from a stop to turn the larger tires. When shifting, however, you'll be able to go a little faster in first and second before changing gear. Also, your tires and wheel bearings should last longer because your wheels will make fewer revolutions.

In competitive situations, wheel width is very important, as it determines how much pavement

Pictured are six different 3G RX-7s, with five different wheel styles. When it comes to expressing your personality, selecting wheels for the street is a safe place to exercise your individuality. In other performance areas, you often must choose function over form.

you are rubbing the strut (inside) or running over curbs (outside). For 8-inch-wide wheels, the maximum offset should not exceed 35 millimeters (front and rear). For 9-inch rims, that max offset is 45/40 millimeters (f/r), and for 10-inch it is 45 millimeters for the rear. A 10-inch rim is not recommended for the front.

For height, you need to follow the guidelines we'll discuss in the next section to insure that your 17- or 18-inch rim/tire combination does not rub on the bottom lip of the fender well.

Tires Basics

What tires are best? As you no doubt guessed, the answer depends in part on what type of driving you want to do. Generally, you get what you pay for. But if you buy expensive tires expecting them to be good for both street and occasional track use, you will probably be disappointed. Tires come in different compounds. A softer compound will offer better handling, but will wear out sooner than a harder tire—think of all the tires race cars go through in a single race. And a racing tire may handle well on dry pavement, but not on wet.

So how do you decide? Forget the hype claiming that one tire is so much better than another. We have been participants and judges in many tire tests, and when comparing tires of similar design and compound, we have usually found no significant difference among the major brands. That is not to say that purpose-built tires don't excel, or do poorly, in particular applications. A Bridgestone Blizzak will outperform a Pirelli P6 on an icy road. But the P6 will do better on dry pavement.

The real difference between tires occurs within a particular company's product line, rather than across major brands. The cheapest Goodyears offer only a fraction of the performance of that company's best tires. But the top-of-the-line performance tire offered by BFGoodrich (BFG), Goodyear, Yokohama, Michelin, and Nitto all compare favorably. Once you narrow down all the brands that make a tire for the particular use you have in mind, go pick the tire that is on sale, or that has a "cool" name. It's very similar to choosing which sneaker you want. And forget that crap about Japanese tires performing better on Japanese cars, because it is just not true. Some of the best-handling RX-7s

in the country run on Hoosier racing tires. Anyway, many of the so-called "American" tire companies are actually owned by companies outside the United States. With all the mergers among the world's big companies, you really need a scorecard to keep track of who owns whom.

So the first thing to do before choosing a tire is to decide what type of driving you want to do. If you don't plan on doing any racing, then a harder compound will fit nicely. You won't compromise traction in the rain and snow as long as you stick with good name brands. If you care more about handling than tire wear, select a softer compound performance tire. Be careful, however, when using these softer compound tires on your daily driver. Performance in the dry will be superior—if not exhilarating—but under any other conditions, you could be putting yourself at risk. If you live in California or Arizona, go for it. But for Seattle and Pittsburgh residents, a more conservative compound would be a better choice. Ask your tire dealer about available compounds before buying.

Trying to compare figures for wear among brands can be difficult. Each manufacturer has its own system

The two wheels pictured were both Mazda OEM alloys for 1993 RX-7s. Viewing the back of each wheel reveals that the one on the right seems slightly more reinforced. Mazda changed wheel subcontractors halfway through the 1993 production year, since the lighter rims had a tendency to crack. The stronger wheel weighs 1.5 pounds more than the earlier wheel. *Dale Black*

Excellent examples of high-performance street rubber (left to right): the BFGoodrich g-Force T/A KD, Yokohama AVS Sport, and Bridgestone Potenza S-02. *Courtesy of the Tire Rack - www.tirerack.com*

of grading wear, which is an indication of how hard or soft a tire may be. There is no standard. A "250" wear rating on a Goodyear tire may not compare to a 250 on a BFGoodrich. But within the same brands, the ratings are more useful. For example, a BFG tire rated at 250 is softer than a BFG rated at 300.

Tire sizes can also be very confusing. Take, for example, a 225/50/15 tire, compared to a 205/50/15. The second number in this tire formula—"50"—is called the series, or more technically, the aspect ratio. It indicates the tire's sidewall height as a percentage of the tire's tread width. A 50 series tire has a sidewall height equal to half its tread width. A tire is wider, or the profile is lower, or both, as the series number decreases. The first number in the size code is the tire width in millimeters. The first tire is 225 millimeters wide, while the second has a tread width of 205 millimeters. From here, we can figure out the sidewall height, or profile, of the tire. Being 50 series tires (profile is 50 percent of tread width), the first has a sidewall height of 112.5 millimeters, and the latter 102.5 millimeters. Both fit on 15-inch wheels but the first tire is

both wider and bigger around—total tire and wheel diameter is 20 millimeters more (10 millimeters taller in profile at both the top and bottom of the wheel) for the 225 tire.

The bigger your wheels, the smaller the profile you're likely to require. To fit 19-inch rims on your car, you need to go to a series 40 or even series 35 tire, so that the entire package will actually fit under your fender well without rubbing. The Michelin Pilot SXL MXX3 or BFGoodrich Comp T/A ZR, both excellent tires, come in the popular size 255/40/19, which is only 102 millimeters tall. The sidewall is therefore a full 10 millimeters shorter than the above 225/50/15. As a comparison, if you did not want to go as radical as a 19-inch wheel, the Nitto Extreme Performance ZR and the Goodyear F1 GS (again, excellent products) make a 255/45/17, which has a sidewall that is approximately 115 millimeters tall. Michelin, BFG, Pirelli, Dunlop, and Yokohama also stock similar sizes.

Let's play with a few numbers to show what's involved in an informed tire decision. Let's say you and your friend have identical RX-7s. He has 17-inch wheels mounted with a set of

255/45/17 tires, and they look great. There doesn't seem to be any way to fit a larger wheel under the car without running into problems. But you want to go one step more radical than your friend, and wonder if somehow there's a way a 19-inch rim could fit.

In order to calculate the overall diameter of your wheel and tire combination, you need to convert your wheel size from inches to millimeters. One inch equals 25.4 millimeters. The wheels you want to buy are 2 inches larger than his, but in reality, only 1 inch will stick up into your fender well. The other inch will lift your car off the ground by an extra inch. That's because the distance from the center of a 17-inch wheel to the outer edge of the rim is only 8.5 inches. The radius of a 19-inch rim is 9.5 inches. So overall, your 19-inch wheels will only reach up an extra inch toward the top and sides of your wheel well.

Now for the hard part. In order to retain the same overall look, what tire size must you use? Your friend's 255/45/17 tires have a 115-millimeter sidewall (255 millimeters x .45). Add 216 millimeters to this (8.5 inches x the conversion factor of 25.4

millimeters) and you get a 331-millimeter radius. With a 255/40/19, you add the height of the sidewall (102 millimeters) to the radius of the 19-inch wheel (9.5 inches x 25.4 millimeters) and you get a radius of 343 millimeters. That's an extra 12 millimeters, or a little less that half an inch. If you don't think that will fit, you could raise your suspension an extra half-inch (if you have an adjustable suspension), get different springs, or consider an 18-inch wheel with a 255/40/18 that will be essentially the same size. But here's the kicker: some tires "seat" lower in wheels than other tires (like the Michelin Pilot). Also, if you buy a wider wheel, the tire will usually seat lower than if you chose a narrower rim.

So decide how you want to use your tires and wheels. Then measure the opening you have to work with, do the math as above, and call a reputable dealer and ask questions. Feel free to then shop around, but don't immediately go with the best price. Good customer service on your tire purchase is important. If the company with the cheapest prices can't answer your detailed questions, look for another shop that makes you comfortable. If you run into problems, the shop that gave you good service can probably help you more than the shop that knew nothing more than its own low prices.

Wheels and Tires for the Track—Autocrossing

Generally, if you want to compete in a stock class, you will be restricted to retaining your stock rim size. But check with the SCCA first before spending any money. The SCCA is also known for making changes in the competition rules from year to year that could make the wheels you used last year (or even your entire car) either ineligible or uncompetitive the following year.

Since alloy wheels are lighter than steel wheels, we recommend them. The factory 3G RX-7 alloys are excellent for autocrossing in stock classes. You would think that some of the more expensive aftermarket wheels would be lighter, but you would be wrong. Stick with the stock wheels.

Interestingly enough, there were two different wheel manufacturers of OEM 1993–1994 3G RX-7 wheels. You have to know what to look for to see any difference from the outside. It's unclear why this happened, but our best guess is that they opted for a different design because of complaints that some wheels were actually cracking. Both wheels were still used on 1994 cars, probably because Mazda wanted to use up its stock. The stronger wheel looks the same on the surface, but on the backside reveals a reinforced spoke design.

For stock classes, use the wheel you have; just mount up a low-profile tire, and you are ready to go racing. Some clubs offer "street tire" classes, so you can use the same rubber on the track that you use on the road, saving you from changing wheels when you get to the track. Even the older first-generation alloys (as ugly as they are) make good choices for stock Solo II competition.

If you want to be more competitive, here is the short list of tires with the highest percentage of recent stock-class wins: BFGoodrich R1, Hoosier Autocrosser, Hoosier Radial, Kumho Victor, and Toyo Proxies. The Nitto R-type drag radial also shows some promise, but Nitto is still behind BFG and Hoosier in soft compound race tire development. During the 1990s, Yokohama made some changes in its first-generation A008R, but chose not to keep pace with the top dogs. The race tire market changes from year to year, so you may want to check with your local autocross club to see what the current hot tires are, or you can go online with one of the autocross discussion forums, such as www.team.net.

There are several differences among the top three brands of

Revolutions are among the most popular wheels for autocross, Solo I, or IT racing. Reasonably priced ($450–$650/set depending on size), strong and lightweight, this three-piece alloy is a sure bet for the track.

autocross tire—BFGoodrich, Hoosier, and Kumho. Kumhos wear better and last much longer. For that reason, they are an excellent choice if you decide to add some track events to your autocross schedule. Hoosiers and BFGs tend to be too sticky for driver schools and track time events.

BFG lays claim to the most stock class wins since the mid-1980s, but unless your tires are properly heat cycled (it's complicated; ask BFG), they could develop the dreaded "groove of doom." Your brand-new tire could begin to separate near the center tread-line, exposing the steel cord below. Once any of your tires shows cord anywhere, you will not be allowed to compete until the tire is replaced.

Hoosier radials made an impact on autocrossing in the late 1990s, but will sometimes wear inconsistently, or wear out too quickly. The most consistent performer of the group, and in our opinion the stickiest gumball you can buy, is the Hoosier Autocrosser.

This tire's non-radial, bias-ply construction has clear advantages over a radial, the best of which may be its weight. For a 1G RX-7, the very popular 225x45x13 size weighs nearly 5 pounds less per tire than the BFGoodrich R-1, Kumho, or Hoosier Radial. All these tires are excellent examples of racing rubber, but they are heavier and add rotating weight to your car, which for a racer is the worst kind of weight.

For the heavier 2G and 3G RX-7s, however, the Hoosiers may tend to wear out too quickly and they could get "greasy" when pushed to the limit. A good principle to keep in mind is that the more horsepower you have, the quicker your tires will wear. The rears will give up some rubber trying to get the power down to the pavement, and the front tires will be working even harder maintaining traction in the turns. The faster your car can make that turn, the more wear your front tires will

see. Add the weight of the 3G car to that equation, and the degree of wear increases. So for most turbo 2G and 3G RX-7s, a BFG or Kumho could be the better choice, but buy the "heat-cycled" from a reputable place like the Tire Rack.

If you decide to leave the stock class and move up to street prepared, there are no restrictions on wheel size. SCCA street prepared history has proved that for most 1G RX-7s, the best choice in wheel size is 13 inch. For a 2G car, your choice should be a 15-inch, as opposed to 16 or 17. This is because the smaller diameter wheel will provide better low-end torque, which is a very valuable commodity in autocrossing.

Specifically, 15x8 for the front, and 15x10 for the rear seems to be a successful combination for a 2G car, while 1G RX-7s are very happy with 13x8 rims all the way around. One of the best wheel distributors, in our opinion, is the Taylor Corporation. Bryan Taylor distributes Duralight and Lite Speed modular racing wheels, which in the sizes above weigh less than 14 pounds each.

We chose our wheel sizes carefully based on extensive testing with RX-7s. Although Revolution Wheels are the most popular choice among autocrossers, the Taylor rims are the best-constructed wheels we have ever seen. The problem is that they can be pricey—nearly $300 each. On the other hand, a used set of 15x8 or 13x8 Revolutions can often be found for around $450, and this would be a great choice to get started. But don't go smaller than 8-inch, unless there is a wheel restriction in your class (as in SCCA's IT road racing).

If drag racing is your bag, you may want to select your wheels based on the rpm at which you cross the finish line (see the racing

We wish we could get free tires for saying this, but we can't. We only say it because it's true: Hoosier bias-ply tires are the best for a 1G Solo I or II race car. The 2G and 3G cars are heavier, so radials would be a better choice for them.

chapter). A set of 13-inch wheels will always give you faster 0–60 times, but they may cause you to make an extra shift before reaching the 1/4-mile mark.

There are times when a larger-diameter wheel would be preferable. Some high-speed courses may require an extra downshift before a particular turn. That can waste precious time. In this scenario, a larger-diameter wheel could be used to change your final drive in the other direction, helping you to avoid that extra shift. The only problem with putting this theory into practice is that you have to bring along different-size wheels and tires to events.

For third-generation cars, 16- or 17-inch wheels work extremely well. The car was designed to use 16-inch alloys, and the gearing was carefully calibrated to give good torque throughout the entire rpm range at this wheel size. Even the most competitive modified 3G cars don't go higher than 17x10 rims. The stock 16x8-inch wheels with a 245/45/16 work well for most autocross applications. Higher-powered 2G turbo cars could also successfully use 16x8 or 16x10 wheels in the Street Prepared and Prepared classes (remember, it is harder to rotate a 16-inch wheel than a 13-inch one).

Racing Slicks

At events or in classes where the use of DOT (Department of Transportation) -approved tires is not required, then racing slicks are the best choice. They can also be much cheaper, especially if you buy used. It is not often that one service stands out above all others, but when it comes to used slicks, we have to mention John Berget Tire (414) 740-0180, out of Wisconsin. The price of a new slick is usually around $130-plus each, but you can get two for that price through Berget. John also has access to new slicks at discount prices. They are sent COD (cash on delivery) to your door in only a few days, and for good customers, he will often throw in a free tire from time to time.

Are slicks that much better than the DOT-approved autocross tires mentioned above? Yes, and for one good reason. They have no tread. The tread on a tire will flex when you throw your car into a hard turn, causing some tread squirm and loss of traction. Since slicks have no tread, they avoid this problem.

If you are new to the sport, we recommend that you don't go out and buy a new set of street tires for autocrossing. A full-treaded tire will slip and screech all over the track, and although this can be entertaining for the spectators, it does not translate into fast times. If you are on a very tight budget, then use the baldest, used street tires you can find, as long as they don't show cord (this can be dangerous, as exposed cord can cause a blowout). You won't be competitive, but you will sure have fun.

There are several good slicks on the market, but despite our love for Hoosier Autocrossers, we have to give the nod to Goodyear when it comes to pure race tires. Over the years, the Goodyear slicks have demonstrated two big advantages over their competitors. First, they resist heat-cycling. This is a problem for the BFG DOT R1 tires. And unlike Hoosier Autocrossers, Hoosier slicks seem prone to harden once they have been heated and cooled several times throughout the season. The other problem with Hoosier slicks is that they tend to leak air.

As far as rubber compounds go, both Hoosier and Goodyear offer some excellent choices. From super sticky (used for qualifying or autocrossing) to endurance tires (harder, tend to last longer), there are several compounds from which to choose. Typically, the lower the com-

Goodyear slicks are one of the better choices for full-blown racing. Pictured here are cantilever tires that "wrap around" the rim, extending the contact surface by several inches. That way, you can use a smaller wheel (often specified by SCCA for "prepared" classes) but still get the benefit of a much wider wheel.

pound number, the stickier the tire. Of course, the stickier the tire, the quicker it wears out.

For the racers who have 13x7-inch wheels and feel like they can't be competitive because their budget won't allow for 15x10-inch slicks, there is an alternative. Cantilever slicks are designed to fit on a 7-inch rim, but actually extend around the wheel and have up to a 9.5-inch contact patch. Instant rim enlargement! The new Michelin Pilot street tire uses similar technology. Even if you only have a 6-inch wheel, you can end up with an 8-inch contact patch by using a 13x8-inch cantilever tire. These are the two most popular sizes in cantilever slicks and that's what Formula Ford (FF) racers use. The slicks were designed to compensate for the wheel restriction imposed on the FF class by the SCCA, but now we all can benefit from it. What size you use depends on the offset of your wheel. A 13x9.5-inch cantilever will also extend inside your fender well and possibly rub on your struts, so if you want to use this size tire to get the biggest possible contact patch, you need to decrease the backspace of your wheel. A wheel spacer can do that up to 1/4 inch, but to do more you need custom wheels. When rules allow, you can skip this whole discussion and just throw on 10-inch-wide wheels with regular 10-inch-wide slicks.

Road Racing

You shouldn't run the same tire for autocrossing as you would when road racing. After several hot laps, a sticky tire will often overheat and become "greasy," thus losing traction. The softer compound tires also won't last the entire race. Autocross compound tires, however, are often used for qualifying.

When you can run a fast qualifying lap, there is less chance of getting taken out by one of the many passing mishaps common in road racing. Most of the manufacturers already mentioned make tires for road racing. The only difference is the compound. Road racers using slicks have additional choices about how soft they want their tires to be. Besides the super sticky autocross compound, there is usually an intermediate soft and full hard tire.

Sometimes, mother nature will challenge a road racer's driving abilities. For this purpose, there are rain tires. Made out of a very sticky compound, rain tires have grooves (it would be a stretch to call it tread) that are designed to channel rain and optimize contact with the pavement. Despite these grooves, rain tires are not DOT approved. Class permitting, autocrossers also use these rain tires when the going gets wet.

Drag Racing

When it comes to tires, drag racers have choices similar to those of autocrossers. Do you go with a street/drag tire, or with a pure race tire? Or do you just use what you have, and head out to the strip? Entry-level drag racers can have tons of fun with little or no money in their wheel/tire budget. But in order to bring down those quarter-mile times, a good drag tire is needed.

The most popular drag tire with the Japanese Import crowd is the Nitto Drag Radial. This tire is constructed with "R" compound rubber, and is the stickiest DOT-approved tire that Nitto makes. The only problem is that only a few sizes are available. In the tire testing that we conducted, it was no faster than the BFGoodrich R1 or the Hoosier Autocrosser, which come in a greater variety of sizes, thus allowing you to

use 13-, 14-, or 15-inch wheels. With the Nittos, you often need to buy 16- or 17-inch (or larger) rims. If your goal is to reduce your quarter-mile times, and you want to use an "R" rated tire (which will wear out quickly on the street), then you should have an extra set of wheels so you can more easily change over from your street tires to the racing rubber.

If this is the case, you should try to fight the urge to look cool with a 17-inch wheel, and stay with a 16-inch rim (3G), 15-inch rim (2G), or 13-inch wheel (1G). These sizes will maximize your low-end torque and give you faster quarter-mile times than if you used the larger-size wheels. The only problem

BFGoodrich now makes a great street drag tire. If you are getting excessive tire spin off the line, either your drag tires are too hot, not hot enough, or your pressures are too high. Try decreasing pressures 1/2 pound per run. If you experience some instability at the end of your run, either your wheels are not balanced properly, or you have lowered your pressures too far. *Courtesy of RS Racing - www.rsracing.com*

It's not likely that you will ever need a wheel or tire like this one. Designed specifically for high-speed record attempts, this combination helped keep Racing Beat's 3G RX-7 straight during its record-breaking 242 mile-per-hour run. *Racing Beat*

with smaller rims is that they may require you to make an extra shift before the finish, which will cost you some time. If you've not yet started drag racing seriously, just bring your car to the track in street trim, and observe the cars that are similar to yours. What size wheels and tires are they using? Are they crossing the line under high or low rpms?

If they made their final shift just before the finish line and end up crossing at lower rpms, a smaller-diameter wheel may provide them with enough time to hit the car's power band after that final shift before crossing the line. It will also provide more torque at the starting line. On the other hand, if the car you are observing is crossing the finish under high rpms (without bouncing off the rev limiter), the owner probably has just the right wheel/tire combination for his car.

When it comes to pure drag tires, there are only a few choices. Mickey Thompson has long been one of the most popular slicks among drag racers. And even though there are sizes available for the formula cars that compete in autocross, you rarely see them among the pylons. Slicks require much less tire pressure than standard racing rubber, so discuss this with your tire dealer before starting out. Third- and second-generation cars tend to use higher pressures since they are heavier than the 1G RX-7s.

Tire Pressures

A whole section related to tire pressures? You've got to be kidding? In the previous chapter, we covered many ways to improve your car's handling, all of which involve spending money. In this section, we'll discuss one of the most effective and cheapest ways to fine-tune handling.

Many people both overlook and underestimate the effect that tire pressure can have on handling. But when it comes to changing handling characteristics, adjusting pressures is one of the best tools you have at your disposal.

For racing suspensions, a good starting point for most 1G RX-7s using bias-ply tires is 35 psi-front, 25 psi-rear. The 3G cars tend to require slightly higher pressures: 40 front and 30 rear with 2G cars falling somewhere in between. Radials require slightly higher pressures (2–3 pounds). If you find your car pushing itself around the track, you should change your settings by decreasing the rear or increasing the front.

If the car's tail is loose (oversteer—common with RX-7s that have installed stiffer rear sway bars), then lower the front pressures and add air to the rear. The theory to keep in mind for most motorsports is: Increased pressures result in increased traction (however, for some reason, dirt-trackers find the reverse is true). Adding air to the front tires will cause them to stick better, and your car will pivot around that point and cause the tail to swing out. Increasing pressure to the rear will cause the back end to stick better and will induce some plowing (understeer).

As mentioned earlier, drag racers tend to run very little air in the rear tires (contrary to the theory above). But drag tires need to flex so initial grip can be maximized.

For the most part, RX-7s are slightly biased toward understeer in stock trim, but not nearly as much as most cars. This is no mistake by the factory, because in normal street driving, an average driver has an easier time correcting for understeer than he or she does oversteer—which can put you into a spin. But by following the guidelines outlined in this chapter, your Mazda can be transformed into a well-balanced and more predictable creature that you can learn to four-wheel drift through turns.

CHAPTER SIX

Intake Systems

Every "instant bolt-on perfor-mance" product claims to enhance the performance of your car—what else would it claim? Often, however, the return on your investment is modest, if any. A well-established exception to this rule is an upgraded intake system. We've seen the results ourselves, and retested and reanalyzed them to be sure they were correct. They were. Using a chassis

Air velocity intake systems can often give a 3-7 percent increase in horsepower. Units, like this Peter Farrell custom system for a 1993-1995 RX-7, are one of the easiest and least-expensive ways to get a true boost in performance.

dyno—not an engine dyno, which gives you an isolated look at performance—we measured how much power actually got to the wheels with an enhanced intake setup.

We had to check the dyno several times to make sure that the numbers we were reading were correct. We double-checked our baselines, installed and tested different intake systems, then removed them. After that, we restored the cars to stock and retested the baselines. The result was a 3–7 percent increase in real horsepower from a product that costs less than $200 and takes only minutes to install. And this increase was consistent all along the torque curve, not just above 7,000 rpms.

Why do these intake systems work so well? The main reason is not that these products are highly advanced technological marvels. It's mostly that the stock intake systems they replace are restrictive and inefficient. That's right: stock intake systems in most cars are not designed for optimum performance. Is this to give engines longer life? To lower insurance rates for drivers? To cheat performance freaks just to get their goat? No. The main reason is noise. The

average car buyer wants a quiet car. A stock intake manifold is therefore designed with resonating chambers, much like a muffler, to keep noise to a minimum. If you don't believe that air intake can be noisy, then you don't already have one of these performance air velocity intake systems. The first time you start your car after installing one, you'll think someone is running a vacuum cleaner.

Because intake manifolds are designed for quietness, rather than performance, car makers often use the same intake manifold on the "sport" versions as the base models. This uniform approach also saves them money because they only have to manufacture one part for all the versions of the car. A good example is the second-generation non-turbo. The base model, SE, used the same intake as the GTU, which was supposed to be the performance model.

As engine people often note, an engine is just a fancy air pump. Therefore, allowing the engine to take in more air increases the engine's ability to do its job. Better breathing equals better performance—with certain qualifications. The airflow still needs to be smooth and consistent, so you get a

If you want to keep it simple and maintain a stock appearance, a K&N replacement filter may be all you need. You can gain a 1–3 percent increase in power from an item that costs around $50. SCCA Solo II stock class and Showroom Stock road racers are prohibited from using anything but this type of replacement air filter. *Racing Beat*

uniform air/fuel mixture and steady combustion. In other words, shortcuts like ripping off the existing air filter and box and putting a sock over the plastic intake tube won't be as effective (or as smart) as buying a kit specifically designed to do what the stock intake system does, only better. A freer flowing K&N filter could net you a few horsepower, but won't provide the same jump in power offered by these products. Aftermarket intake systems reduce air turbulence while increasing the velocity of the air (sometimes as much as twofold) on its way to the injection system. This provides more air, delivered just the way your engine needs it for better performance.

If you are driving a 1G RX-7 and want a little extra power, you can look for the stock intake manifold from a 1976 12A or 13B (depending on your engine). They have the best flow characteristics of any stock intake up to 1985. The 1976 RX-3SP also had a special intake manifold for improved breathing, so 1976 was a good year for rotary intakes. And here's a final tip for all 1984–1985 GSL-SE owners: if you substitute a 1986–1987 EGI airflow meter for your current one, you can gain a few horsepower.

Two carbureted first-generation solutions to get more air into your engine. To the left is a popular Holley conversion and Racing Beat air cleaner unit supplied with the Holley kit. This is a great option for improved street performance. For racing, however, the K&N air cleaner system on the bottom maximizes air flow. Note the fuel-pressure regulator placed in line just before the fuel enters the carb.

Second-generation owners also benefit from air intake technology. Pictured is an HKS Powerflow unit on a Turbo II engine that can net an average of 5 percent more power for your 13B.

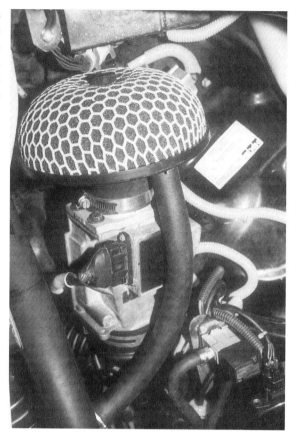

Heat Shielding

Giving your engine cooler air is another way to improve performance. That's because cool air is denser than hot air and holds more oxygen for combustion. For street use, a heat shield or box that surrounds and isolates your air intake from engine heat should give you slightly better performance. This rule of thumb may not apply on the track, where more, cooler outside air is rushing into the engine compartment. Stop-and-go driving can sap street performance, since it allows time for the engine compartment to heat up. A standard air-velocity system will have no choice but to suck in that hot air. A heat shield box will keep some of the hot air away from the air intake. The best boxes are made out of non-heat-absorbing material, such as plastic, rubber, or carbon fiber. You can also make your own if you have the time and patience.

One of the best things you can do for a second- or third-gen RX-7

There are no readily available parts for heat-shielded air intake systems. This one was custom designed and machined by Mark Halama for his 1984 GSL-SE. Note that the cool air enters through the mesh of the stock grill and is directed to the K&N-type filter. The hotter engine compartment air is not able to reach the filter. Aluminum is the most popular type of material used in heat shielding since it disperses heat well, and is easy to work with when doing custom fabrication.

Third-generation owners have several options from which to choose. They range from lower-priced units like this one, about $200, to units about $500. The difference between the lower- and higher-priced systems may only be 2 to 3 horsepower, depending on what other modifications are on board. For a stock 3G, there will likely be even less difference in net horsepower for that extra $300.

is to fabricate a heat shield to fit between the turbo manifold and the intake manifold. There is currently no one making such a product at this time, but there are a few custom units being made. The idea we are trying to drive home is that dispersing as much heat as possible will improve performance. This principle is important with any hopped-up car, but it is critical for a rotary engine. High temperature air in the intake can cause detonation, and thus serious engine damage. Then it will be time to check the limit on your Mastercard! So is a heat shield or a performance intake the best thing for your car? It could boil down to a matter of individual preference, price, looks, color, or how you use your car. The bottom line is that you really can't go wrong with any of them.

Other Cooling Tricks

Competitive drivers, who are always on the lookout for a few extra horses, have additional ways to put cooler air into their engines. Some RX-7 drag racers have been known to install a nitrous-oxide system (NOS) for cooler air. Instead of directing it into their air intake, they give their intercooler an occasional squirt of freezing NOS gas to help keep the incoming air cooler.

As we discuss in chapter 12, the drawback of any turbo or supercharging system is that it compresses the air, and that generates heat. Turbos use exhaust gases to compress the air, so the result is even hotter air. Since heat is any engine's enemy, it makes an intercooler a valuable performance addition. An intercooler simply acts like a radiator to cool this compressed, hot air much like the engine's radiator cools the water flowing through your engine. You can read more about intercoolers in chapter 12.

This GT-3 3G RX-7 had to be converted to carburetion in order to compete in SCCA road racing. Notice how the intake manifold is wrapped in insulated, reflective aluminum foil (shiny side out). If you look closely, you can see the top two nuts of the exhaust manifold. The rest of the manifold is hidden under—you guessed it—more reflective aluminum heat shielding.

Air inlet technology is rather complicated when it comes to the 3G. This free-flow air inlet duct kit replaces the inefficient stock system and allows turbo boost pressure to rise faster and recover more quickly during the turbo "switch over" sequence. This Racing Beat kit draws only cold air from outside the car and is made out of ABS plastic. Minor cutting of the stock air filter box is required to insure a proper fit. *Racing Beat*

Fuel-injected RX-7s have intakes that are right on top of the motor. RX-7 autocrossers routinely put ice on the manifold to cool it between runs, or they squirt it with cold water. Autocrossing doesn't really get your engine too hot since you are only out on the course for one minute at a time. But that's long enough to get the turbo and intake hot. Be careful where you spray the water, however: keep it on the intake and away from any electrical components.

Your intake manifold and engine block will also remain cooler if your exhaust system efficiently clears hot exhaust gases away from the engine and out the tailpipe. A better exhaust system will also help keep the intake slightly cooler. Exhaust systems are covered fully in the next chapter.

Autocrossers know the benefits of cold, denser air when it comes to improved combustion and horsepower. Often, between runs—especially on hot days—they put ice bags directly on their intake manifold. In the heat of battle, just don't forget to remove the ice before taking your next run.

For aftermarket fuel-injection conversions, the ITG air filter system is a great solution. This 1G 13B uses a special manifold that wraps around to the top of the engine, similar to the one that was used on the discontinued Racing Beat Weber/Dellorto/Mikuni carb conversion kits. Note the Electromotive ignition mounted against the firewall, and the fuel-pressure regulator at the entrance of the fuel rail.

Phillip Garrott has a unique solution for getting more air into his intake manifold. He built a special air box (like the one pictured earlier in this chapter) to help feed his Paxton-Nelson supercharged engine. He cut holes on top and below the passenger side headlight assembly to allow the cooler outside air to directly enter the intake. *Phillip Garrott*

CHAPTER SEVEN

Exhaust Systems

Installing a high-performance exhaust system is one of the easiest, most common, and most beneficial modifications you can make to a street or race car. No matter what rotary you own, the most cost-effective way to increase horsepower in this non-piston engine is to open up the exhaust. A wide-open exhaust in a four-cylinder engine rarely yields anything other than loss of low-end torque (and hearing), unless major modifications have been made to the fuel-management system to complement the increased airflow through the engine.

But when it comes to rotary engines, noise is not just for show; it's for go. As much as 30 horsepower can be gained by the addition of a header and performance exhaust system, depending upon the degree the engine has been ported. Even in an older stock 12A, a 5 to 10 horsepower improvement is common.

And the newer your RX-7 is, the more emission equipment is likely on board, hence the more power you will find by letting the exhaust gases exit more efficiently. Race car drivers don't have many restrictions when it comes to noise levels; however, most of us can't afford that luxury. We have

The key to a high-performance exhaust system is an efficient exhaust manifold mated to a header. In this case, we see a custom Peter Farrell turbo exhaust manifold for a 3G RX-7. It is lighter and flows much better than the stock manifold. Horsepower varies depending on what other modifications are on board, but on a stock vehicle you can expect a 2–5 percent increase in power.

The Supertrapp, manufactured by Kerker Performance, is a unique muffler, or should we say "spark arresting device." It does reduce decibels without compromising power, but has, on occasion, been known to shoot flames out the tailpipe with the best of 'em, which can happen with any ported rotary engine. The Supertrapp is also unique because it can be "tuned" by removing or adding discs to maximize either low or high-end torque.

to live by rules that keep us from going too far. We therefore need to strike a proper balance between power, noise, and emissions.

Any of the good, brand-name performance exhaust systems are designed to help get the most out of your car. Select your system based on the experience and reputation of the aftermarket tuner, not based on horsepower claims. Remember that those claims were made with the exhaust attached to an engine that has been built to take full advantage of what a free flow exhaust can offer over the more restrictive stock system. Unless you have made those same modifications resulting in an engine that is nearly choking on its own exhaust gases, begging for a more efficient way out, your actual horsepower gain will be much less than what is quoted. You can't really blame the manufacturers. They're just trying to demonstrate their product under the best possible circumstances, and are facing competition that employs the same practices.

When it comes to basic design, most of these aftermarket systems are relatively similar. That is, except for one. Originally a manufacturer of motorcycle exhaust systems, Kerker Performance, makers of the Supertrapp, have taken a different approach. That is not to say that this system is better than the others, but it does help demonstrate the concept of back pressure.

The business end of a Supertrapp utilizes disks that function as baffles and fit over the tail pipe canister muffler. Often, a stack of between 1 to 15 baffle disks are used to either restrict or open up the flow of escaping gases. When a high number of disks are used, there are more spaces between the disks for exhaust gases to escape, thus decreasing back pressure. Removing disks,

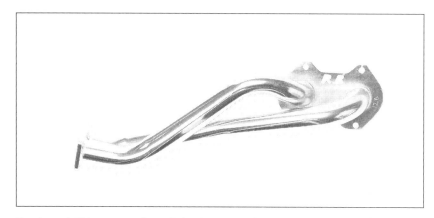

For the early RX cars, as well as 1979–1992 non-turbo RX-7s, Racing Beat offers its popular road race header designed to fit the 12A and both the four and six-port 13B. This is a quality unit that uses 2-inch O.D. pipe and 1/8-inch thick walls. Headers are also available for full race engines with peripheral exhaust ports. When it comes to horsepower bang for the buck, it's hard to beat a header. *Racing Beat*

however, creates the opposite effect, as there is less space for the gases to escape, effectively increasing back pressure. To explain it in simple terms, if you increase back pressure (restrict flow), you can experience an increase in low-end torque. Allow more gas to escape, and you get more power above 6,000 rpms. A Supertrapp is one of the only exhaust systems that can be tuned to adjust back pressure, while still decreasing decibels.

Once a standard performance exhaust system is on your car, you have no real options to adjust torque. But here's a reality check before the folks at Kerker Performance get swamped with phone orders. The tunability of a Supertrapp covers a very small range of torque (plus or minus 1 to 5 ft-lbs of torque). On the other hand they are relatively cheap (under $150) and work with your stock pipes (replacing the much heavier OEM muffler). So why doesn't every RX-7 owner use a Supertrapp? Since rotary engines generate such a high degree of heat, anytime you try to restrict flow, you get a buildup of heat in your system that could back up into the header, causing the

exhaust temperature to reach critical mass. So when you see a Supertrapp in use with a rotary engine, it usually contains either a maximum number of disks, or none at all (wide open). A common glass-packed, "Cherry Bomb" system from your local muffler shop will save weight and still cut down on decibels without sacrificing too much power. However, glass pack mufflers are not tunable like the Supertrapp systems.

Header Performance

Contrary to popular belief, for most new Japanese piston-powered cars, a header will not substantially improve performance. How can we say that? We performed dyno testing with all the major brand-name headers, and found that at best, on a stock engine, you can gain 2 horsepower, and at worst, you can lose 1–2 horsepower. Actually, the most expensive brand we tested performed the worst! Headers do offer substantial weight savings and look cool, but gains (if any) are minimal.

When it comes to a rotary-powered RX-7, however, even the cheapest header can offer considerable gains in both low and high-end torque, as well

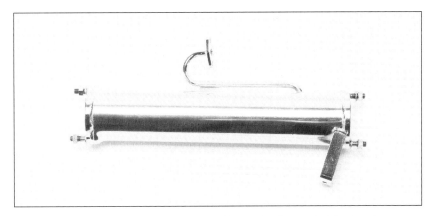

Racing Beat manufactures this pre-silencer, designed to be used with a header as part of a complete bolt-on exhaust system for all rotary engines up to and including 1992 (including the Turbo II). It is a subcomponent, along with a catalytic converter replacement pipe, that eliminates the high-frequency pitch of the exhaust tone. *Racing Beat*

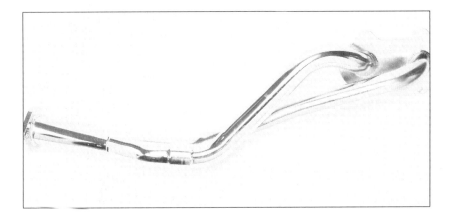

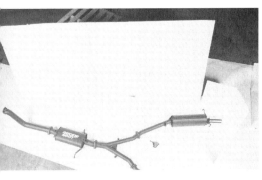

For 1981–1992 non-turbo RX-7s (12A and 13B engines, including automatic transmissions), this is an excellent solution for increased horsepower. As always, these Racing Beat headers are bolt-on installations, and this unit replaces the catalytic converter and any intermediate pieces of tubing. *Racing Beat*

as overall horsepower. OEM non-turbo rotary exhaust manifolds were designed not only to remove exhaust gases, but to keep engine noise to an acceptable level. And since a Wankel is not the most efficient engine on the planet, as pollution standards became more restrictive in the 1980s, so did the exhaust manifolds and catalytic converters found on RX-7s. It seemed only logical to target one of the most polluting power plants being used in production vehicles. For full-blown race cars, the solution is to replace the entire stock system with a header and a straight-through exhaust.

Unfortunately, environmental laws in all states make it illegal to remove your catalytic converter from a car driven on the roads. But even if with your cat, a good header unit can still help your car to breathe better by allowing the exhaust gases to escape more efficiently.

The Downpipe

For turbo cars, the exhaust manifold does more than send your exhaust to the tailpipe. First, it

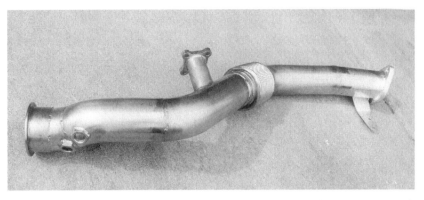

For turbo cars, which can't use a simple header, an aftermarket "downpipe" is a quick and easy solution. This Peter Farrell unit—larger than the stock pipe—will help keep exhaust gases from building up in your system, essentially reducing heat in your engine. A tuned downpipe such as this will increase the efficiency of your exhaust system, especially at high rpm.

sends some of the exhaust gases on a mission to power a turbine or two. As the turbine spins, it compresses air that is then sent to the intake system. This special manifold cannot be replaced with a header because headers can't redirect exhaust to your turbocharger(s). But that doesn't mean you can't improve the way your engine eliminates exhaust gases.

The remainder of your exhaust gases—not sent to the turbo—must still be efficiently released out the tailpipe. If this is not done properly, heat will build up in the manifold and cook the engine. A poor-flowing exhaust system creates increased back pressure, which can inhibit the engine from functioning properly at higher rpms. The key component that removes the exhaust gases in a turbo system is known as a downpipe.

Many turbo owners have discovered that by replacing the stock downpipe with a larger aftermarket unit, they can make their engines run cooler and have more power, especially above 6,000 rpm. The theory at work here is similar to replacing a non-turbo exhaust manifold with a header. An aftermarket downpipe is more efficient at helping the exhaust gases to escape from the engine. The main reason for this is simply that it is larger than the stock unit. But performance downpipes are also "tuned" to flow better, while at the same time maintaining adequate back pressure. More-efficient release of exhaust gases allows the engine to develop more power.

Heat Management

The main enemy of a rotary engine is heat (with a close second going to dirt). There have been spots, especially on the older Wankel designs, where overheating can occur. This excessive heat can cause the coolant to form bubbles. Once formed, they are nearly impossible to break up. The 3G RX-7s come equipped with a device to do just that; however, even with a bubble separator in place, the problem can persist.

A good way to detect heat buildup in your engine is to install an exhaust temperature gauge. Nearly all RX-7s came with this option, so pay close attention to what it is telling

One of the biggest (and heaviest) pieces of an RX-7's emission control system is the air pump. That's why racers remove them, along with the catalytic converter, before just about any other non-essential part on their cars. The unit is designed to pump air (oxygen) into the mix of carbon monoxide and hydrocarbons to help "clean up" exhaust gases before they exit the tailpipe. The 1G racers can just remove the pump and throw both it and the belt away, since the fan pulley turns separate belts for the air pump and the alternator/water pump. You can see where the inside groove on this 1G 13B no longer supports the air-pump belt.

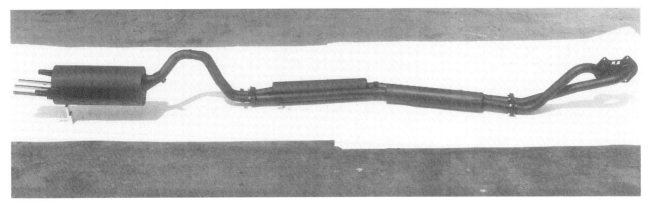

This complete exhaust system, including header, is for 1979–1985 RX-7s that have either non-ported or street-ported engines. *Racing Beat*

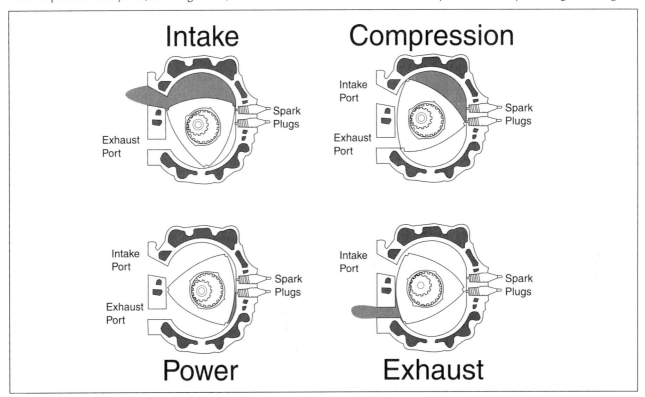

Intake. To better visualize the four strokes of a rotary powerplant, it helps to think of the rotor moving in a clockwise rotation. As the rotor begins its journey, the leading edge (designated by 3a2) is at the bottom tip of the intake port. The intake stroke of a rotary engine occurs when our leading edge closes off the exhaust port and the vacuum in the chamber draws the mixture of air and fuel into the engine.

Compression. The mixture of air and fuel is compressed as the leading edge approaches the spark plug array. As the rotor continues to spin from left to right, the chamber's size decreases, forcing the same quantity of air and fuel to occupy a smaller space. This excites the molecules, and the fuel charge increases in density.

Power. As the leading edge approaches the spark plugs, they fire. The heavily compressed air and fuel mixture is ignited and the released energy pushes the leading edge of the rotor toward the exhaust manifold.

Exhaust. The rotors leading edge has now rotated nearly 180 degrees. Edge (3a2) pushes the spent gases out through the exhaust port as the momentum from the power stroke carries it toward the intake port to begin the sequence all over again. Remember, there are two other edges in different strokes of the cycle. Edge (3c2) has just completed its power stroke, pushing our edge even harder toward its intake port. At the same time, the edge directly in front of it (3b2) is already compressing its mixture of air and fuel in preparation for a power stroke of its own.

you. If the exhaust system you installed is causing your exhaust temperature to rise, there is a problem. Fortunately, most aftermarket exhaust systems help reduce the backup of gases and can decrease the operating temperature of your engine.

The Infamous Air Pump

The air pump is part of an RX-7's pollution-control system and is designed to feed air into a valve. That valve, in turn, directs air to one of three places (or two, depending on the model): 1) the "thermal reactor," otherwise known as the exhaust manifold, 2) the main catalytic converter, and 3) the throttle body. It receives information from a solenoid or vacuum source that provides data regarding engine rpm, temperature, and throttle position (for computer-controlled engines). Designed to operate under 4,000 rpm, it adds oxygen to the exhaust gases before they exit the tailpipe in an attempt to decrease pollution. At higher rpm, the air pump is not needed since the exhaust and catalytic converter become hot enough to remove excess emissions.

Most racers remove their air pumps to save a few pounds and reduce drag. This is not recommended for the street because, honestly, you don't gain much power (maybe 1 horsepower), and it violates emission laws. The racers remove them because they also remove their catalytic converters. Once you do that, there is no need to keep the air pump, since CO and hydrocarbons will be pouring out the tailpipe anyway. Adding a little oxygen to that polluting mix may dilute it in the exhaust system, but it all goes into the environment anyway.

Removing the air pump poses no real problem for 1G racers because a separate belt, connected to the cooling fan, turns the pump.

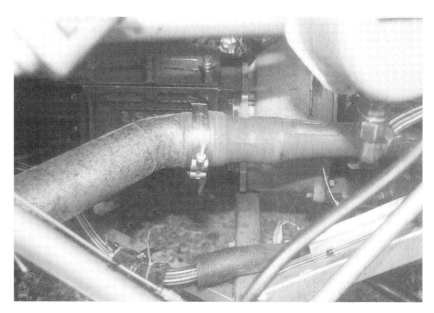

Shown here is a custom exhaust pipe used in a 3G GT-3 road racer, which was forced to convert to a carbureted 12A engine. The pipe gradually increases from 2-inch outside diameter (O.D.) to 3-inch O.D. in an effort to reduce back pressure—ideal for high rpm applications.

Some highly modified RX-7s have their exhaust exits just below the rear of the passenger side door. This saves weight, decreases back pressure, and also, when the driver lifts his foot from the throttle, keeps the flames from shooting into the front end of any car in pursuit.

You just take out the pump and throw away the belt. In 3G cars, however, you will need to buy a different belt, since the one you already have turns the air pump, alternator, and water pump all at the same time. Take the pump out of the loop, and your belt will be too big. GReddy has a pulley kit that also contains an overdrive (larger) alternator and water pump pulleys, plus the right size belt to fit your new configuration. The reduced drag from these pulleys alone (over the stock ones) will net a couple of horsepower, especially down low.

Bargain Hunting

Pacesetter headers aren't exactly the best on the market, but they are certainly affordable, especially through the J.C. Whitney Co. A plain header for a first- or second-gen 13B RX-7 is only $98 (prices at the time of this writing). If you have a 1G with a 12A, it will cost you a little more ($108). Of course, these do not match the quality of a Racing Beat header, which has been specifically tuned for RX-7 performance. But if you opt for saving money, here's a great option that can help make your Whitney header last forever. Pacesetter offers a ceramic-coated header for all 1G cars for just $224. It costs at least $150 to get your header coated if you send it out, so this is a bargain. An entire cat-back "Monza" type exhaust system (Pacesetter again) is available for all first- and second-generation cars for $110 (1G) and $210 (2G). How long they can hold up under the extreme heat generated by a rotary engine, however, is a question we cannot answer.

Conclusions

So what have we learned? First, that headers are a great modification to a non-turbo car that will increase the overall efficiency of your exhaust system. Check to see if local emission laws permit their use on the street. Second, performance exhaust systems are one of the coolest bolt-on hop-up presents you can give to your car. Don't just go to the local muffler shop, however, unless you bring them your new Mazdatrix, Racing Beat, or GReddy system. Call one of your favorite RX-7 performance shops and order an exhaust that will match the capabilities of your car. For highly modified

A custom exhaust rounds out George Dodsworth's 2G RX-7. The car is equipped with an aftermarket turbo and an Electromotive TEC-II injection system.

engines, you can get away with a wide-open exhaust system, but without additional modifications to your fuel-injection system, a wide-open system can hurt performance, espe-cially at low rpm. If you can afford stainless steel systems, and you plan on keeping your car for a while, then the extra expense—often twice the cost of soft steel—is worth it.

CHAPTER EIGHT

Engines and Engine Transplants

Mazda's design of the WRCE (Wankel Rotary Combustion Engine) produces an impressive amount of power per cubic centimeter. Most cars aren't running rotary engines because the early engines were very dirty from an emissions standpoint, and not particularly fuel efficient. They also had carbon apex seals that had a tendency to become brittle and crack. And if that wasn't enough, the oil seals often leaked, resulting in smoking tailpipes.

When serious pollution standards went into effect in the mid-1970s, it became impractical for most auto manufacturers to try to clean up the rotary engine enough to satisfy government standards. For the most part, compared to a piston engine, rotaries produce a much higher level of both carbon monoxide and hydrocarbons. Even though these levels are significantly reduced when exposed to the high heat generated by the rotary's exhaust gases, U.S. manufacturers had problems

enough trying to clean up their current piston engines. They all chose to put their energy into bringing their traditional power plants up to standard, rather than splitting their efforts and resources by trying to get two engines to satisfy government regulations. It was this decision, made at this critical time in history, that killed the rotary development programs at most of the major automobile manufacturers.

The only company to roll the dice and actually attempt to mass-

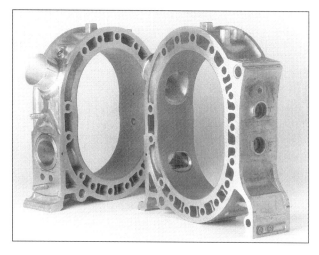

Most RX-7 fans have to keep themselves from drooling when exposed to images like these. The reason is obvious: these babies translate into neck-jerking power. Special race rotors are available for all 1979–1992 RX-7s (including Turbo II), and housings with peripheral intake ports can also be ordered for those same cars. Read about porting later in this chapter. *Racing Beat*

produce an automotive rotary power plant was, of course, Mazda. NSU's original design underwent extensive development after Mazda bought the rights to produce the engine. The company immediately replaced the brittle cast-iron apex seals with a carbon-aluminum composite. This move instantly increased reliability. Next, it concentrated on reducing vibration at low rpm. This was accomplished by modifying the way the engine took in fuel and air. Mazda altered NSU's design by changing to side ports for the intake. With one port on either side of the rotor, the combustion sequence functioned with greater harmony. Choosing to concentrate on a twin rotor design, Mazda added twin spark plugs in 1961, which made for a smoother-running and more efficient engine. Headed by Kohei Matsuda, "project rotary" really began to take form in 1962 when a chassis was designed to showcase the new engine. The 1962 Cosmo Sport was born just to serve this purpose. The engine underwent numerous other changes until it finally reached mass production when Cosmos began to trickle out of Toyo Kogyo's Hiroshima plant in 1967.

Rotary Engine Chronology

L10A, 10A - 982cc (60 cubic inches)
108–110 horsepower
Cosmo Sport (1967)

There was actually one rotary engine that preceded the L10A, and that was the L8A. It displaced only 798cc and was never put into any vehicle other than the Cosmo Sport prototype. The first rotary engine actually to appear in a mass-produced Mazda was the 10A. Many non-RX-7 fans believed that this engine was a single rotor design, but

that is not the case. This first production Wankel had two rotors and a total of 982 cubic centimeters of displacement. The recipient of this lightweight power plant was a car that would set the automotive world on its ear: the 1967 Cosmo Sport. Sadly, fewer than 1,500 of these vehicles actually got into the garages of the American public.

L10B - 1146cc (70 cubic inches)
128 horsepower
Cosmo Sport (1968–1972)

The following year, a new Cosmo was introduced. Although it looked the same on the outside, there were many changes over the previous year's version, as Mazda continually tried to make a car that would have international appeal. From 1968 on, the L10A motor was slightly tweaked along the way. It eventually was capable of 128 horsepower (thanks mostly to an aggressive change in port timing) when it was retired in 1972.

10A - 982cc (60 cubic inches)
100 horsepower, 92 ft-lbs of torque
R100 (1970–1972)

Basically the same engine that first appeared in the Cosmo Sport, this version of the L10A was detuned for the U.S. market. By changing the port timing from wild to mild, the company was able to develop a smoother-running engine. Finally, by replacing the four-barrel Hitachi carb with another that had more conservative fuel delivery, engineers made the old L10A behave like an entirely different engine. This prompted Mazda to drop the "L" designation for the R100. It was never to return.

12A - 1146cc (70 cubic inches)
90–120 horsepower, 96–105 ft-lbs of torque
RX-2, RX-3, RX-3SP, (1978–1985)
RX-7 (except GSL-SE)

The first full-production rotary was the 10A, which came in this great little car known as the R100. Along with the RX-2, this was the car that first helped give Mazda a foothold in the U.S. market. The 10A had a decent power rating at 100 horsepower, and displaced 982cc. Unfortunately, the car was only made for two years (1970-1972), replaced by the RX-2. *John McBeth*

Further refinement to the basic 10A resulted in one of Mazda's, and therefore one of the world's, most popular rotary engines. The 10A's

One of most popular sports car engines for racing is the 12A, which in stock trim is only capable of 90 horsepower and displaces 1146cc. IT racers, however, remove emissions equipment, install a header and exhaust, racing carb (Holley shown), etc., and get power increases to 120-plus. Porting (not allowed in IT, but O.K. for GT) will add up to 70-80 more ponies. For the most part, 13B engines are excluded from competition in most SCCA road racing classes. In autocross, however, anything goes, depending on which class you choose.

rotors were widened by 10 millimeters (from 60 to 70 millimeters) to form one of the most popular rotary engines in history: the 12A. The only disappointment was that Mazda only produced the 12A with greater horsepower than the 10A design for one year. Following the initial year of the RX-2, the 10A was gradually detuned to a low point in 1973–1974, when all it could manage was 97 horsepower. The company had a practical reason for dropping the engine's power. Mazda was convinced that in order to compete in the U.S. market, its cars would have to drink less fuel and generate less pollution. So the 12A was purposely restricted, losing 20 percent of its power from 1971–1974.

Port sizes on the 12A were further reduced in 1976 in an attempt to gain some additional fuel economy, but the RX-3SP countered with a cool intake design that flowed better than any previous (or future) 12A intakes. The end result, however, was a low point in performance. The RX-3 could only produce 92 horsepower. If you want to do a complete engine swap, 1976 is the year to avoid. Taking the 1976 intake, on the other hand, is a good move. Any of the 1976 intakes (12A, 12A/RX-3SP, 13B) were superior. For pure horsepower (without porting), the 1971 12A still has the edge, but reliability is somewhat compromised over the later 12As.

Although the 12A lost horsepower as it matured, expert Mazda tuners were able to undue what the factory had done. Racing Beat's Jim Mederer is a good example. Competing in the 1973 IMSA RS series, he helped build an RX-2 12A that was capable of more than 210 horsepower. Mazda

didn't improve 12A performance until the RX-7 was introduced.

In 1978, Mazda concentrated on making the 12A a little more reliable by fitting new apex seals that resisted cracking. Although horsepower ratings were at 100, with some porting and the right carb, this little baby could easily crank out 150 horsepower.

In 1981, 12A cars were further restricted, mostly as a result of the exhaust system. Twin catalytic converters were fitted to the RX-7. They not only cut down on emissions, they allowed for a leaner setting on the carb (Mazda's "lean burn" system). No real loss of horsepower occurred, thankfully.

If you were living in Japan in 1983 and you didn't buy an RX-7 12A Turbo GT-X, shame on you. With this conservative turbo system, horsepower ratings were increased by 35 ponies. In the United States, we benefited slightly from the GT-X development project when the 12A received lightened rotors and a better oil pump.

In its final two years of production, the 12A got some healthy competition from the newly introduced GSL-SE's 13B. Despite that, many 12A RX-7s were sold in 1984–1985. The 12A is still one of the most popular engines in racing, as hundreds of 1G RX-7s compete successfully in the SCCA's ITA (Improved Touring) class.

13B - 1308cc (80 cubic inches)
110–135 horsepower, 117–133 ft-lbs
    of torque
RX-4, RX-5 Cosmo, (1984–1985)
    RX-7 GSL-SE

In case this isn't apparent, the designation 12A and 13B is a direct abbreviation for each engine's

The 13B is the largest of all rotaries sold in the United States, displacing 1308cc and producing anywhere from 110 (early designs) to up to 255 horsepower (3G). This six-port motor out of a GSL-SE found its way into a Triumph Spitfire. Add Electromotive TEC-II injection, a street port, and various other goodies and you have a reliable 225-plus horsepower, normally aspirated.

displacement. (Mazda made a 13A motor, as mentioned in chapter 1, but used it only in a car that wasn't exported to the United States.) The 12A is 1146cc (rounded to 1200cc), while 13B comes from that motor's 1308cc. Although the housings that contain both are the same general size on the outside, the 13B is a different creature altogether on the inside. With a combustion chamber a 10th of a liter larger per rotor, the first 13B was instantly capable of 35 more horsepower than the 12A.

The 1974 RX-4 was the first production Mazda to come with a 13B. This was such a good motor that even though there are few RX-4s around, there are lots of

A newly designed 13B finally found its way into a 1G RX-7 in 1984. The GSL-SE is one of the highest rated RX-7s among collectors since it has great power, handling, and value. Mark Halama's SE has a custom air intake, MSD ignition, and several other of the most popular upgrades that can help it compete with more modern and powerful cars.

RX-4 and RX-5 engines. They live on as one of the most popular engines for transplantation into a 12A-equipped 1979–1985 RX-7. The first 13Bs had a four-port intake, but when the engine was reintroduced in the 1984 GSL-SE, two more ports were added. Actually, the old 13B's secondary ports were slightly enlarged and split in two, to produce the six-port version. There was a complex intake system put in place to take advantage of the twin secondary ports. When the tach would wind up beyond 5K, a pair of rotary valves opened the two new ports, allowing more air and fuel into the engine. With these new secondary ports doing the work when the motor was at high rpm, fuel mix and ignition timing for the primary ports could be designed to optimize low to mid-range performance. The result of this engineering was an easy 135 horsepower out of only 1.3 liters! And things were about to get even better.

13B - 1308cc (80 cubic inches)
146–160 horsepower, 138–140 ft-lbs
    of torque
RX-7 (1986–1992)

When the 2G RX-7 came along in 1986, output rose again, to 146 horsepower, thanks to an improved intake and fuel-injection system. This was also the year of the new thinner, three-piece cast-iron/alloy apex seals. The result was a tighter seal for the combustion chamber, less friction, and longer life. The motor was also better lubricated, as separate pumps squirted oil directly on the inner surface of the rotors, right into the intake manifold, and on the eccentric shaft/bearings. This also served to cool the engine. A friend and long-time RX-7 mechanic who lives in Florida has completely replaced the coolant that circulated through his Turbo II motor with a very light oil. That's right, he adds oil to the radiator, not water. This simple change has significantly reduced his car's engine temperature. Of course, he's an RX-7 mechanic—we don't recommend your making this

Redesigned again in 1986 for the 2G RX-7, the 13B was given more power (146–160 horsepower) without increasing displacement (although the latter was considered, and rejected). Improvements in fuel injection, the intake system, and better apex seals were mostly responsible for this improvement. Lighter rotors came along in 1989, helping boost the power up to 160.

change. Mazda made a final revision in 1989, which included lighter rotors, higher compression, and yet more refinements to the intake. The result was 14 more horsepower, for a total of 160, without compromising fuel economy.

13B Turbo II - 1308cc (80 cubic inches)
182–200 horsepower, 183–196 ft-lbs
    of torque
RX-7 Turbo (1989–1991)

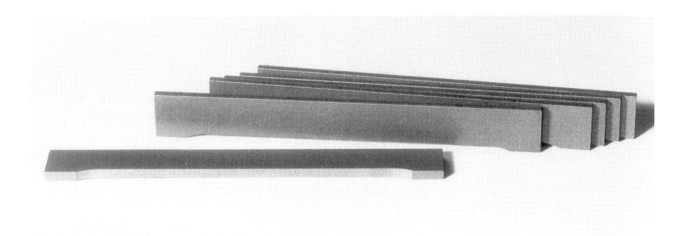

In 1986, new apex seals were introduced for the redesigned 13B powerplant. Revised three-piece seals replaced the previous two-piece units. A three-piece aftermarket unit is pictured here. *Racing Beat*

As shown left and below, the Turbo II engine added more horses to an already competent power plant. The engine was introduced in 1987, rating initially at 182, and it rose to 200 horsepower by the end of production in 1992.

As mentioned in chapter 1, there was no Turbo I engine. No matter—the Turbo II is one great engine. When first introduced in the Mazda Turbo, this power plant cranked out 182 horsepower with only 5–6 pounds of boost! But the best was yet to come.

If you are looking for one of the all-time great turbo power plants, look no further than the 1989–1991 13B. The 1989 base engine was given an increased compression ratio and lighter rotors. When it was combined with a slightly more efficient turbo unit in 1991, its power finally hit the 200 horsepower mark.

13B Twin Turbo - 1308cc (80 cubic inches)
255 horsepower, 217 ft-lbs of torque
RX-7 (1993–1995)

One of the best things about Mazda is the company's persistence. It always seem to be on a mission to make its cars better and faster. Most sports car enthusiasts' prayers were answered in 1993 when the 3G was released. The power plant was nearly completely redesigned. Although still a 13B at heart, this baby came packing a pair of Hitachi turbochargers. Referred to as the 13B REW engine, which believe it or not, stands for "Rotary Engine Double-turbo," this new power plant was originally conceived as a three-rotor design. Mazda scrapped the triple rotor prior to production due to the higher weight of the engine, as well as the frame needed to support it. To keep performance at the desired level, the company went with twin turbos instead, for maximum power-to-weight ratio. To keep things cool, there is a large turbo intercooler and dual oil coolers located at each front corner of the car.

The turbos are powered by exhaust gases that are initially diverted to the primary turbo for quicker off-the-line performance with minimal hesitation. The initial problem with the secondary turbo was that, during constant acceleration, there was considerable turbo lag from the time that the majority of exhaust gases were switched over from the primary to the secondary turbo. This was corrected

If you wish you had a turbo on your 2G GTU, no problem. Just add an aftermarket kit like George Dodsworth did.

Left: The engine that nearly ended up in the 1993 3G was similar to this 20A motor found only in Japan. Powering the Mazda Cosmo since 1992, this puppy can crank out 280 horsepower. But the absolute most impressive thing about the engine, and the main reason to transplant it, is that it has nearly 300 ft-lbs of torque— previously unheard of for a rotary engine.

The 13B Twin Turbo (1993–1995 in the United States) was the most powerful rotary to date, producing 255 horsepower with a whopping 217 ft-lbs of torque. An aftermarket single-stage sport turbo is a popular upgrade. This conversion was performed by Peter Farrell Supercars on Gordon Monsen's 3G.

by having some exhaust gases diverted to the secondary turbo even at low throttle. With the secondary turbine already spinning, it was ready to kick in much quicker as the rpm increased into its power range.

Of course, ignition and fuel-management systems were programmed to make this transition as smooth as possible. The third generation's ECU needed to be able to monitor all systems to keep this complex system running properly. For that reason, there is a huge network of bypass valves and solenoids to enable the entire system to communicate and respond to the whim of our right foot.

20B (triple rotor) - 1962cc (120 cubic inches)
280 horsepower and 296 ft-lbs of torque!
Japanese domestic market Mazda Cosmo (1992–present)

Available in cars only in Japan, this engine has made its way across the ocean, but without a body attached. Offered on the Japanese Cosmo, this is an extremely popular motor for transplantation. But we don't recommend having one shipped to your doorstep. The process of putting this beast into your second- or third-gen chassis successfully is complex, and only recommended for experts.

Power output for the triple rotor is impressive: 280 horsepower with a whopping 297 ft-lbs of torque! The 20B REW (nearly 2 liters) first made its debut in 1992 in the luxury Sedan that borrows its name from the first production rotary-powered Mazda: the Cosmo. This is Japanese technology at its peak. The 20B has a large primary turbo that is designed to reduce turbo lag. The exhaust gases contact the turbine at an 80-degree angle, cutting down on response time after you initially punch the gas pedal. A

Nowadays, you can just call one of the RX-7 tuners listed in the back of this book, and they will put together an engine to your specifications. *Excellent Performance/Pettit Racing*

What is your goal when it comes to building an engine? How many horsepower do you want—150? 250? 350? More? How fast do you want to go? How about 242 miles per hour? That's what this engine did for Racing Beat's 3G, which took its class at the Bonneville Salt Flats Challenge. *Racing Beat*

smaller secondary turbo forces air into the combustion chamber at a much higher velocity than the primary unit via six separate tracts (two for each rotor). The secondary, or second stage turbo, is designed to kick in at higher rpm.

Porting Yields More Power

There are several ways to get gobs more power out of a rotary engine. As mentioned in chapters 6 and 7, two such ways are improved intake and exhaust systems. If you own a car that has factory fuel injection, chapter 10 explains how an ECU upgrade can really give your car a boost. And speaking of boost, chapter 12 discusses turbos and supercharging. There are two other common tricks for finding extra horses: engine porting and transplantation.

The one thing that all rotaries have in common, from the 10A up to the triple rotor 20B, is that skillful intake and exhaust porting can unleash the engine's true potential.

No matter what type of engine you are talking about (piston or rotary), porting is a universal term. The term "port" simply refers to an entrance or exit hole in your engine, intake or exhaust.

Remember, an engine is basically an air pump. The more efficiently air gets in and out of an engine, the more power you can generate. Porting refers to opening up a hole, or to matching that hole precisely to the hole on the part you are planning to attach to it. One kind of porting is matching an intake manifold or exhaust header exactly to the intake or exhaust ports on an engine, so that there is no disturbance in air flow. Widening the passages in your intake manifold through either custom machine work, or a process such as Extrude Hone,

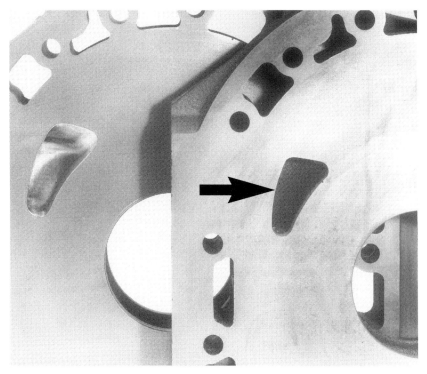

On the right of this photo is an excellent example of a stock intake port, and on the left is a street port. The port on the left has been enlarged and polished for street applications. *Racing Beat*

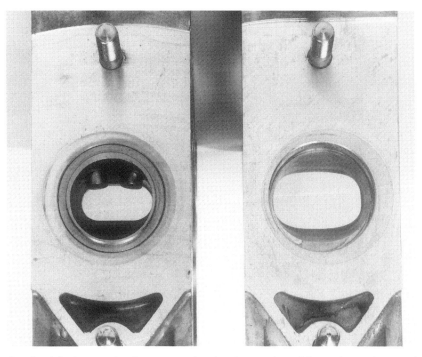

On the right is a stock exhaust port that has been enlarged for racing. It is one of the best bang-for-the-buck modifications you can perform on a rotary engine. *Racing Beat*

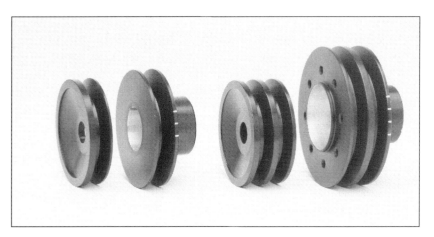

Lightweight and oversize pulleys can reduce drag on a rotary engine, and give you a little bit more power by decreasing rotating mass. They are inexpensive and relatively easy to install. *Racing Beat*

will result in better air flow. An extrude hone process involves forcing an abrasive medium through the part to be modified. This polishes the inner surface and produces a slightly wider opening in that particular part and/or chamber. Air flow increases considerably when it doesn't get hung up on minor casting imperfections that will cause turbulence.

When looking at a standard piston engine, porting is a simple concept to explain. The intake and exhaust ports can easily be seen from the outside. With a rotary engine, however, the ports are harder to visualize. Even Wankel experts sometimes have to stop and think before they can get a good perspective on what is involved in engine porting. But even though a piston engine works in a completely different manner than a rotary, the concept of engine porting is a common variable, with one difference: rotaries respond to it much better than piston engines do. Often the key to big power gains on a rotary lies with an expert porting job.

As the previous sentence suggests, porting a rotary engine is a task reserved for highly skilled rotary engine mechanics. You can't just take a

rotary grinding tool to the intake and exhaust ports. The stock intake port edges are dangerously close to the oil control rings, so you must use extreme care. And you can only enlarge certain areas. The shape and smoothness all the way through the port are very

important, and only an expert is likely to get them right. What we have therefore set forth are the principles of porting, so you can understand its benefits to your engine. When it comes down to getting the job done, check your budget, determine your needs (fast street, autocross, drag, full-blown racing), and hire an expert to do a first-rate job on your power plant. The better the porting job, the more power you'll gain.

Grassroots Motorsports has generated possibly the best discussion of porting the rotary engine that we have ever read. When it comes to explaining the different types of engine porting, publisher Tim Suddard has succeeded where others failed because he has approached the discussion from a layperson's point of view. That's because he was learning as he wrote. Following is Suddard's discussion of this important performance enhancement.

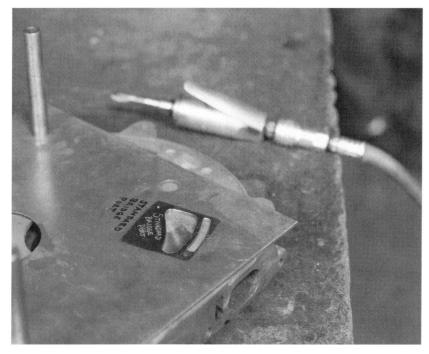

If you insist on doing the job yourself, porting templates are available from many of the tuning shops. Just stay within the lines, or you could get into some serious trouble. *Racing Beat*

Understanding the Art of Rotary Porting
By Tim Suddard and Mike Ancas

The term "porting" is thrown around a lot when people talk about rotary engines. So why is porting so important? The answer is simple: The more fuel you pump in and the more exhaust you pump out, the faster the motor will turn and the more power it will make. Because the rotary has so few other parts compared to a piston engine, there's not much else you can do if you want to increase horsepower. With a piston engine, you can play with the camshaft, bore the cylinders and put in bigger pistons, grind the valves, modify the rocker arms, balance/lighten the crank, etc. None of that is possible with a rotary.

But theoretically, if you double the port size, you can double the performance if you give the engine enough fuel, then find a way to get the exhaust gases out of the engine with similar efficiency. Doubling the port sizes on a piston engine does little or no good unless you beef up the rest of the drivetrain to withstand the increased rpm. You also need to highly modify the valve size and cam gear to take advantage of this increased fuel flow. Of course, this is an oversimplification, but the rotary's simplicity and inherent design make increasing port size a very cheap and effective way to make extra power. There are three basic types of porting you will see on an RX-7 engine and one specialized type of porting used only for racing RX-7 engines. Listed below, they go from mild to wild:

Street Port

This is the simplest and most common type of porting you'll see for a rotary engine. The idea is to enlarge the intake and exhaust ports to increase horsepower. How much power are we talking about? A good street port job combined with a decent performance intake and exhaust system will give a stock rotary engine an increase of about 50–60 percent. Nowhere else can you get so much improvement over stock for so little work and money.

The downside of this improvement (and there is a downside with nearly any performance enhancement), is that afterwards, it is nearly impossible to get a rotary to pass most states' emissions testing. Add an aftermarket intake and exhaust system, and you can kiss that emissions sticker goodbye.

Although fuel mileage and emissions are impaired, a properly street-ported engine still has excellent drivability and low-end performance. When done right, you can even run your car's air conditioning at idle with no problems. Street porting essentially causes the intake ports to close later, thus allowing in more fuel. The exhaust ports will open earlier and close later as well. The exhaust ports are simpler to modify, but if you make them too wide, you will lose support for the apex seals, which can then get into your combustion chamber and cause real problems. Although it's called "street porting," it does not necessarily mean that when you are finished, the exhaust gases will remain in compliance with state and local emission laws.

Bridge Port

Bridge porting is very similar to street porting, but the machining is taken a little bit further. So far, in fact, that you leave only a "bridge" for the corner seal to pass over so it doesn't fall into the hole you've created. When bridge porting, you actually cut an additional intake port into the edge of the housing, leaving some material between the new port and the original port on the surface of the housing. Underneath that bridge, however, the new port is enlarged to actually join up with the original port. This procedure causes the intake ports to open earlier and close even later. It compromises sealing and is impractical for the street as low-speed driveability, emissions, and economy are greatly compromised.

Remember, these are generalizations. You could conceivably make a bridge port so small as to retain some semblance of streetability, or a street port so large that you lose almost all low-speed driveability.

1/2 Bridge Port

One of Tri-Point Engineering's favorite modifications, the 1/2 bridge, combines the best aspects of a good street port with a full bridge port. The primary intake port is opened only an additional 15–20 percent, but as in a bridge port, a third port is cut near the very edge of the housing, leaving a bridge (as above) for the corner seal to cross over. The advantage over a street port is more power. But the best thing about a 1/2 bridge port for an autocrosser is the fact that the power is available much earlier in the rpm range. In a typical full bridge port, the best torque is only achieved between 6,000–9,500 rpm, while the 1/2 port has usable power between 4,000 and 8,500 rpm. In Solo II, that means getting off the line and coming out of a turn with more torque.

Peripheral Port

Peripheral porting does just what the name implies. It takes the intake ports out of the side housing (these original ports are then filled with epoxy) and moves them to the periphery of the engine in the rotor housing. Why go to all that trouble? Because this greatly alters port timing and moves the power band way up, like from 4,000–8,000 rpm on a street-ported engine to 8,000–10,000 rpm for a peripheral-ported engine. This type of porting is obviously reserved only for all-out race cars because it creates overlap like a radical cam does in a piston engine.

Porting Summary

Keep in mind that any of these port jobs, when performed on a rotary engine, will change the engine timing to a certain degree. Also remember that the key to taking full advantage of your new port job is by improving fuel and exhaust flow as well as ignition timing. Porting works on any rotary engine. Just be sure to plan out your project carefully, making sure you get the right balance in your carburetion/fuel-injection, exhaust, and ignition systems.

Engine Transplantation

This book describes many ways to get more power out of your engine. Often the extra power comes at a cost of some degree of comfort on the street—such as increased noise or reduced low-speed performance. That's why some owners opt to improve their engines by replacing them altogether. An engine transplant can add power without detracting from road comfort.

Owners of 1979–1985 RX-7s that are equipped with the small-chambered 12A motor can instantly gain 50 horsepower by upgrading to a 13B. Of course, they could keep the 12A, do a street port, add a header and exhaust, Weber carb, etc. This could net 50 horsepower. But it would also produce a car that is loud, gets really poor gas mileage, won't start easily in cold weather, and won't pass emissions—not the sort of vehicle you'd want to drive back and forth to work.

By swapping over to a 13B, you get the same extra 50 horsepower, without having to do all the modifications, keeping your car as pleasant to drive on the street as when you had your stock 12A under the hood. Except now, your car is faster!

You can clearly see the bridge formed by the extra port created to the outside of the original port. What is harder to see is that the two ports are actually connected underneath the bridge. *Racing Beat*

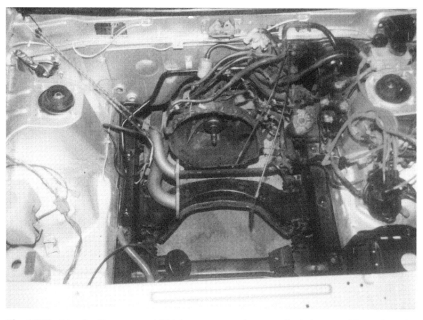

The 1970s Mazda Cosmos and RX-4s are great places to find 4-port 13B engines for 12A-powered first generation RX-7s. They are starting to get a little hard to find, so if you locate one, pull it out before someone else beats you to it. In the case of this Cosmo, you're too late.

If, on the other hand, you have come to take for granted your 160-horsepower 2G non-turbo, or even your 255-horsepower 3G RX-7, and want some extra pop, your options for engine swapping are considerably more complex. Adding a turbo unit to your normally aspirated 2G car is an excellent way to get a 40-plus horsepower increase without compromising your street cruising comfort. If you have a turbocharged 2G or 3G, the answer may be to create more boost for your stock turbo units (see chapter 12). Engine swapping should be a last resort for these cars.

Popular Engine Swaps

1978–1985 - The First-Generation RX-7

When the RX-7 reached U.S. shores in 1978, it weighed in at a little over 2,400 pounds and was fitted with a 12A motor capable of

100 horsepower. The big weakness of this power plant is the lack of torque, which is an anemic 105 ft-lbs. If you own a GS model and are looking for a new engine, you have several options. All 12A motors from this long production run are interchangeable—and there were over 300,000 cars made with this engine, most of which were imported to the U.S. market. But how does 35 extra horses and nearly 30 ft-lbs of torque sound? That's what you can get by upgrading your 12A to a 13B. For that reason alone, this is one of the most popular and simple engine swaps.

But before you head off to the junkyard, you should consider a few things. If your present RX-7's body is not in good enough shape, don't use it (even though you may love it). There are many RX-7s with good bodies and bad engines that can be found for under $1,000, mostly in the South and West. If you are going to take the

time to do this kind of project, it is very important to start with a good body (see chapter 3), and pay particular attention to the unibody. Are there holes in the floor or around the rocker panels? Inspect the rear fenders. No matter how much you love your car, don't start off with trouble. Find one with a good body in need of an engine, then you can sell yours once the swap is completed.

Assuming you have a good donor car, it's time to search for an engine. You essentially have three choices when it comes to a 13B engine: an early four-port from an RX-4, a six-port from a 1984–1985 GSL-SE, or a six-port from a second-generation car.

There were a couple pre-RX-7 Mazdas that came standard with a four-port 13B that will easily replace your 12A. The 1974–1978 RX-4 and 1976–1978 Cosmo were both equipped with what you need to boost horsepower in your 1978–1985 car. Here are the relatively simple modifications you need to make in order to perform a successful swap.

The first thing to keep in mind is that the 12A block is slightly shorter than the 13B. That means that you need to change two things right up front: the engine mounting plate and the exhaust system/manifold. The motor mounts in your 12A chassis will work just fine, but since there's a few millimeters difference in width between the two engines, you have to either slot the two holes on the 13B mounting plate (bad idea) or use the plate from your 12A. They interchange rather easily.

If you just bought a new exhaust system for your 12A, here's the bad news: The exhaust ports are the same, but since the old engine block is shorter, you will either need to get a different header/13B exhaust manifold, or shorten the exhaust system itself. Then there's the oil pan. You will need to retrofit the pan and oil pick up tube from your 12A to the new engine, or get a pan from a 1984–1985 SE, as the early 13B pans won't clear properly. Of course, if the 13B you've lined up is from a 1984–1985 SE, you won't have a clearance problem.

You can't get the engines out from underneath, so you will need to rent a cherry picker to pull the motor, if you don't own one. The swap itself from this point on is rather straightforward. You may run into one other complication, however, in that there were two different carburetors made for the four-port pre-RX-7 13B and the 1978–1985 four-port 12A. The good news is that either block will work with whatever carb you have. A 12A carb fits on a 13B intake manifold with just a little modification (redrilling and tapping mounting studs). This is common practice and saves you money if the 13B you secure doesn't come with a carb.

The 13B engines are usually available at your local import junkyard. But that doesn't mean the engine you get there isn't in need of a rebuild. It would be a shame to do all that work and find that the boneyard engine's apex seals are shot. The best approach is to call an engine broker or a rotary performance shop, like Pettit, Mazdatrix, or Peter Farrell Supercars. Your guaranteed rotary engine will be shipped directly to your garage door, ready for transplantation.

1986–1995 - The Second and Third Generation RX-7s

There is only one swap we would consider for these newer cars. It started with the 3G driver who yearned for supercar performance, and has gradually trickled down to the 2G community. We are talking about the 20B triple

Peter Farrell Supercars (PFS) attempted one of the first triple rotor transplants into a 2G RX-7. With a greater availability of the 20A from Japan, you will see many more over the coming years.

rotor swap. We don't recommend this to anyone but an expert, and only a few transformations have been successfully completed. The cost is staggering, which is why this is mostly a "rich guy" 3G project. We took a trip over to Peter Farrell Supercars to learn more.

What we really wanted to understand is why anyone would want to upset the fragile balance of one of the best sports cars ever made. The 3G offers an excellent mix of both power and handling. But when we met some of Farrell's customers, we started to get the picture. These are typically guys who are accustomed to driving high-end sports cars, but like the classic yet beautiful lines of the 3G RX-7. No matter how fast your Lamborghini is, it still looks like a kit car. And while the 911 has gained a lot in technology, luxury, and grunt, some fans of the marque feel it has lost the pure and elegant lines it had early in life. The killer

looks of the 3G RX-7 is inspiring some of these wealthy sports car buffs to buy a 3G RX-7 and then opt for a triple rotor conversion.

Despite its cost and complexity, this swap is gaining in popularity and is being performed almost as fast as the engines can be imported. This, however, is not one that should be left to the casual mechanic. Its no bolt-in swap, like the 12A to 13B conversion. It would almost be as easy to swap in a V-8 as to shoehorn in a triple rotor.

Fresh out of the newer Japanese-only Mazda Cosmos, the 20B engine produces more horsepower and tons more torque than the 3G 13B. The torque improvement alone is incentive enough to consider this swap. But there are serious obstacles to overcome before you can drive your hybrid down the street for the first time.

Since the 20B has one more rotor, the engine block is longer by the length of a rotor housing plus the

The most popular candidate for a 20A transplant is the 3G RX-7. PFS has performed several of these over the past few years, the people involved accumulating valuable knowledge in the process.

One of PFS's first attempts at 20A transplantation used the same motor mount location (for the most part) as the 13B. The problem with that was that the 20A has an extra rotor that makes the block longer, and that length has to go somewhere. With the car shown above, the length went toward the front of the car. You can see the difference between Farrell's first attempt and his second, which shifted the entire engine back toward the cockpit. Notice how the air intake filter is crunched up against the front of the car shown above, but is in its normal position on the 20A transplant to the right.

width of the intermediate housing (160 millimeter total). One of the experts performing this conversion is Peter Farrell Supercars, who has done two different versions of this transplant.

Version One: Add that extra 6 inches toward the front of the car. This produces exceptional power but with a cramped engine compartment. Also, there is more weight ahead of the front wheels, resulting in a less balanced car overall. The advantage is that it's a simpler conversion and requires a minimal amount of cutting.

Version Two: Add the extra 6 inches toward the rear of the car. This approach corrects both of the problems encountered above. The balance of the car is not compromised, and the engine compartment is not crowded. The problem is that there's no room to add 6 inches toward the rear of the engine compartment. The solution is to get out the cutting torch. This conversion requires that the transmission be moved 6 inches toward the rear of the car. That's no easy task, and should be left to a professional like

The drawback to moving the engine 6 inches toward the rear is that you have to move the tranny as well. That means cutting a new hole in the floor and creating a new mounting position for the shifter. You can see where it was located—approximately 6 inches to the right. This transplant also benefits from better weight distribution, and has triple the power it used to.

Farrell or Pettit. The result, however, may actually be worth the $15,000-plus cost of the conversion.

The first time I drove a triple rotor 3G RX-7, I was immediately impressed with the engine's good low-end torque compared to that of the 13B motor. When I put my foot down, the aftermarket single-stage turbo kicked in, and the horizon blurred. I felt like Han Solo making the jump to lightspeed. Time was suspended for an instant before the 20B's turbo smoothly rocketed the sleek 3G body into hyperspace. This is a 911 killer, with style. No wonder 3G lovers are opting more and more for this transplant. Expensive, yes, but if your budget can handle it, you can convert your RX-7 into one of the most competent supercars on the planet. Given the sticker on the 911 Turbo, you might even convince yourself that the swap would be cost-effective.

Oddball Swaps

One of the most unusual swaps we have ever seen was inspired by the SCCA (Sports Car Club of America). You start out with a beautiful 3G RX-7, yank out the 13B and turbo, replacing them with a 12A and a carb. Well actually, the guys who run GT-3s don't really start out with a complete 3G car. They build a complete or partial tube frame chassis, then put a fiberglass/plastic 3G body around the chassis. Under the shell, however, the car looks more like a 1G than a 3G RX-7. The engine is also restricted to 200 horsepower, but to be able to get that kind of power out of a normally aspirated 12A is impressive. Unfortunately, these cars are not as competitive as they could be if the SCCA decided to loosen up on the rules a bit.

Another swap that is growing in popularity is the Chevy V-8. Frankly, we don't get it. Sure, when done correctly this will cure one of the only weak points of the RX-7: poor low-end torque. That V-8 will shake the wheels off the car at the starting line, but can you imagine how it sounds? Turning the key on an RX-7 and hearing a V-8 is like blowing into a trumpet and hearing a drum solo. Gone would be that beautiful high-pitched whine, replaced by a ground-pounding, low-pitched rumble. Why not save the trouble and just buy a Camaro in the first place? Then again, most of us would rather have a car that had the fine lines of an RX-7, as opposed to that U.S. cookie-cutter design used on most GM and Ford products (Corvettes and most Chrysler vehicles are the exception). One additional problem with a transplant is that you may not be allowed to run in some SCCA classes. We observed a 1980 RX-7 with a V-8

engine get turned away at a Solo I. The transplant forced it to be classed as a "Special" (reserved for home-made vehicles and formula cars). Since it didn't have sufficient safety equipment to compete in that class, it was not allowed to run. Without the transplant, it would easily have fit into one of the "Street Modified" or "Street Prepared" classes.

The rotary engine has been turning up in the strangest places lately. Other than the Honda transplant phenomenon, one of the most popular transplants is to put the 13B or 12A into a British car. Sprites, MGs, and Spitfires are cool-looking cars to start with. But the reason most people don't use them as a daily driver (or a race car, for that matter) is that they are underpowered and unreliable. I recall that the TR4 I raced for several years was no exception to this rule. It wasn't until I installed an Allison ignition, SK racing carbs, U.S.-manufactured header and exhaust, KYB shocks, etc., that the car finally became reliable and race ready. The rotary engine and tranny can change all that.

In our opinion, a Triumph Spitfire with a 13B in it is more of an RX-7 than an RX-7 shell hiding a V-8. One of the most talked-about transplants of this type is the *Grassroots Motorsports* magazine Project Ro-Spit. With a six-port 13B mated to an RX-7 tranny, this little pocket rocket can really fly. Add some street porting, plus an Electromotive ignition and fuel-management system, and if it had wings it could probably take off just like a real World War II Spitfire. How does 0–60 in under 5 seconds sound? It sounds like a tricked-out 3G, but for half the price. Another extremely successful British rotary was the Bob

Some 13B power plants have found their way into most everything, but most don't seem at home in anything but an RX-7. That is not the case with Ron Moreck's Hillclimb Special. In this case, the car was built around the engine, similar to the way the RX-7 was originally designed. This is one oddball swap that works both mechanically and philosophically.

King-built Ro-Spit that dominated its class (E Modified) in Solo II during the late 1980s and early 1990s.

But by far the fastest 0–60 and 1/4-mile rotary-powered land vehicle at the turn of the century was the special-built turbo-powered formula car belonging to the Moreck clan. This father-son racing team with son Ron as the driver has been setting course records at almost every Hillclimb in the East. The vehicle itself is something that must be seen firsthand, as photos cannot do it justice. The bodywork, paint, and wings are so aesthetically pleasing that you get the impression this car could sim-

ply fly to the top of the hill like a bird. The huge Trust intercooler mounted behind the 13B appears bigger than the engine itself. The turbo does not seem to function well in the low-rpm band, and turbo lag is measured in seconds. You get the feeling that Moreck needs a push to get the car going off the line—that is, until it reaches around 5,000 rpms, when the turbo begins to spool up. At that point, the thing hits warp drive, and for a few seconds until Moreck is forced to shift, the car and the space around it seem to blur as if it's about to enter another dimension. The tree branches outlining the

course shake as the huge wing displaces enough air to knock a grown man off his feet. Rotary lovers would revel in the power. Even muscle car fans, who constitute the majority of the spectators at an East Coast Hillclimb, are speechless (except for muttering "Holy $&%@" under their breath) as they watch the car hit its stride and vanish up the hill.

Finally, the SCCA is also the home for Formula Mazda, a spec road racing class that attracts some of the country's best drivers. Powered by a tuned 13B, these lightweight Indy-type cars handle like they are on rails and make for some of the best racing

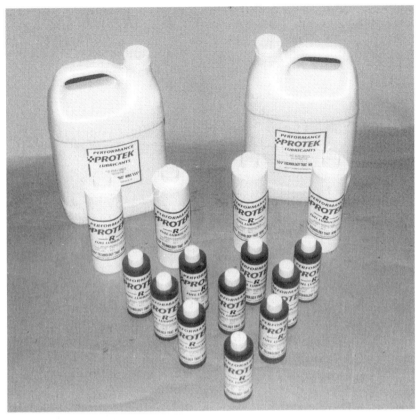

Racers can't afford an interruption of the oil injected into the engine by the oil metering pump. To avoid that possibility, some racers remove the oil metering system altogether and throw it away. They then premix fuel with oil, just like with two-cycle lawn mowers and most chain saws. It's like Mazda going back to its roots. Even with street cars, especially ones that have been ported, it is a good idea to add an additional protectant to the fuel such as Pettit's Protek. *Excellent Performance/Pettit Racing*

you could ever hope to watch. As we said, rotaries are turning up in some of the strangest places.

Engine Cooling

As mentioned in several of this book's chapters, a cool engine is a happy engine. But there are some things that are working against keeping your rotary happy. For a third-gen car, one of these things is the stock air separator tank (AST). The AST's task is to break up air bubbles in the cooling system. The problem is that the stock unit has been known to burst, and is not very efficient at dispersing heat even when it's working. Both Excellent Performance (Pettit) and Tri-Point offer a solution to this problem—a more efficient, aluminum AST that disperses heat better and won't burst.

A variety of aftermarket radiators and oil coolers are also available. Both will provide added cooling, possibly just enough to keep your car out of the red when it's hot outside. As an added precaution against heat,

Keeping your engine clean and cool is a good thing. Changing oil at least every 3,000 miles is a must for RX-7s, because the oil seems to accumulate more contaminants than with a piston engine. If you don't change the oil on time, this could happen. A typical scotched rotor next to a brand-new one. It's likely that the apex seal(s) cracked and got dislodged, taking a few turns around the combustion chambers before they were ground up into little pieces, ruining the rotor and housing in the process.

Racers often use a device like this, called an accusump, that will keep forcing oil into the engine even under the high g-forces that can be experienced in racing. Without one of these, a long, high-speed sweeper could move the oil out of contact with your sump, meaning the death of your engine from oil starvation.

we recommend replacing your stock radiator hoses with stronger silicone ones. Some racers can even use steel braided hoses, which also help to radiate some heat (it all adds up). Water Wetter (radiator additive) has also been proved to reduce coolant temperatures.

Finally, 3G owners may need to replace the sending units for oil pressure and water temperature, as they are prone to failure. If your car doesn't have a temperature indicator, get one. They're a must for a rotary-powered engine because if you overheat an RX-7, you will likely do irreversible damage. You need to be aware of any increase in either engine or exhaust gas temperature before it is too late.

Even though autocrossers only run their cars for a minute at a time, they must cool their engines before the next run. The benefit is both added power and longer engine life. Seriously consider the many tips throughout the book concerning ways to reduce engine temperature.

CHAPTER NINE

Ignition and Timing

An aftermarket ignition system is an important upgrade for a carbureted or race engine. But most stock RX-7 ignitions provide a strong hot spark, especially ones fitted to the 3G cars, and don't require an upgrade. You should base your decision on the intended use of the car. For example, if you plan on hopping up a 1987 GTU for the street, you don't need to spend money on an aftermarket ignition, as it could be spent in better ways. For the track, however, it could be well worth the investment.

As you know, there are two coils powering two spark plugs each in the RX-7 ignition system. Earlier rotary engines actually had two distributors as well. In reality, one coil and one plug per rotor is all you really need. The second, or trailing, coil, which fires the secondary spark plugs, is only intended to burn the mixture more efficiently by igniting gases that may have escaped the primary plug's spark. This also serves to push the rotor along its way with a little more force.

The first RX-7s (1978–1979) didn't even have electronic ignitions; they used the old-fashioned points and condenser setup. An electronic ignition was standard beginning in 1980, but the igniters were separate from the distributor. Igniters were finally incorporated into the distributor in 1981.

There are basically two types of aftermarket ignition systems on the market, and they can be distinguished by their method of timing and distributing the spark. The most popular add-on ignitions use a Capacitive Discharge (CD) mechanism. Most RX-7s (except 1979–1980) come stock with inductive systems that are designed to burn fuel more efficiently by supplying a long spark duration. A CD system, however, builds up energy in its capacitors, then discharges the spark

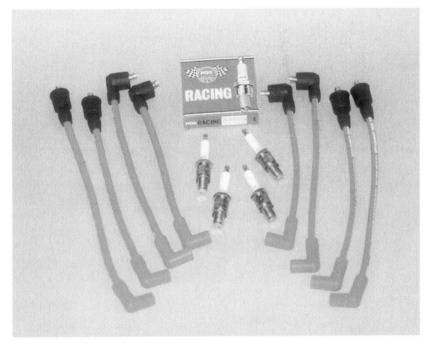

A good set of aftermarket wires, like these by NGK, is just one component of a high-performance ignition system. Most RX-7s won't benefit very much from updating the stock system; however, it's a must-do if you are running more fuel and air through your rotary engine.

in one short, powerful burst of energy. A CD system will tolerate a larger spark plug gap and tends to generate a more consistent torque curve at higher rpms.

One of the best ignition systems for a carbureted 1G is the MSD 6AL. It delivers multiple sparks to your rotary's combustion chamber, effectively burning more fuel than your conventional ignition setup. There is also a built-in, modifiable rev-limit feature that allows the driver to change "chips" to adjust maximum rpms.

We have tested a variety of the systems over the years, and for the most part, they are all the same. There are many different systems on the market, but the ones we will discuss in this chapter have been proved to be an asset to most applications. A multiple spark-type ignition, such as the MSD, is the preferred ignition for rotary engines. MSDs fire the plug several times instead of just once (or should we say twice due to the RX-7's twin-plug design?). They will also burn rich mixtures more efficiently than your stock system. MSD has a dual box system with a built-in rev limiter that is perfect for a first- or second-generation car, even though a multiple-spark ignition is not always the most reliable design out there. If you have a 1979 RX-7, you should replace the points/external igniter systems with an aftermarket electronic ignition.

The other type of system to consider is the same one that revolutionized

amateur racing in the 1990s. It is difficult to install and can cost $300–$500, but if you have the time and patience, there are rewards. This system is the Electromotive HPV1.

This ignition distinguishes itself from the others in two ways: 1) you won't need your distributor (great, save some weight), and 2) it uses a multi-coil setup. This allows one coil time to recharge while the others are working. It's a great system, but a little more challenging to install. And it looks a little odd. Your friends will probably ask, "Hey, what *is* that thing?"

The hassle of installing an HPV1 involves converting your engine to a crank-fire (or in this case, eccentric-fire) system. This system provides a much more accurate distribution of spark than a standard distributor can achieve. And with the money you save on caps and rotors, this system could pay for itself in 50 years! With a crank-fire system, you

eliminate this entire loop, because the Electromotive ignition receives its information directly from the eccentric shaft (see below for a more complete description of how an RX-7 ignition works).

The shaft has to be fitted with a magnet, and then you may have to fabricate an aluminum mounting bracket for the engine block to support the crank trigger mechanism that can monitor the position of the eccentric shaft. As the magnet on the shaft pulley turns past the magnet in the crank trigger, timing information can be passed directly to the Electromotive system to tell it precisely when to light up the spark plugs.

Getting the mounting bracket and magnets aligned can be tedious, but once your system is set, look out. Talk about a flat torque curve, even at 10K! Only the Electromotive system can offer that. Of course once you have installed the HPV1, you will

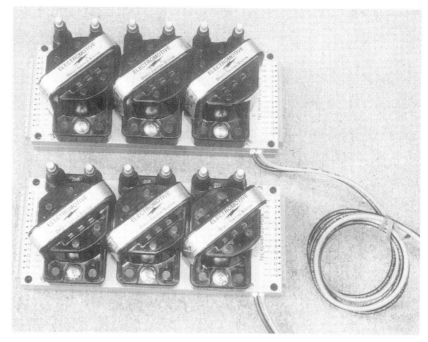

The Electromotive system uses a multiple coil setup so that one coil can re-energize before it is called on to fire the plugs again. With this ignition, you can throw away your distributor, and for that matter, your coils. The stock RX-7 distributor relies on a gear to turn the rotor, which in turn distributes the spark. The Electromotive system senses the rotation of the eccentric shaft directly, and fires accordingly.

Crane's Fireball ignition is a popular mod for fuel-injected RX-7s. It provides a hotter spark and also has an easily adjustable rev limiter on board.

want to convert to Electromotive fuel injection. We will discuss the pros and cons of this later in the book.

In conclusion, all the systems outlined here should give you more horsepower, better gas mileage, and move you up a few notches on the "cool" list. But which should you choose? If you are looking at doing some serious racing, then the Electromotive should be your choice, as it is probably the best system. For performance street or autocross applications, we would choose one of the others. Yes, we know that many Street Prepared and Prepared Solo II National Champions have the Electromotive system on board, so if you plan on becoming a National Champ, then by all means, indulge yourself. If not, go with one of the other CD systems. The free time you save on installation can be spent with your family, when they help you wax your RX-7.

Wires and Coils

Adding aftermarket ignition wires and plugs is a very common modification to RX-7s and many other cars. But can these products really improve performance?

Many race car drivers who compete in stock classes feel that they do. These classes don't allow many of the changes outlined in this book, but they do permit replacement of the stock ignition coils, wires, and plugs. There is much debate as to whether it's worth it to buy Splitfire plugs, high-performance wires, or super coils. Stock power plants typically do not respond as well to these ignition upgrades compared to the more modified engines.

Carbureted cars will benefit more from ignition modifications than their computer-controlled, fuel-injected counterparts. Fuel-injected cars have an oxygen sensor that provides feedback to the computer that controls the injectors, and therefore can provide a more accurate and consistent mixture of air and fuel into the cylinders. A carburetion system is much more crude, and in the event that the mixture becomes too rich, a stronger and more consistent spark can result in a more efficient burning of the mixture.

Fuel-injection systems that have been modified can also derive some benefit from these products. Depending on what modifications have been performed, as much as 5 horsepower can be captured by using a high-power ignition module, wires, plugs, and a coil. The extra power results when your stock ignition cannot keep up with the needs of the richer fuel mixture the modified injection system puts into the combustion chambers. In fact, you may experience a decrease in performance if you install bigger injectors without making any other changes to balance out the system.

High-power coils and special spark plugs are often overkill on standard RX-7 EFI systems. Most later-model ignition coils can easily supply

Hot wires installed on two highly modified 13Bs. These bridge-ported engines need all the spark they can handle.

the energy needed to fire a spark plug. Providing more juice to the plug will not necessarily create a hotter or bigger spark. This would be similar to putting 94-octane gas into your rotary engine when it only really needs 87 or 89. If you're already getting complete combustion with your present system, a stronger spark won't change anything. And for 3G owners, changing wires can be an all-day experience, especially when it comes to the coil wires. It's probably not worth the effort, as the gain for most stock 3G motors will be negligible, and in certain circumstances, "hot" wires can do more harm than good (see below).

Racing Beat offers an 8 millimeter set of wires specifically designed for rotary engines. These "Ultra Red-Hot" wires come either shielded or unshielded—for racing RX-7 drivers that could care less about radio interference. We have tried these, and they are great. But in our opinion, the leader in ignition wire technology is Magnecor. This manufacturer con-

centrates on making high-quality wires that are designed not to interfere with the vehicle's electronic fuel-management system. One of the side effects of using some of the "low resistance" wires on the market today is that many will emit electromagnetic interference. This can cause your EFI computer to misinterpret some of the signals it receives, which can produce anything from an occasional misfire to a rough running engine. The Magnecor wires (8.5 millimeter and 10 millimeter) are designed to eliminate electromagnetic interference altogether, and are constructed better than most of the other products on the market. The company also makes no claims that its wires will increase horsepower.

For this, Magnecor should be applauded. Most other companies state that their products have been proved to increase horsepower. That may be true under certain circumstances, but they have yet to pass our chassis dyno test. Over the years, we have tried many brands of wires on RX-7s that have had

both stock and modified fuel-injected engines, and found little evidence to support these claims.

So where does that leave you? Probably confused, and that's because most ignition products can, at best, add only a couple of horsepower under certain circumstances. OEM, Mazda, or NGK wires are excellent products, and usually never need to be replaced unless they wear out. If you install a high-power ignition system, however, there is some evidence to support upgrading to a high-performance wire. Some stock wires have been known to fail under the more extreme conditions imposed by a hotter ignition. Then again, so have some high-performance wires, so check all your wires at least every 50,000 miles. And speaking of heat, as with most other items in the engine bay, your battery should be protected from the heat. This will result in better charging performance and longer life.

If you choose to invest in any of these ignition products, the "bang for the buck" quotient is not as favorable as with other modifications described in this book. One additional bit of advice: Don't use solid-core wires on fuel-injected cars. They are meant for carbureted race cars, and can play havoc with an EFI system.

Ignition Basics: How a Rotary Engine Works

An RX-7 ignition system's timing can be adjusted to maximize torque at a given rpm. If you want to do this, it's important to be able to visualize how a rotary engine works. Your basic Wankel design calls for the same "strokes" as a piston engine: intake, compression, combustion (or power), and exhaust. (Nearly all of you reading this book have seen this before, so we'll be brief.) Assume that the rotor is rotating in a clockwise direction with

MSD Blaster coils are used here in conjunction with an MSD 6AL in Mark Halama's 1984 GSL-SE. The "Blaster" coil delivers a stronger charge to the spark plugs, and they in turn, can deliver a hotter spark.

If you are running "hotter" coils and wires, you should use a spark plug designated to withstand that extra charge. In turn, the system will produce a stronger spark. NGK offers several different plugs, depending on what you have done to your engine. *Mazda Competition Parts Department*

the intake and exhaust ports on the left, and the spark plugs on the right. Don't worry about visualizing this in three dimensions. For a while, let's forget that a rotor has three points and three sides, just like a triangle, and concentrate on just two points and the one side between them.

If the rotor is turning clockwise, the first point will be leading the way around the housing while the second point will dragging along behind it. First, the leading edge of the rotor passes by the intake port and "sucks" in an air/fuel mixture (thanks to a vacuum effect). Shortly afterwards, the trailing edge on that side of the rotor passes by that same intake port and closes it off, thus isolating one chamber between the two that has been filled with the air/fuel mix. This completes the intake "stroke."

Next, as the rotor continues to move in a clockwise circle just passing by the first spark plug hole, the volume in the chamber is greatly reduced in size, compressing the air/fuel mix up against the right side of the housing. This is the compression stroke. Igniting an air/fuel mixture that is not compressed won't generate as much energy as when the molecules of air and fuel have been packed very tightly together.

Then, the moment we've been waiting for. The spark plugs fire and the rotor is pushed along its merry way by an explosion of expanding gases (power stroke). That pressure will be enough for the leading edge of the rotor to spin all the way around, turning the eccentric shaft, tranny, and wheels in the process.

Finally, as the leading edge of the rotor passes by the exhaust port on the left side of the housing, exhaust gases begin to escape. When the trailing edge of the rotor approaches the port, nearly all of the gases are forced out through that small hole that leads directly to the header.

Then it starts all over again very quickly since the exhaust port and intake port are only millimeters apart from each other on the same (left)

side of the housing. To keep a tight seal in the chamber created by the movement of the rotor, springlike pieces of metal push up against the rotor housing to keep gases from escaping until they are supposed to. These are the apex seals, and there is one for each point.

The engineering beauty of a rotary engine lies in its triangular design. We were following the exploits of two edges and one side of our rotor above. But add just one more edge/point to complete the triangle, and you get two more sides—the side between our leading edge and the new triangle point, and the side that is formed by our trailing edge and the new point. That also means that there are two other chambers that are formed. So as the rotor revolves around the housing, three different things are happening in the three different chambers. It is hard to think in terms of "three" if you are used to dealing with a piston engine that does things in "four." But those same "four strokes" are present in a rotary engine, as we explained above. It's just that only three of these four strokes are happening at one time, as opposed to a piston engine in which you can find all four things happening simultaneously somewhere in the engine.

But technically, with three strokes happening in each rotor, it is essentially equivalent to a three-cylinder engine. Put two rotors together, and you have a six-banger. For this reason, rotary engines are sometimes treated like a V-6 engine when it comes to racing classifications.

Rotary Engine Timing

As discussed above, both 12A or 13B power plants have a "two spark plugs per rotor" configuration, and they fire once every time the eccen-

To correctly time any engine, you should use a timing light that incorporates an advance dial into it. That way, all you need to do is set the dial to the exact amount of advance you wish to dial in, then turn the distributor until the timing mark lines up to TDC. With a standard timing light, you have to guess how far past TDC you want the timing mark to go, and unless you have a degree wheel, this is virtually an impossible task. This advance light can be found at most Sears stores for under $75. Once you learn how to use it (and it's simple), you'll never want to use the old type of light again.

tric shaft makes a complete rotation. The shaft performs three rotations each time the rotor turns 360 degrees (remember, there are three chambers that fire each time the rotor makes one trip around the inside of the housing). The second rotor is doing the same thing, but is 180 degrees out of phase with the first rotor.

Racers and mechanics with all levels of expertise recognize that distributor (ignition) timing is one of the many components that can be adjusted to change the characteristics of how your engine performs.

Your car's engine produces a fixed number of horsepower, and changing the timing will usually not affect this, unless someone adjusted your timing and put it seriously out of whack. In that case, returning the timing back

to the factory setting should recapture your lost performance. What changing the distributor timing will do is tell the engine when you want that horsepower to work for you.

If you want more power at low rpms, you will likely have to sacrifice some power and torque in the higher rpm band. It's simply a matter of whether your ignition is advanced or retarded. The distributor determines when current will be sent to the spark plugs. Once the plug fires, there is still a minute delay before the air/fuel mixture ignites. This interval remains constant (unless you use a slower-burning, higher-octane gasoline, or are supercompressing the mixture). What changes, based on rpms, is the position of the rotor at the time the air/fuel mixture ignites.

By moving the distributor in order to retard ignition timing, in essence you are allowing the rotor to get closer to top dead center (TDC) on the eccentric shaft before the spark plug fires and ignites the air/fuel mixture. But as rpms increase, this relationship changes. A faster-moving rotor's leading edge travels toward TDC at a higher rate of speed. Since the time it takes to ignite the air/fuel mixture remains constant, by the time you put spark to the mixture, the leading edge could be on its way to the other side of the rotor, heading toward the exhaust port. To "catch" it in time, you need to advance the timing so that the mixture is ignited earlier, before the leading edge is gone.

To retard the timing, you adjust the distributor so the spark begins to ignite the fuel when the leading edge of the rotor is much closer to TDC, or in some cases, after it moves past. But why put a spark to the fuel when it isn't fully compressed?

Remember that even if you have your distributor timing set at -10 degrees BTDC (before top dead center), that doesn't mean that all the fuel will burn before the rotor reaches TDC. The spark plug may fire at -10 degrees, but initially only part of the fuel ignites, which in turn causes the main mixture to explode. During that time, the leading edge has advanced much closer to (or just beyond) TDC. The point in time (relative to TDC) at which you choose to push the rotor along its way will define certain torque characteristics along the eccentric shaft.

Autocrossers often tend to retard their timing to increase low-end torque, enabling them to get more power coming out of a low-speed turn. Depending on the track and gear selection, road racers spend much more time in the higher rpm band, and are willing to sacrifice power at 3,000 rpm to gain power at 6K. For this reason, they *advance* the ignition timing. By advancing the timing, the plug fires sooner, so that only at higher rpms has the rotor gotten ten close enough to TDC to derive maximum force from the explosion. Drag racers follow the same philosophy as the road racers.

As with any adjustment you make to your car, you should initially experiment with small changes and measure what effect they have on horsepower and torque throughout the rpm range. The only reliable way to do this is on a chassis dyno. You should only need about an hour to accomplish the fine-tuning necessary to obtain your desired torque curve. This is probably the best thing you can do on a dyno. Most RX-7 owners can usually find between 2–5 horsepower depending on what they have done to their engines.

CHAPTER TEN

Fuel-Injection and Carburetion Systems
by Dale Black and Mike Ancas

This chapter will focus on second- and third-generation RX-7s, as most 1G cars, except for the 1984–1985 GSL-SE, were not fuel injected. If you do own a 1978–1983 RX-7, you don't need to feel left out. The bulk of the next chapter is devoted to you.

Before making a single change to your injection system, you should consider getting your stock fuel injectors cleaned or balanced and blueprinted. You will be surprised just how much difference this can make. Second-generation RX-7s are now between 7 and 14 years old. Unless you've just had your injectors replaced, we guarantee that they are not functioning at 100 percent—no matter what type of injector cleaner you are using. Cars with especially high mileage may be experiencing even more inefficiency. And even if they are flowing at 99–100 percent, the spray pattern may be less than 360 degrees, which will rob your engine of low-end torque. Marren Motorsports and RC Engineering both offer a balancing and blueprinting service that can restore your car to its original performance.

Sometimes you may need to replace an injector or two, especially

Want some more juice? Most 3G aftermarket turbo setups require the addition of extra injectors. Note the expert job (braided-steel fuel line) performed on this 3G by Peter Farrell Supercars. Just like a bad carburetor will rob performance, an EFI engine is only as good as its fuel injectors. Don't assume that they will perform like new forever. They need to be removed and professionally cleaned or replaced with time, just as a carburetor needs to be rebuilt.

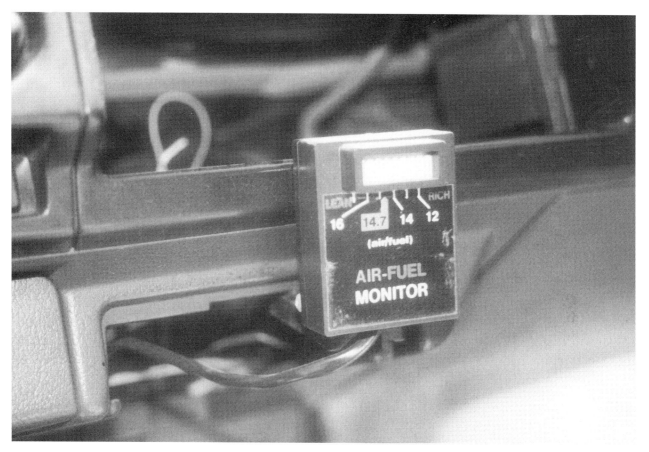

All fuel-injected cars that become performance projects should get one of these inexpensive (around $100) air/fuel meters. This one is sold by Racer Wholesale for less than $100. *Courtesy of EFI Systems*

if have an early 2G. This is a must-do for a 1984–1985 GSL-SE that has never had its injectors removed, cleaned, and blueprinted. Experts remind us that even after only four to five years of service, your injectors can become worn or partially clogged, so even 3G owners should take notice. Heck, we've seen performance variations with brand-new injectors right out of the factory. The reason balanced injectors are so important is that your stock EFI system may decrease flow to your good injectors in an attempt to match the poor performance of one or two of the worn injectors.

The cost for balancing and blueprinting can vary from around $125 to $400 depending on how ineffi-

cient your injectors are or how many you need to replace. You will be able to notice the extra low-end torque as soon as you put the new or cleaned and balanced injectors in.

While properly functioning injectors are essential to good performance, many owners of fuel-injected cars think the way to increase power is to get more fuel into the air/fuel mixture by either raising the fuel pressure, installing larger injectors, or by installing additional injectors. Remember, more fuel is not necessarily the goal. What *is* essential is to get the right amount of fuel for the volume of air being brought in. An air/fuel ratio monitor can help you establish the proper mix. Inexpensive monitors are available through compa-

nies like Racer Wholesale (800-886-RACE) for $100–$150. These units easily tap into your existing oxygen sensor and are highly recommended for determining whether or not the desired effect has been achieved when a change is made to the injection process. Keep in mind that the setup that works for one RX-7 may not be best for another. Even stock fuel-management systems vary slightly (since individual engines operate in various stages of efficiency), so the results may vary even between vehicles of the same make, model, and year.

Fuel mixture control is separated into two modes: closed-loop and open-loop. During closed-loop engine operation (idle and low load—2,000 rpm and below),

99

the ECU uses the oxygen sensor to trim the air/fuel ratio to the chemically ideal value of 14.7:1 for best emissions performance. Thus, any adjustments you make within this range get canceled out by the stock ECU. Open-loop fuel adjustments are not canceled out and are generally considered to affect medium- to high-load operation (4,000 rpm and above, and wide-open throttle). Since emissions at these loads and speeds are essentially unregulated, engineers generally choose a very rich fuel curve to protect the engine against knock and thermal stress and to ensure that fuel pump and injector wear will not result in dangerously lean conditions over the life of the engine. In doing so, they compromise peak power and harm fuel efficiency. Stock vehicles generally respond to fuel subtractions in these open-loop ranges. For modified engines, the guidelines above also apply; however, heavily modified engines may need extra fuel in the upper rpm range. Since timing becomes a critical variable in power tuning, a device that can measure injector "duty" cycle is helpful as well (for example, if you find the stock injectors frequently hit 90–92 percent or above, then larger or additional injectors are probably needed). More on that later.

Fuel-injected rotaries can be a real brain teaser to set up just right. Any serious maladjustment can cause your engine to knock, which is a sign of detonation, which can cause excessive heat and quickly ruin your engine. That is why it is always best to start with either the stock programming or an extra rich air/fuel mixture as a baseline. From there, you should be able to add and subtract fuel to tune performance.

Reprogramming the Stock ECU

Aside from the additional injectors/controllers, which will be discussed later, there are basically three ways to retune a second- or third-generation RX-7's engine for optimal performance. First, you can exchange the stock ECU for one that has been specifically programmed for your modifications. There are a number of performance companies with the

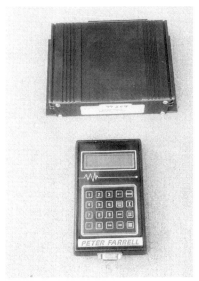

A Programmable Management System (PMS) like this one from Farrell (manufactured by EFI Systems) reads the stock fuel injection and spark timing signals from the engine's control unit, then changes them to the settings that you specify via terminal or PC laptop entry. This allows different fuel and timing adjustments to be made for idle, partial throttle, and wide-open throttle. There are also two user-programmable switches that allow the PMS to activate power adders like nitrous oxide, with two stages that need to be activated at different times. The PMS also can monitor your stock engine control unit and give you the ability to control the engine's timing and fuel curves. It controls the timing in 1-degree increments and the fuel in 2 percent increments. It makes the use of aftermarket performance "chips" unnecessary. Farrell also reprograms the stock computers (above) for injected RX-7s.

right amount of know-how to do this, often without even having the car on site. Among those are Pettit Racing, Mostly Mazda, XS Engineering, and Rotary Performance of Texas. One downside to this type of engine management is that its programming is not changeable without removing the ECU and sending it out along with a list of modification changes.

The second way to go about tuning an engine by reprogramming is by using what's called a "piggyback" system, which is an external computer that plugs inline of the stock ECU. The piggyback system changes the input/output variables of the stock ECU. Here, it is possible to incorporate various program settings for different venues of performance. Plus, it becomes possible to change the programming with changes made to your car. Two good piggyback systems currently available for the third generation are the Peter Farrell Supercars' Programmable Management Computer (PFS PMC for short) and the Wolf 3D System. The PFS PMC is the same as EFI System's PMS (Programmable Management System), but cannot be obtained directly.

The third way to retune the engine is with an aftermarket ECU, discussed below.

Installing an Aftermarket ECU

If you've made modifications beyond that of popular bolt-ons, such as porting of the internal engine, throttle body, intake, and/or turbo manifold, then you might consider a complete ECU replacement, if your goal is to race. Often referred to as a "stand-alone" because its sole purpose is to control the engine's functions and nothing else, it is a popular option among racers, especially those competing professionally and whose cars are not driven on the

David Lane has added two additional injectors to his turbocharged GSL-SE. You can spot the "Y" wire just to the right of the Mazdatrix oil cap that leads to the injectors installed at the bottom of the stock RE-EGI intake. *David Lane*

George Dodsworth has also installed two additional injectors on his aftermarket turbo 2G RX-7. All these photos of extra injectors makes my car seem inadequate. It must be a case of injector envy.

street. This is an extreme performance method of optimizing power and is not legal for street use—and is extremely difficult to program for the street, anyway. We do not recommend that you pursue this avenue unless you intend only to race your vehicle. It does not provide any compromise between high performance and streetability.

Adding Additional Injectors and a Controller

If you discover that you need more fuel delivery, additional injectors or controllers may be the answer. But there is a drawback if you choose to follow this path. Separate air/fuel controllers are not always a good idea in addition to a stock or modified ECU. That's because their reaction time is too slow, and if knock occurs, you could easily experience detonation. In most cases, they don't even react to knock, just boost levels. In other cases, a separate boost controller can be used in conjunction. Either way, it's just not reliable enough to protect the engine against harmful knock. During our trip to Peter Farrell's shop, we did see examples of how these systems can work, and work well. Most of this work should be trusted to a professional, however, and will not be cheap. But after personally driving one of these babies, we can say that you get what you pay for.

Too Much Boost?

Mazda built in a defense system to avoid problems associated with overboost. On the third generation, if a certain high level of boost is sustained and observed by the ECU, it will cut the fuel to the rear rotor as well as bleed off as much boost as the air bypass valve will allow. This is also done in an effort to protect against detonation, and may occur as a result of input from the knock sensor.

Proper fuel pressure is very important on EFI RX-7s. To insure that this 20B triple-rotor Cosmo motor is getting just the right amount of fuel, Peter Farrell Supercars installed this regulator. Fuel pressure is even more critical on cars incorporating forced induction (turbo supercharging).

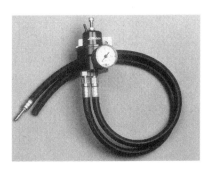

Often, a fuel pressure riser can slightly boost the output of your stock injectors. That can make them act more like bigger injectors. Risers, like this Stillen unit, are particularly useful on cars equipped with a header, exhaust, and air intake, which help the car breathe better without providing the extra fuel for which the car may now thirst. *Stillen*

For a second-generation turbo unit, you can buy a Fuel-Cut Defenser (FCD). This simple little electronic device can defeat the factory-set fuel-cut-out program, and help get you the boost you want. Your Mazda computer is not prepared to deal with people like us who try to manipulate parameters in an effort to

increase boost. The stock EFI computer is designed to decrease the fuel mix, which, when working in conjunction with the stock system, will limit boost. But when you shut down that failsafe system by manually adjusting the boost, you can imagine what would happen to your engine if the computer couldn't deliver enough fuel to compensate for the more oxygen-rich intake charge. The result would be an overly lean mixture, and detonation would occur. An FCD will keep the computer from cutting down the fuel in its effort to reduce boost. If you use an FCD, it is highly advisable to use a proven boost controller as well. In fact, Apexi recently released a state-of-the-art combined system that is so sophisticated, it falls just short of being a PFS PMC replacement! This product has not yet developed a reputation in the marketplace, good or bad.

Another way to keep from having the degree of boost you desire limited by your stock EFI feedback system is to port out the wastegate. It

is designed to handle only a small amount of preset factory boost, and will be a weak link in your system once you have overcome the situations above that also attempt to deprive us of the boost we want.

Carburetion Versus Fuel Injection

Carburetors were masters of the air/fuel mix for most of the last century. That reign was challenged in the 1980s and 1990s, as manufacturers began to switch more and more cars over to fuel injection. You can still buy both systems for your RX-7, and both were used on the cars—carburetors on the 1Gs until 1984, and fuel injection thereafter. Which system gives the best performance is still a subject of debate, though aftermarket suppliers have followed manufacturers in the move from the old technology to the new.

Fuel-injected cars start easier, idle consistently, and allow you to set the fuel mixture with great accuracy—particularly with aftermarket programmable fuel injection. On the other hand, carbs are what gives a car its personality. They're a simpler concept reminiscent of simpler times. You feel more connected to the car because there isn't a computer chip separating you from performance adjustments. If the mix is too rich or too lean, you can whip out a spanner (otherwise known as a wrench), a screwdriver, and your shop manual, and put the problem right. Which system you choose will depend on your budget and sympathies, although your hand may be forced in certain competition classes.

You would have to be a carburetor fanatic—or an SCCA member—to convert a 2G or 3G car to carburetion. Why else would you rip out one of the most efficient fuel-management systems ever developed for a street car and replace it with a carburetor? If you're not

Two completely different approaches to achieving "full-blown performance." At the right is one of the most popular carb conversions for 1G RX-7s: Racing Beat's 465 CFM four-barrel Holley setup. It's relatively easy to install and tune. At the other end of the spectrum is an Electromotive TEC-II aftermarket EFI system. Once you have it set, you can forget about it, but getting to that point can be a long—and costly—journey.

This GT-3 third-generation RX-7 had to convert to carburetion in order to compete in SCCA road racing. Note the huge aluminum air intake, custom designed to keep the hotter engine compartment separate from the denser, cooler air coming in from the outside (probably at around 100 miles per hour). This is an excellent example of function over form.

This is an excellent example of function over form. Actually, this car just looks like a third gen from the outside. Underneath the removable skin, however, it has about as much in common with a real RX-7 as Dale Jarrett's Winston Cup car has with your dad's Ford Taurus.

The inside of a stock 1G carb seems competent enough, but it would need to be completely reworked to approach the performance of an aftermarket conversion such as a Holley, Weber, Delortto, or Mikuni. It's just easier to buy the upgraded carb—if you can find it. Holley and Weber are the only current manufacturers, but Webers don't work as well for non-racing applications (rough idle and poor cold starting).

a fanatic, then you must be a GT-3 competitor in the SCCA. Incredibly, the present rules of this division require 2G and 3G owners to replace their fuel-injection systems with carburetors. Even the "regional" road racing circuit, known as IT racing, restricts many fuel-injected cars from competition. The SCCA Solo program, however, is more of an entry-level racing effort. Classes are structured so that you can maintain, or even modify, a fuel-injected RX-7 and still compete successfully.

The SCCA policy is an anomaly on this issue. Both within the Mazda line and among aftermarket suppliers, the momentum has shifted from carburetion to EFI. In the early 1990s, there were more aftermarket carburetors to choose from than EFI systems. Probably the most popular conversion was replacing your stock unit with a high-performance carb. There were actually a few Delorttos to choose from, offering the enthusiast options ranging from reliable street performance to pure racing. When Delortto stopped producing side

draft carbs, Mikuni and Weber offered an alternative. Distributed mainly by Racing Beat in the United States, this "over the top" manifold and side draft setup not only looked cool, but worked very well. Mikuni was the best choice if you planned on driving your RX-7 on the street. The Japanese-made carb idled better than the Weber, and could match its performance on the racetrack as well. The jets were easily accessible by removing a small cap on the top of the carb, making tuning a simple task. The Weber was cruder. Because it didn't idle well, it was recommended only for racing purposes. Even though the Weber carb is still listed in some RX-7 performance catalogs, it has been discontinued and is hard to find. Mikunis are even more scarce.

Today Holley is the only manufacturer offering carbs for the RX-7. As this book was going to press, Holley made a new commitment to the RX-7 community by working closely with Racing Beat to further develop their line of carbs. Holley

offers down-draft carbs for both 12A and 13B power plants, whether they're stock, street-ported, and even bridge-ported. If you want to go carbureted, Holley has what you need.

By the early 1990s, the tide was shifting away from carburetors and toward EFI systems. Enthusiasts now have more options with fuel injection than with carburetors. Haltech used to be the only player in fuel injection in the mid-1980s, followed by Electromotive in the late 1980s—but now there are so many EFI brands on the market that it's hard to keep track. The systems range from low cost (SDS-Simple Digital Systems under $1,000) to big buck (Motec, costing over $4,000 when all is said and done), with many in between. The cheaper systems don't seem to have the range adjustability that's necessary to effectively smooth out "dead" spots in their EFI programming. You may be able to tune the systems for great low- and high-end torque, but for a few seconds during the transition, your RX-7 may feel like it's pulling a trailer. The mid-priced systems are an excellent alternative to a Motec. One of our favorites is the Electromotive TEC-II, which publisher friend Tim Suddard just used to power his Ro-Spit rotary-powered Triumph Spitfire. The TEC-II is very well suited to a rotary engine, and with enough of them out there on 12As and 13Bs, there are fuel maps to help give you a starting point when it comes time to fine-tune your new system.

Tuning ease is an important factor when you're choosing among aftermarket EFI systems. Most have a self-contained programming pad included in the conversion kit, while others, like Haltech, require the use of a laptop computer to change parameters. The system you choose should be based on your budget, as well as the other local resources you have at your disposal. If there's an EFI dealer near you that offers installation and technical support, one of its units may be the most practical for your needs.

If you decide to install an EFI unit yourself, you will probably end up at your local EFI dealer eventually because they're so difficult to tune properly. If you have more than one dealer near you, choose the one with a chassis dyno in its shop. A dyno is essential for correctly tuning a new EFI system, and could be valuable when you perform other non-EFI related modifications. As a good customer, you may be able to buy future dyno time at a discount. Even if the local distributor's price is $100 more than you can purchase the system for on the Internet, we recommend spending the extra money to get it from the dealer, even if you attempt to install it yourself. Try to develop a good relationship with the EFI dealer, as it will come in handy later. It's true that once you get your new EFI

system tuned properly, you can basically forget about it. But if, over time, you add more bolt-on performance parts to your engine, your EFI system may need to be tweaked to reap more benefit from the improvements you made. Given the hassle of setting up the unit, however, it would be wise to make all your other modifications first, so you don't have to retune it.

Installing a Performance Carburetor

If, after looking through the previous chapter, you have convinced yourself that fuel injection is something you can't live without, perhaps this section and the next will change your mind.

Most readers have heard of the problems that can arise with high performance carburetion. This poor reputation, however, dates back to a time when carbs were generally unre-

liable and difficult to adjust properly. There is a new generation of carbs that are much more user-friendly and can always be set up quicker and easier than installing an aftermarket EFI system. This is especially true of Holley's carburetors—which is convenient, since they're the only manufacturer still making carbs for RX-7s.

The carb we selected for our conversion was Racing Beat's Holley 465 cubic feet per minute (CFM) four-barrel, which was specially modified to work on a rotary engine. Our project car had a four-port engine from an RX-4.

The kit from Racing Beat comes with a new intake manifold, foam air filter assembly, linkage, and all the gaskets you will need. We also ordered the optional heat shield to help isolate the intake from the hot exhaust header—remember, cooler air is denser air, which is more combustible and provides more

If you perform a 13B transplant for your 1979–1985 RX-7, but find that the carb that came with the engine is shot, you can reuse the good-working 12A from your current engine. Just drill out the top of the intake manifold and tap new holes, then relocate the studs slightly inward. With that slight modification, you can put your 12A carb right onto that newly transplanted 13B.

A Weber conversion is great for racing, but Webers are getting harder and harder to find. They have poor idle and are hard to start in cold weather, but at higher rpm they really come into their own. Delorttos and Mikunis are even harder to find, although much more streetworthy than the Weber. Holley is the best option for dual duty/street/autocross/drag/track time.

It's a good idea to use a fuel pressure regulator with a carb conversion. That way you can gain just a little more control over your carb setup, depending on what kind of driving you will be doing (street vs. race). At sustained high rpm, your carb could need a touch more fuel, but for street driving, too much fuel will cause the plugs to foul quickly.

horsepower. We had an aftermarket electric fuel pump and Purolator fuel-pressure regulator installed, which is highly recommended if you want to deliver a more consistent fuel flow to the carb.

Removing the old manifold and carb is the first step in the process and turned out to be the most time consuming—it took about an hour. Then the new manifold, carb, and linkage were secured into place. Everything just bolts right on—it really is that easy. Our new carb required no adjustment other than setting the idle. At this point in the conversion, we knew we would be way ahead of the aftermarket EFI project as far as ease of installation and time commitment, since the carb project only took one afternoon to complete.

Installing Electronic Fuel Injection
by Dennis Witt

When fuel-injected cars first appeared at the racetrack, they were expensive and mechanically complex—not an obvious threat to the carburetor's dominance. As the systems improved and the costs came down, however, they became attractive to a much wider market. Today, fuel injection is available for almost anyone with a little money and the inclination to make the switch. Our comparison should validate the theory that a carburetor conversion "sucks" when compared to an electronic fuel delivery system that "injects."

The heart of our fuel-injected project comprises an intake manifold, 40-millimeter throttle bodies, a fuel rail kit, and linkage supplied by TWM. Injectors and technical advice were provided by RC Engineering,

which has just about any size injector in stock and can tailor a "wet" system for any vehicle. Haltech's F7 control module was the electronic brain in our conversion. This is a throttle-position controlled-injection system that computes air flow by monitoring throttle position and engine speed. Based on the resulting "air mass" computation and inlet air temperature, it adds fuel to the intake by electrically triggering a fixed-flow injector for a precise length of time, measured in milliseconds—this is referred to as the injector's pulse width. The more air that flows into the engine, the longer the pulse.

Now a bit of advice for anyone attempting an EFI conversion: start with a fuel-injected RX-7 like a 1984–1985 GSL-SE or any 2G! (We don't recommend converting a 3G to aftermarket EFI, since there are ECUs available that can change parameters without the need for a new delivery system.) We converted a car that was not initially designed for fuel injection, and that's a difficult process. For starters, the standard 1979–1985

RX-7's carb only needs 3–4 psi of pressure from the fuel pump; however, it takes 40 to 50 psi to run fuel injectors. If you start with a carbureted car, you will find that none of the existing fuel lines or hoses are capable of handling these higher pressures. So the first problem you face is how to get the fuel from the gas tank to the injectors without bursting your fuel lines. The solution is to install a larger-diameter stainless steel fuel line from the tank to the engine compartment—a difficult and dirty task. We chose a 3/8-inch diameter steel line to handle the additional fuel flow, connected to a high-pressure fuel filter to insure that no contaminants clog the expensive system.

Once you have the new fuel line in—if you haven't taken a sledge hammer to the car out of frustration—you will need a high pressure fuel pump to feed the injectors. We chose a pump manufactured by NOS and distributed by RC Engineering, but you could go to a boneyard and find a used Bosch from a BMW 320i or a VW Golf. Next, AN (high pressure aluminum) fittings should be attached to the fuel pump and plumbed into the new stainless steel line. Use high quality components throughout, as a high pressure stream of fuel shot onto electrical and hot

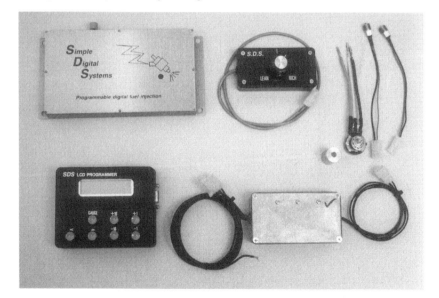

Here is what a typical aftermarket EFI system looks like after you unpack the box. This Simple Digital Systems (SDS) package does not include a direct-fire ignition system, but it doesn't require a laptop computer to make adjustments like a Haltech. It does, however, use a Hall sensor that is mounted on the engine block to sense the rotation of the eccentric shaft. This SDS package uses the stock distributor to distribute the spark, but this magnetic sensor (on right) provides feedback to the EFI's brain to help coordinate that spark with the injection triggering program.

engine parts through a rupture in the system could burn up all your hard work in a hurry. Nothing ruins a performance dream like a charred, smoldering engine bay.

Another frustration we faced was that the individual parts used to install an aftermarket EFI system come from different manufacturers, hence the project is not an "insert part A into tab B" process. We spent a significant amount of time trying to figure out how the entire system would be tied together. Be aware that different EFI systems use different injectors. There are two types on the market—"peak and hold" and "saturation"—and they come in different sizes. Make sure the injectors you have are compatible with the rest of the system—on another project we did, we were given the wrong injectors.

Both RC Engineering and MSD have a formula that will help compute exactly what injector you need for your application. For this project, we used 34 pounds/hour peak and hold injectors. Used injectors will also work (if you can find them), but we don't recommend them. The cleaning and balancing they are likely to require will offset any savings. Used injectors could throw off your fuel computer's parameters and result in decreased performance.

You will also need to run an air filter, and we found that the ITG system fit well in the limited space between the throttle body and the RX-7's inside fender well.

If your header is not fitted to contain an oxygen sensor, then a hole must be drilled so that a 22-millimeter nut can be welded in position. Your EFI system's mapping uses the air-to-gas ratio throughout the operating range of the engine, and modifying the various parameters to optimize performance.

You will also need a fuel pressure regulator to tame the 60-plus psi flow of fuel coming out of the fuel pump. One is available from Essex Industries. At high pressure, sometimes not all of the fuel is needed, but you can tap into the fuel return line that's already on your 1G RX-7 to direct this unused fuel back to the gas tank.

The moral of the story is that there are many things that can and will go wrong when you tackle a conversion like this. If you mentally prepare yourself to face these problems before you start, it could help preserve your sanity. To prevent a stay at the funny farm, starting with an EFI car will help you avoid the dirty job of replacing the low-pressure fuel lines that were designed to work with a 5-psi carb, not your new 50-psi EFI fuel pump.

Time Commitment

The carburetion conversion is much simpler, period. With all components on hand, it can be done in one day. Just make sure, if you are starting with a carbureted car, that your fuel pump can deliver 2–5 psi of fuel pressure, as most RX-7 non-EFI pumps can do. If you start with an EFI car and try to convert to an aftermarket carb, you will have to get rid of the high-pressure stock pump or it will overwhelm the carb. A trip to the local auto parts store can give you several to choose from for under $75. Switching fuel pumps can be a dirty job, and some improvising may be necessary, but an average mechanic will have no trouble with any part of this carb conversion project.

Removal of the stock intake system and replacement with a TWM intake is a no-brainer. You will need to add some fuel hose in the engine compartment, and splice in an adjustable (1–5-psi) fuel-pressure regulator (we also recommend a fuel-pressure gauge). Then, some fiddling with the throttle and choke cables should complete the task.

The EFI conversion, on the other hand, will take much longer. We recommend starting with a fuel-injected car in the first place. That will save hours of labor converting a fuel delivery system that is used to providing fuel at 3–5 psi, to one that must handle 60 psi.

This SDS system allows the operator to change a multitude of parameters so one can find the ideal fuel system setup. This inexpensive system retails for less than $1,000, and it allows the tuner to make adjustments without the use of a laptop computer.

If you have never replaced all the fuel hose in your car, you haven't lived. There is a great sense of satisfaction that comes from completing the task, similar to the feeling you get when you have been beating your head against a wall, and then suddenly stop.

Installing the new intake manifold for EFI is no big deal, but there is more fiddling required than with the carb conversion. Rerouting the throttle cable to the side of the engine as opposed to the top, where it was originally located, requires much finesse (and a longer cable).

Another problem we have seen with some EFI intake manifolds is they require more spring strength to keep the butterflies closed, and many stock throttle cables can't withstand this tension. A day at the track can be ruined when your throttle cable gives way under the pressure (don't ask us how we know this).

Fine-Tuning

Carburetion systems have been given a bad rap when it comes to fine-tuning. Playing around with jetting can drive you a little crazy. But it is, at worst, a trial and error ordeal, something that any moron (even us) can endure. The shop that sells you the carbs should be able to give you a good starting point, and you can take it from there. Plan to spend anywhere from a few weeks to a few months to get the setup that best fits your application.

On the other hand, the EFI systems are not easy to set up, either. The problem is there are so many parameters that you don't know where to start. Even when you get some initial guidelines, the number of variables you need to manipulate can be mind-boggling.

It takes a great deal of experience (again, mostly through trial and error) to get the hang of it. And in the end, you will find that you are speaking a different language than your friends. When you tell them your car is running a little rich today because your water temperature and manifold pressure seem to be affecting the duty cycle of your injectors (which is dependent on the MAP sensor and degree of dialed-in knock/retard), they may say you need to spend some time on something other than your car. If that happens, just scratch your head, declaring that you figured out that your closed-loop high parameter needs to be 14.1 inches in order to obtain stoiciometric balance. That'll shut 'em up.

The Bottom Line: Horsepower and Torque

Aftermarket performance carburetion on a rotary engine, if done correctly, can net 200-plus horsepower and 200-plus ft-lbs of torque, depending on porting. Dyno tests show that much of that power isn't achieved until after the tach goes above 5K. On the other hand, a fully sorted-out aftermarket EFI conversion will usually add about 5–10 percent to that number. So when it comes to raw power, the Haltech system will nearly always beat a Holley conversion. And although the best-built carbureted RX-7s get good torque, there is more to be had with an EFI system. That's because even a stock fuel-injection system can deliver better low-end torque than a car sporting a performance carb. And when it comes to aftermarket programmable EFI systems, your torque curve can be customized to deliver power wherever you need it. This is where EFI systems really stand out.

So the bottom line is that the EFI systems can deliver slightly more horsepower, and even a stock EFI system inherently will provide better low-end torque than a carbed car.

Which system is best for you will depend on what type of racing you want to do. The Solo II Street Prepared class is infested with aftermarket EFI cars, but to run an aftermarket EFI system in a Prepared class will cost a 150-plus pound weight penalty. Most drivers feel that this is too much weight to spot the carbureted cars. That's why the Holley carb conversion remains the hot setup for the Prepared classes.

Tunability

Due to the multitude of parameters to consider, which in turn gives way to an infinite number of programming combinations, initially setting up an aftermarket EFI system is a long, tedious undertaking. There are initial "start-up" maps provided in the software, but most of the tuning needs to be done on a dyno with

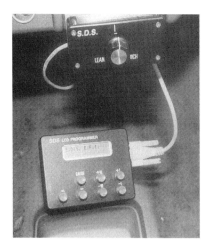

This small control panel is all you need to change parameters on the SDS package. The problem is that there are so many parameters to consider, the tuning process can take months. The best way to do it (if you don't have access to a dyno), is, once you have the system up and running O.K., get a friend to drive your car while you fine-tune the parameters from the passenger seat. That's why it's important to mount the control pad where you can both get at it.

The famous *Grassroots Motorsports* magazine's 1979 project car rockets up the Giant's Despair Hillclimb in Wilkes-Barre, Pennsylvania. Built by publisher Tim Suddard, this baby is packing a Haltech-injected four-port 13B power plant. With 240 horsepower on tap, pilot Norm Chute has all he can handle as he rounds turn 1 on his way to "Devil's Elbow," and 1,000 screaming fans who are hoping he will misjudge the braking point and wrap it around a tree. *Michelle Chute*

an air/fuel meter within view. A carb project is much simpler to set up, but precise fine-tuning is difficult. Once you get the knack of an EFI system, you can get it to do just about anything you want.

For example, if you get to the track, and it is a hot, humid day, no problem. Your programming adjusts for this scenario. You will be crossing the finish line ahead of the carbed cars whether you race in Texas or Alaska.

If you have ever seen the Pike's Peak Hillclimb, you may have heard that most of the fastest vehicles have EFI computer systems on board that can adjust the air/fuel mixture dozens of times per second! They get to the top first because the atmospheric conditions at the starting line are much different than they are at the top. With an altitude change of over 7,000 feet, you could start out with a hot, sunny day and end up in the sleet and snow. And don't forget what 15,000 feet does to the air pressure. If you have a hard time breathing at that altitude, it is a sure bet that your car does, too. The computer in these aftermarket EFI systems (and in the stock EFI system) can adjust for this variable, and carburetors can't.

Reliability

With today's modern carburetors, reliability is not as much a problem as in the past. We had a Mikuni that ran great for years, but eventually the throttle bodies began to wear and very small vacuum leaks developed around the shafts. This is the same kind of problem that many British cars develop.

But throttle bodies on the EFI engines can also wear, and often they are under more stress. An EFI system can be more sensitive to the loss of vacuum that will occur if your throttle doesn't completely close. For this reason, owners often use larger throttle return springs, which tends to put more tension on the entire linkage assembly, thus increasing wear to the components.

And injectors don't last forever, either. They can clog, wear, and once the spray pattern and flow rate have been altered, you must have them cleaned. Professional cleaning will cost over $100 per set, and sometimes cleaning won't help. New injectors are even more expensive. Remember to replace your fuel filter (also more expensive on an EFI car) every year or two. Your injectors will be grateful.

Then there's the higher-pressure fuel pump, which works harder and is more expensive than the low-psi unit on the carbed cars. If one of those wears out, the EFI pump will put a bigger dent in your wallet.

So when it comes to reliability, maybe we should call it a draw. But if something goes wrong, it will typically cost more money to replace components in an EFI system.

Conclusions

Watching both systems at work on the same car, the results were not surprising. With the Holley, 0–60 times were around 7 seconds, but after the EFI system was properly tuned (and that took six months), it shaved over a full second from that time, plus there was slightly improved gas mileage. The EFI system was also much better at start-up on cold days.

As we've said, you should base your choice on your budget for your car and the car's planned use. If you have the money, need low-end torque, tunability, and have plenty of time on your hands, get an aftermarket EFI setup. If, however, you are in more of a hurry and only want to spend hundreds instead of thousands of dollars, then a Holley carb may be your best choice. Either conversion will give you a killer RX-7, and let you experience high-end performance.

CHAPTER ELEVEN

Turbocharging, Supercharging and Nitrous-Oxide Systems

A turbocharger will supply a naturally aspirated RX-7 with a serious boost in performance—but at substantial expense. A boneyard stock RX-7 engine is all you need to begin your project. As long as the engine is healthy (a turbo won't cure the problems associated with a weak engine), you are ready to go. And you can get about the same boost in horsepower as you would by religiously completing the projects outlined in all the previous chapters. Also, the cost in dollars may actually be less than your other performance options. And there is one big advantage: your car will be more streetworthy than a car that has been ported, and is running a racing carb or aftermarket fuel injection. And if you already drive a turbocharged RX-7 and still want more power, there are several reputable Mazda tuners across the country that can help you replace your factory turbo with a more powerful and efficient aftermarket unit.

But there are a few things you need to know before you get out your wallet. First, your stock clutch may not be able to handle the 50–100 horsepower increase your engine will generate with the new turbo system. If you have a relatively new heavy-duty Mazda clutch, you're probably in good shape. Otherwise, be prepared for this additional expense. RX-7 trannys, on the other hand, are extremely strong and will likely be able to handle the extra power. Many of the sub-10-second rotaries are successfully using the stock transmission with no problems.

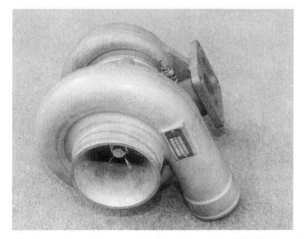 

The heart of a turbo system is the turbo unit itself (left). In order to cool down the hot exhaust gases before they get to the intake manifold, they are sent through an intercooler. Just as your car's radiator cools the antifreeze/water mix, an intercooler (right) sends the hot air through a maze of small chambers. By the time it exits, the overall temperature has dropped considerably. The bigger the maze, or intercooler, the cooler the air—but the farther the air has to travel, the more "turbo lag" the driver will experience. Both photos show trick aftermarket units for a 3G RX-7 distributed by Peter Farrell Supercars.

It's often hard to visualize how a turbo system works because many of the components are hidden from view inside the engine compartment. But there's no hiding anything in Ron Moreck's killer 13B turbo hillclimb formula car. And no need for bodywork, either. Maximum cooling is the goal, because the cooler the engine, the more power it can make. First, exhaust gases turn the turbine unit, seen here to the left of the K&N filter system. If you look closely, you can see the oxygen sensor attached to the exhaust pipe just before the turbo.

Turbocharging Theory
by Dennis Witt

In a standard intake system, air enters (or is drawn into) the engine through the intake manifold. If there is a cold-air induction system in place, or if your car has any type of "ram-air" intake, the air entering the intake manifold will be cooler and will be moving slightly faster with less turbulence than a stock delivery system. The effect can be slightly increased horsepower. A forced induction system takes this theory a lot further.

Turbocharging involves the delivery of air into the intake manifold. What distinguishes this air from that delivered by a normal induction system is that this air is compressed, containing more oxygen molecules to combine with gasoline. This releases greater energy during combustion.

Turbochargers compress air with a spinning turbine. This turbine is driven by exhaust gases that are relayed back to the turbo by the exhaust manifold. The faster the turbine spins, the greater the compression and the more turbo boost is produced. The system is capable of reaching a point where so much boost is created that your engine blows apart. To prevent this, the turbo system has a release valve to keep boost within acceptable limits.

The 2G Turbo II engines originally were restricted to 5–6 pounds of boost. That's a conservative limit to set, representing only a fraction of the boost the system is capable of delivering. To determine how much further your system should go, it's best to consult the tuning shop where you purchased the turbo. It all depends on your engine. The more fortified it is, the more boost it can handle.

The system that limits boost is a small valve known as a "wastegate" or "pop-off valve." This device diverts exhaust gases away from the turbo unit once the turbine is spinning fast enough to reach the desired boost. When the volume of forced air

The first RX-7 to come with a factory turbo unit was the second-generation 1987 RX-7 turbo. Pictured is the intercooled "Turbo II" engine that, by 1992, was producing 200 horsepower.

encounters a closed throttle plate (as happens between shifts) it must go somewhere other than into the engine. If there was no way of relieving this pressure, it would either back up in the system and damage the turbo or blow out through the weakest link in the turbo system. The wastegate allows the excess pressure to be vented from the system by opening at a preset level of boost, thus avoiding a pressure spike in the system.

When it compresses air, a turbo creates an unwanted side effect: heat. Since hotter air is less dense than cool air, this heat reduces the benefits produced by the turbocharger. A superheated intake charge also increases the chance of unwanted detonation of the air/fuel mixture. Detonation occurs when the mixture of air and fuel ignites before the plug fires. This means that the rotor has not yet completed its compression cycle before the fuel mixture is ignited. If the frequency and severity of this occurs too often, an expensive rebuild will soon be in order, because the force created by early detonation is working against the spinning rotor instead of driving it in the correct direction.

In the next step in the turbo sequence, hot, compressed air is sent through the intercooler. In this photo, the dense hot air is traveling clockwise. In the next photo, the air is sent through this huge intercooler, and by the time it emerges, the air is both much cooler and denser. That can only mean one thing: big time power.

As the air exits the intercooler, it makes its way to the intake manifold. Excess pressure is expelled by this large blow-off valve.

The solution to this problem is an intercooler. Intercoolers are nothing more than glorified radiators, but instead of cooling the water circulating through your engine, they cool the incoming air charge to the cylinders. There are two basic types of intercoolers: air-to-air and air-to-liquid. A general rule that can be applied to the incoming air charge is that an 11-degree Fahrenheit decrease in the temperature creates an increase in power of about 1 percent. To maximize your power output, you want to chill the incoming air as much as possible. Air-to-air intercoolers can operate at up to 80 percent efficiency, meaning that you still have 20 percent hotter than normal incoming air charge. Air-to-liquid intercoolers can easily operate at this level and higher, but just how efficient they will be depends on the size of the intercooler you use, and how cool you can get the water that will be flowing through the system. Air-to-liquid intercoolers are a little more complex than the air-to-air type, because they require a pump and a tank for the liquid to be circulated through the system—but the payoff comes in more potential power from the engine. Inserting an intercooler between the turbo and the throttle body does cause somewhat of an obstruction, but this is more than offset by the denser charge of air the rotors receive as a result of the cooling process.

Now that we have a compressed and cooled incoming air charge, it must be properly mixed with a precise amount of fuel to insure the maximum horsepower and torque. Since a stock non-turbo RX-7 ECU was never designed to compensate for the increased air flow provided by a turbo, a method to provide increased fuel delivery at boost must be spliced into the system. Depending on the amount of boost you plan to run, an additional computer can be piggybacked onto the stock unit, or a separate aftermarket unit can be used in place of the existing factory computer. Aftermarket computers can be specifically tailored for your application and have an almost infinite number of variables that can be modified for every imaginable combination of conditions you may encounter. You can find a range of these units, from very basic to top-of-the-line models. Your budget, and a little common sense, will indicate which system is for you. Buying the very cheapest model of a complex device may not be prudent. If your research indicates that the only part you can afford is of marginal quality or functionality, you may want to hold off altogether, and return to this item when you have a little more money.

Finally, the cool, dense air reaches the intake manifold and is mixed with fuel and combusted in the rotary's chambers. Total time it takes the hot air to get from the turbine, up the pile leading to the intercooler, through the intercooler, past the pop-off valve and into the intake is about two minutes. At least that's what it seems like when you are watching Moreck's car accelerate up a hill. But when that cool dense air/fuel is finally combusted, look out. Ron's formula Mazda seems about to enter another dimension when "turbo lag" transitions to "warp speed."

Modern computer-controlled cars are tuned for minimum emissions and maximum fuel economy. In general, your factory computer is always trying to achieve a stoiciometric ratio of 14.7 parts air to 1 part fuel. This is the point at which the engine generates the least amount of emissions and the car will still perform in an acceptable manner. This may be fine for running at a steady speed down the interstate, but if you want real power, more fuel must be introduced into the system. A turbo system without a fuel enrichment program would result in a very lean mixture (30 parts air to 1 part fuel). Therefore, any turbo setup must have a way to enrich the fuel mixture as

boost increases. This is accomplished either through an aftermarket computer system, or by using a fuel-pressure regulator to increase the fuel flow relative to increasing boost. Often, additional injectors are added to the intake of high-powered 2G and 3G RX-7s to add more fuel at higher rpm to mix with the compressed air. These injectors must also be controlled by a computer. Running a little rich at 12:1 or 13:1 may foul your plugs, but if your fuel delivery system comes up short, major engine damage can occur. We strongly recommend that an air/fuel ratio meter be installed, along with a boost gauge, and that you have your car run on a dyno to insure that the

engine is getting a proper dose of fuel. Monitoring your boost and air/fuel ratios while on the dyno will allow you to make any changes to your car before you blow it up on the strip or the street.

Turbo Upgrades for Second- and Third-Generation RX-7s
by Dale Black

If you already own a turbocharged 2G or 3G RX-7 and feel the need for even more power, there are several things you can do to further boost your horsepower. The first is to ditch your stock turbo unit and replace it with an aftermarket system. There are several reasons why you

This third-generation RX-7 has received many of the turbo upgrades discussed in this chapter. This includes a single-stage turbo, bigger intercooler, extra injectors, and related parts.

might want to upgrade your turbo. At the same time, there are good reasons not to make a switch. For every modification, there is a trade-off, the biggest of which is usually a reduction in streetability.

The stock turbochargers on the third-gen RX-7 are Hitachi H12s with different blade configurations between the primary and secondary units. They are controlled by numerous actuators and solenoids tied together with more than 40 feet of vacuum lines! This alone is one big reason for changing out the turbos—to simplify things. When working properly, the stock setup can't be beat for streetability, smooth power delivery, and low-end torque. However, unless the car has never been driven hard (and who could contain themselves?), then

chances are, things aren't 100 percent. A reliable boost gauge properly connected gives all the tell-tale indications as to whether or not things are "right."

From idle, boost should build smoothly to about 3,000 rpm. At this point, the secondary turbo begins pre-spooling to 4,500 rpm when the charge control valve opens, bringing maximum power and torque to bear until redline.

The turbo blades are configured such that the primary blades deliver maximum boost at the lower rpm range. The secondary turbo blades take full advantage of the powerful exhaust flow in the high rpm range. The transition at 4,500 should be hardly noticeable.

If things aren't 100 percent, then more than likely it is a problem in the

control system, not with the turbos themselves. So many times owners have spent thousands of dollars replacing turbos, only to experience the same problems afterwards. Enter the single turbo option. Replacing the stock twin-turbo setup in the 3G with an aftermarket single turbo eliminates much of the seemingly unnecessary complexity of the control system. Gone are more than half of the solenoids and vacuum lines. Gone are the charge relief and air-bypass valves in favor of a single blow-off valve. Gone is the extra piping that would route boost pressure from two turbos to the intercooler. Gone are the added oil and coolant lines. In fact, the lower friction and heat of a single turbo could be beneficial in the form of longevity and power gains. But the trade-off with a single turbo is the lack of low-end torque, often referred to as turbo lag. Single turbos simply require higher rpms to build boost as fast as twin turbos. In fact, if a large enough single turbo is selected, even more boost is possible, but at the cost of low-end power. Also, single turbos can potentially create higher amounts of boost in the high rpm range because there is less friction and heat. This is why single turbos are ideal for race cars since they spend most of their time driven at high rpms with hardly any stop and go.

Another option is to get your stock turbo rebuilt. If you want to

A typical aftermarket "pop-off" valve for a third-gen conversion.

An aftermarket Peter Farrell turbo unit installed on a 1993 RX-7.

keep all the bits and pieces in place and like the idea of having respectable low-end torque, then you might want to go this route. Essentially, the low-end power/torque is only hindered slightly. The idea is to port the turbos and manifold using a process called extrude-honing. This smoothes out the passages through which the boosted air and exhaust flow, and in the process, makes them slightly larger as well. Also, to take full advantage of this type of modification, the exhaust system itself should be modified to allow greater flow. Keep in mind that the turbo manifold itself is the greatest restriction in the exhaust system.

There are a number of reputable turbocharger rebuilding companies from which to choose, whether you decide to keep things stock or go with a modified setup. Both Peter Farrell Supercars in Manassas, Virginia, and Pettit Racing in Fort Lauderdale, Florida, offer units that are based on the stock assembly, but with slightly improved performance. Turbonetics out of California also offers an economical solution. Others include: Turbo City in Orange, California, (offers rebuilt stock unit/assembly), and Rotary Performance in Garland, Texas (offers two single turbo upgrade options using GReddy turbos).

Keep in mind that the power gains from any turbo are based on many things: restriction and temperature in the intake air, pressure and temperature drop from the intercooler, control system components such as solenoid valves, blow-off-valves, pop-off valves, and actuators, wastegate, cooling and oiling, and exhaust flow restriction. Simply pulling out the factory turbos and bolting in a single turbo won't add performance and reliability. You need careful planning to ensure that all systems will complement each other from the first time you fire up that engine.

Finally, all turbo-charged engines should have a turbo timing control

Aftermarket intercoolers neatly lined up waiting for a good home. These Pettit units are designed to be highly efficient when it comes to both air flow and cooling. *Courtesy of Excellent Performance/Pettit Racing*

unit. This will keep your car running for up to 10 minutes after you turn off the ignition. Much damage can occur to the turbo unit itself if you shut it down too quickly after getting the turbines hot.

Colder Is Faster (and Vice Versa)

Another thing to consider, whether or not you trade up for a more potent turbo system, is to install an aftermarket intercooler. Your stock Mazda unit is designed to cool down the compressed air before it enters the intake manifold, and for the most part it does a good job. But good automotive engineers never sleep. They always seem to find ways to improve on a good thing. And thanks to the growing popularity of the import drag movement, the motivation to find ways to go even faster has given birth to a new breed of intercooler technology.

Again, the more you can cool down the compressed air before it is mixed with fuel, the more horsepower your engine can generate. Denser air makes for better and more complete combustion. So if you can

replace your stock unit with a more efficient, racing-type intercooler, your engine will respond with more lively performance. One of the best examples of aftermarket intercooling can be found in the Manassas, Virginia, home of Peter Farrell Supercars.

Farrell has designed a unit for 2G and 3G cars that works better than the stock system. It is less restrictive, provides denser air to the intake, and looks cool all at the same time.

Supercharging Theory

Supercharging achieves the same effect as a turbo but in a somewhat different manner. The energy used to turn a turbocharger is spent exhaust gases that would normally be lost to the atmosphere. By inserting a turbine in the exhaust stream, you are essentially getting a free source of power to compress the incoming air charge, and this power is not mechanical or electrical. The trade-off, however, is that a turbo represents a substantial restriction in the exhaust system, numerically similar to the boost you get in psi.

So horsepower is essentially being rerouted to run the turbine.

A supercharger, on the other hand, is driven by a belt running off the engine, much the same as a power steering unit or air-conditioning requires. Since this belt can only turn by using some of the power of the engine, a supercharger will also result in a power drain on the engine, but it does not restrict the exhaust. The power drain is similar to what you lose when running an air-conditioning compressor.

The big difference is that a turbo unit must wait for exhaust gases to spin its turbine. Then the compressed air must flow through an intercooler before eventually getting to your intake manifold. The interval from when you first stomp on the throttle to when the compressed air finally reaches the engine is what is referred to as "turbo lag." This can cause a delay in the delivery of power. Since this is not the case with a belt-driven supercharger, the power delivery is nearly instantaneous.

Due to the high power output of a stock 3G RX-7, plus all of the great turbo enhancing and aftermarket turbo kits on the market, most 3Gs are not supercharged. It may not be worth the effort, but for 2G and especially 1G cars, supercharging may be the best way to get power. Note that we didn't say the cheapest way, because superchargers are not cheap. They are, however, the best way to get a big power gain while maintaining streetability.

Installing a Supercharger in a 2G RX-7
by Travis Shrey

Rotary engines love force-fed air, and superchargers are a great means of delivering it. If you limit the amount of

Turbo kits are even available for 1G cars. David Lane has just such a system installed on his 1G. The custom intake plumbing was done by Hahn Racecraft, and that's an HKS Super Pop-off valve. His mild, street-ported engine was built by Rotary Performance in Manassas, Virginia. *David Lane*

One of the best supercharging kits on the market for second generation RX-7s is offered by Nelson. Included in the kit is a Paxton supercharger unit, an aluminum mounting bracket, a fuel pressure riser, new serpentine pulleys and belts, a top radiator tube (with aluminum water neck), and a new throttle body elbow and horn. The flexible air pipe from the air filter to the rubber elbow for the supercharger intake, as well as a heat shield for the front of the engine compartment are also included.

First, remove the aluminum mount from the air pump and use the three bolts to mount the new supercharger/air pump bracket. It's critical to align the pulleys for the serpentine belt in this step. Mount the supercharger on the bracket, and using a straightedge, project it from the face of the supercharger pulley to the alternator pulley. You'll find that the supercharger may need to be spaced back quite a bit. Using the spacer washers, mount the supercharger so that the faces of the pulleys are lined up. In our car, because it had to be spaced so far back, the mounting bracket needed to be modified to allow room to fit the oil fill tube.

The same thing must be done with the air pump, if you're using one—not that we endorse removing it. Mount the rubber elbow on the back of the supercharger and run the 3-inch flex tubing up the air flow meter and connect it. Mount the new throttle air horn on the throttle body, and fit the connecting elbow from the supercharger to the air horn. Install the new top radiator tube, and remember to fill it with coolant. Next, tighten the serpentine belt using the tensioning pulley. Finally, recheck all the connections, fill the supercharger with oil (making sure it is

boost to under 7 pounds, you can even make do without an intercooler. While 7 pounds doesn't sound like much for a Turbo II, the six-port NA engine uses higher-compression rotors and—with the secondary intake ports open—offers considerably larger intake dura-tion and air flow. If you can manage to keep your foot out of it, fuel consump-tion won't increase. And when you want to get on it (not that we endorse breaking any laws), you'll be rewarded by the kind of acceleration only modi-fied Turbo II drivers get to experience.

You can't do a supercharger conversion without a way to get more fuel to your engine under boost. That's exactly what this Paxton fuel-pressure regulator is designed to do. It is the key to avoiding problems associated with running too lean a mixture. *Philip Garrott*

well lubricated), and fire the car up. When the supercharger is new it is very hard to turn. After a couple hundred miles, it gets much easier. Until then it may be necessary to increase the car's idle, especially if you've gutted the throttle body. Make sure you don't have any fuel or coolant leaks before you take it for a test drive.

The Bottom Line

The list of new companies doing street and strip turbocharger and supercharger conversions seems to grow longer as each month goes by, but check the Internet or ask a reputable speed shop before you buy any off-brand system. You want proof that the kit will work for your application. Dyno numbers are not always

to be trusted. You need to speak first-hand with someone who has actually completed the project (magazines don't count either, since they are rarely critical of their advertisers). A good place to start is with one of the popular RX-7 club Web sites.

Prices vary, but a kit can usually be had for around $3,000, although 2G and 3G upgrades are nearly double that figure. So go ahead and put a turbo or supercharger on your RX-7, or upgrade your present system. Then you will have even more opportunity to show your rear end to those pesky 5.0-liter muscle cars!

Nitrous—Radical, Dude!

If you don't want to go to the trouble of installing a turbo or super-charger, but you still want to blow the doors off those Mustangs and Camaros, a nitrous-oxide system should be considered. And even if your car is already "charged," you can still give it some gas (NOS)—that is, if your engine components are equipped to withstand it. An NOS system is simple to install (takes only a few hours), and is absolutely the cheapest way to get horsepower. It's also one of the few modifications that will maintain your car's streetability. But before placing an order, you had better be sure that your RX-7 can handle the extra strain. An older, slightly worn engine may not hold together when exposed to nitrous (or a blower for that matter).

When you push the button, and nitrous oxide gas is mixed with the air as it is entering the combustion chamber, the result is an air/fuel mix that is supercombustible. This is because, per molecule, nitrous oxide gas has more oxygen than the air we (or our engine) normally breathe. Specifically, it contains two parts nitrogen and one part oxygen. As the nitrogen is heated, it releases

"Gimme some juice." A nitrous system can give you an extra 50-75 horsepower for very short periods of time. For that reason, this type of system is great for a drag car. It can shave years off the life of your engine, but it is the quickest and cheapest way to make horsepower. Mount your NOS bottle in your hatchback, out of harm's way where it can be easily filled.

oxygen, which allows an engine to burn more fuel. The resulting explosion will turn the engine's rotors harder than they ever have been turned before. A newer engine can usually take this abuse, but one with very high mileage may not. One need not be afraid when driving a car with a nitrous bottle mounted in the interior compartment. Nitrous oxide by itself is not flammable!

Since nitrous gas is very cold when it is discharged, some RX-7 drag racers have installed an NOS fogging system and aimed it directly at the turbo intercooler. In this capacity, the nitrous system only lowers the temperature of compressed air after it leaves the turbo, but the cooler, denser air provides a stronger fuel charge for better combustion. That's another reason why an NOS system used in the conventional manner will increase power. Much colder air enters your throttle body. Colder is denser, and denser air translates into more power. With a properly installed NOS system, you could experience up to a 3-second decrease in quarter-mile times!

But here are few final thoughts before you go out and get gassed. Nitrous systems are not legal for any form of SCCA (Sports Car Club of America) racing. On the other hand, many of the fastest turbocharged RX-7 drag cars don't leave home without them. Adding the cold nitrous gas to the hot, compressed air coming from the turbo will add

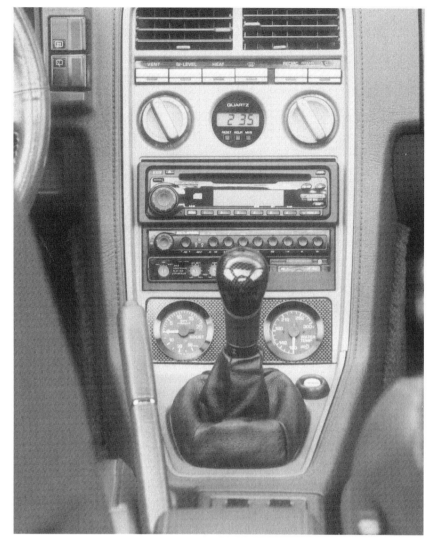

This is an interior control panel on a first generation car. It features easy-to-read water temperature and turbo boost gauges. *David Lane*

even more power and virtually eliminate lag. But again, if used improperly for your application, the result could be a blown engine rather than a fast one. Since you can choose a system that can deliver anywhere from 40 to 100 extra horsepower—or more for pure racing applications—you need to make sure that your engine can handle that extra power. If you get too greedy, an NOS system will actually cause increased wear to your engine components.

Finally, make sure that you don't have your ignition advanced too far before you install an NOS system. Premium fuel should also be used to help avoid detonation, which can kill your engine. And speaking of fuel, you need to ensure that your stock fuel pump can handle the increased pressure needed for full-throttle NOS use. You may need to add a second fuel pump just for use with the nitrous system. Following these simple guidelines will add increased reliability to your radical turbo-, super-, or NOS-charged RX-7.

CHAPTER TWELVE

Transmissions

In a perfect world, when you went around a corner the outside drive wheel would rotate faster than the inside wheel since more distance needs to be covered at the outer circumference of the turning circle. But in the real world, the transaxle and drive wheels on conventional vehicles fight this simple concept of geometry. Since weight transfer is greater to the outside wheel, it tends to generate greater friction with the road, resulting in more grip to that tire.

The inside wheel tries to maintain the same revolutions per minute as the outside, even though it doesn't need to cover as much distance around the inside of the circle. Add to that a difference in friction due to weight transfer, with the much lighter inside wheel being forced to do what it cannot avoid, and you experience a very common problem—lost traction and inside wheel spin. Even a Chevette can burn rubber in this manner on a tight turn.

For years, the solution to this problem has been one of the greatest automotive inventions of all time: the limited-slip differential (LSD). An

The guts of any good racing transmission includes (from left to right) an aluminum flywheel for automatic transmissions, and for the manual, performance discs and heavy-duty pressure plate. *Racing Beat*

LSD limits the speed of the inside wheel, allowing it to create its own pulling force, resulting in much improved traction in a turn. The problem with an LSD is that it tends to create push, or understeer, because it's applying driving force from the inside of the turn. Under hard cornering, this requires some adjustment for someone who is not used to one. But with an LSD, the inside wheel usually will maintain contact with the ground even if you are applying a heavy right foot.

The Limited-Slip Differential

With all of the suspension and engine improvements discussed in the previous chapters, the problem many RX-7 drivers will now encounter when accelerating out of a turn is loss of traction. On really tight turns especially, a driver with a car that has been treated to more horsepower and torque will have a difficult time controlling wheel spin without a limited-slip differential.

A cheap solution for the 1G driver is to do a rear axle swap with a

Traction is extremely important in racing. When Solo I driver Marc Cefalo exits the "Devil's Elbow" turn at the Giant's Despair hillclimb, he needs the grip that only an limited-slip differential can offer, or his 1G's tail will end up sliding into the dirt. Marc competes in both ITA and GT-3 (usually on the same weekend), and tows both cars to events on his flatbed!

1984–1985 GSL-SE. If you can't find a GSL version, the 1984–1985 SE also came with a limited-slip differential. But if you are going to swap out the rear axle, you may as well get the vented rear disc brakes that came on the GSL-SE. Once completed, however, you will find that the stock LSDs wear out quickly. We had to do a rebuild once per year when heavily autocrossing our 1G. The other problem with a rear axle swap between the 1984-plus cars and 1979–1982 chassis was that in 1983, the drive shaft flange changed to a slightly larger unit. This can be matched, but it presents an additional challenge. All swaps between other 1983–1985 cars and the GSL-SE axle are a straightforward procedure.

One of the best rear ends to look for if you have a non-turbo second-generation car is the 4.30 ratio 1989–1991 axle assembly from the GTU or GXL. This axle contains a viscous LSD and is a direct bolt-in swap with all non-turbo 2G cars. The 4.10 rear end out of the Turbo, however, requires that you drill out and machine the pinion flange for all non-turbo conversions in order to use the Turbo halfshafts.

You can also look for an aftermarket LSD. One of the best units is the Torsen, and it is available for all RX-7s including the 3G. This aftermarket unit has gained a reputation as one of the best torque-sensing differentials ever made.

A cheaper option is a rebuilt factory replacement LSD. To keep your LSD functioning at its best, you should use a special LSD additive that can reduce chatter, use either NEO 75-90 synthetic or conventional fluid in the transmission.

Turn, Turn, Turn!

If you begin racing your car with an LSD where once there was none, you will have to make some serious adjustments in your driving style. We found ourselves yelling "TURN!" the first time we raced our project RX-7 after installing the new LSD. Be prepared for plowing, especially if you have also experimented with ride height. An LSD, increased negative camber up front,

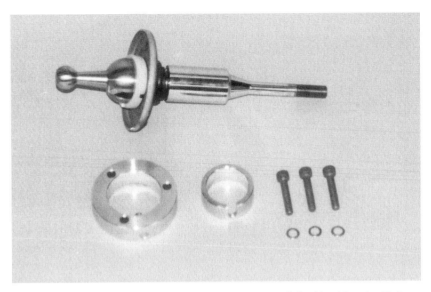

Some 1G and 2G car owners may want to consider a short shifter kit. This unit will shorten the throw of the shifter between gears. It takes some getting used to, but once you have one, you will not know how you ever did without it. The 3G cars already have a nice shifter mechanism, but there are short shifter kits for those, too. *Excellent Performance/Pettit Racing*

and insufficient toe out can cause you to take the scenic route through the first hairpin turn you approach. Keep the windows rolled up so that your friends don't think you're crazy if they hear you yelling at your car to "turn!!!"

With the LSD installed, you may need less negative camber and more toe out. The reason is that, as the car enters a turn, the posi will tend to drive the front wheels further into the turn (especially if you are moving a little too fast). Entering a turn too fast is a common "pre-posi" habit that can be hard to break. Drivers without LSDs expect the rear wheels to slide a little, which they often compensated for by left foot breaking. When done with skill, this will cause the rear end to get slightly loose and result in a nice four-wheel drift.

But with an LSD in place, the rear wheels will maintain traction as you turn the wheel (which is what you pay a posi to do). If you go in too hot, the result will be oversteer. With a posi rear end, you may need to slow

down a little entering the turn. This will pay off big time on the way out, since power can be applied earlier and with more gusto, resulting in a faster exit speed. Fine-tuning the front suspension to match your individual driving style can be accomplished by experimenting with negative camber, toe, sway bars and sway bar bushing material, shock and strut

stiffness, and the easiest thing of all to adjust—tire pressures.

Transmission Swaps

There is a reason why you don't see a lot of 2G or 3G motors or trannys in a 1G car. Not that it's impossible to do—anything is possible with persistence and fabrication skills—it's just that the transmission bell housing is different, as is the flywheel. That makes both engine and tranny swaps much more troublesome. A 1983–1985 tranny will go into an earlier RX-7, but the shifter on the 1983–1985 tranny was moved back by two inches. Other than that, they are a straight bolt-in procedure except that the tunnel shifter hole needs to be changed, and inside the cockpit the console will need to be adapted to compensate for this shift. The redesigned 1986-plus tranny is a better engineered piece and is more reliable than the 1G units.

Clutches

Mazda OEM clutches seem to work well for most applications. In a pinch, we have even successfully used non-OEM clutches (like NAPA, etc.) when we needed a

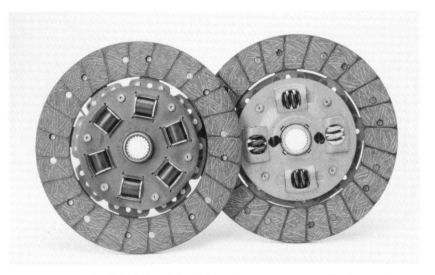

This street/strip clutch is designed for high-performance street applications and occasional drag or road racing. Cars with modified engines should consider a clutch upgrade, and they are available for all RX-7 models. *Racing Beat*

clutch at the track and no Mazda dealer was nearby. If you can afford it, nothing beats a good Centerforce clutch. These babies are designed for maximum hookup at even high rpm. A large majority of racers use the Centerforce clutch. There are two models to choose from. The Centerforce I claims 30 percent more clamping power than a stock unit, and the newer Centerforce II offers a 60 percent increase, making it a favorite among drag racers. There are also several other clutch designs to choose from, depending on what type of driving or racing you want to do, ranging from an OEM design up to full race.

One of the challenges that many RX-7 owners face, especially with the popularity of 1G transplants, is identifying what clutch they need. Between 1982 and 1983 there were two different sizes used, so make sure you know where your 12A motor came from before you order your clutch.

If you have never done an RX-7 clutch yourself, you are in for a treat. It is a rather straightforward task. A clutch alignment tool makes it easier to line up the disc and pressure plate. Most racers also recommend replacing the pilot bearing each time you put in a clutch. The only problem is that it is a difficult bearing to remove. You can do it with some hassle, but Mazdatrix offers a tool that makes removing it a snap. Always make sure that you don't touch the disc or get any oil on it or it will chatter up a storm when it is engaged the first few times until the oil is burned off.

Flywheels

The question always comes up as to which flywheel a competitor uses. Should you just put the original weight unit back in, should you machine it to cut down on weight, or should you buy a trick aluminum

An aluminum flywheel reduces the OEM flywheel weight up to 55 percent, depending on the RX-7 model. Subsequently, inertia (while at rest) is also reduced by a substantial amount (up to 80 percent). You may have to rev the engine a little higher to get off the line, but once you get the hang of it, you will accelerate quicker. The only disadvantage is that less torque will be available when coming out of a turn, since there will be less inertia (in motion) to help with momentum. An automatic transmission aluminum flywheel is shown on the right. *Racing Beat*

unit? Once you have held an RX-7 flywheel, you will understand this controversy. It is heavy—one of the heaviest flywheels we have ever seen. But there are two good reasons why Mazda designed it that way.

First, it helps balance the engine, making it run smoother even at low rpm. Secondly, if RX-7s (except 3Gs and triple rotor transplants) lack one thing, it is torque. This is especially true for 1G cars. The 12A engine only produces 105 ft-lbs. Here is where a heavy flywheel can help. In a turn, a heavier flywheel loses less momentum when you take your foot off the throttle—allowing you better exit speed when you get back on it. It is especially helpful if you just had to shift gears. Cutting it down (not recommended due to engagement problems) or substituting an aluminum unit will cut that available torque considerably. Spinning this heavy flywheel does require power, which is where an aluminum one can come in handy. You

may not be able to have the same smooth starts in first gear since the aluminum units are lighter, requiring higher rpms in order to move forward and maintain momentum. Your engine may also idle as if it has been ported when using an aluminum flywheel. But since you have cut down on rotating weight, your car will accelerate quicker. The trade-off is streetability. A good compromise is Racing Beat's lightweight steel flywheels.

Speaking of flywheels, if you have a four- or five-speed tranny and are planning to transplant an engine that was once mated to a car with an automatic tranny, then you could face some work ahead of you. If the smaller, automatic flywheel is still there, you'll need a special tool to get it off and replace it with the manual flywheel. The flywheel nut is huge on rotary-powered cars, requiring the purchase of a Mazda special tool flywheel remover, or a 2 1/8 inch, 3/4-drive socket to use

Changing a clutch and flywheel on your own is no big deal on a rotary engine. One of the biggest hassles, however, is removing the flywheel nut. For one thing, it is huge. Sears has a socket that will fit, but we thought you may want to see the size of it (2-1/2 inches). It is compared to a typical 10-millimeter one. Even with the right socket, this nut is extremely hard to remove—causing us to speculate that Toyo Kogyo hired King Kong to torque it down. Mazda makes a special removal tool, but we found that if you crank your air compressor up high one quick zip on the gun can get it off.

with your air compressor—cranked up to the max. You won't find this size socket in many places, but Sears carries them. King Kong has torqued the nut on at the factory. You will need all the strength you can muster to get it off. Then putting it back on requires the same amount of muscle. You could use Locktite when putting it back on, but that would require that you heat it if you ever needed to remove it again (to dissolve the Locktite). In all likelihood, you will likely never use that huge socket again. We can tell you from experience that they make great paperweights.

Conclusions

No matter how much horsepower you have at your disposal, it will do you no good unless you can get the power down to the ground. Choose a clutch, transmission, and rear end appropriate for your competition plans. As always, beware of making your car too race compatible to be enjoyable on the street. A racing clutch and an aluminum flywheel will make your RX-7 a less suitable commuter, so you need to be prepared for that trade-off.

CHAPTER THIRTEEN

Street Tuning on a Budget

Now that you have had a chance to review the modifications that can help your car go faster and handle better, you are faced with a choice. Which do you do first? Chapter 2 advises that you set a budget and make decisions based on those priorities. To illustrate this point, we have outlined clusters of modifications that should be done given the amount of money you have to spend.

This will vary based on how you want to use your car, but we assume that most people reading this book are interested in having their car perform dual duty. That is, getting more performance for the street during the week with the potential to participate in mild autocrossing or drag racing on the weekend. Those who are preparing their cars solely for racing must plan for a much higher budget to be

competitive. The exception to this rule may be the first-generation RX-7. A full-blown regionally competitive SCCA Solo I, II, or even IT car can be built for under $5,000. That also may be true for second-generation cars, but the 3G is another story. By the time you buy a roll cage, wheels, and race tires, your budget is nearly shot.

Certainly, most of the modifications listed in this chapter will easily

One of the first things you should do before you even buy your first performance parts is to establish a budget for both money and time. Without a clear look into the future, you could find your modifications getting out of hand, and you could end up doing things to your car that are either unnecessary, perform no real function, or are inconsistent with the planned use of your car. *Dale Black*

Most IT cars are race only, but it is possible to build a project (especially a 1G) that can be used for both street and track. It's just a little inconvenient getting in and out of your daily driver when it has a full cage installed. That's why we haven't done it.

relate to both first- and second-generation drivers who want to go full-blown autocrossing, or drag and road racing. Under each category, several budget amounts are listed: Low Buck, (under $1,500); Moderate Hop-up (under $3,000), and Serious Project (over $5,000). Labor costs have not been considered, since they vary greatly. Most of these changes require only a modest amount of mechanical expertise. For those who plan to go all out, or do not need to consider a financial budget, the Serious Project category is for you.

A 3G car will consume your budget much more quickly than a 1G car. And usually, the "bang for the buck" factor is more favorable for the earlier cars, whether you want a fast street car or want to do some racing. But since the 3G cars are so much more technologically advanced than the earlier RX-7s, often an injection of $5,000 will yield performance that many supercar owners will have a difficult time matching.

Dual Duty: The Challenge to Retain Streetability

Do you need your car to get you back and forth to work during the week, but also want to play with it a little on the weekend? Then a dual-duty project is for you. Often, serious racing modifications will render your car a pain in the @$$ to drive on the street. This section is dedicated to hop-up alternatives that will work on the track, without compromising too much comfort on the street.

You will not end up with a championship race car by following these guidelines, but you will be able to preserve your car's street integrity. If autocross is one of your goals, then refer to the next chapter to decide which modifications will be in your best interest, as some may prohibit you from competing in the stock classes. Since there are so many possible scenarios, we have simply outlined modifications that will add to the overall fun in both street driving and weekend amateur racing, even though some could render your car ineligible for stock competition.

Internal engine modifications or rebuilds are not addressed in these sections, as they can completely eat up your budget. Many RX-7s remain competitive despite having 100,000-plus miles recorded on the odometer. Since a properly cared-for rotary engine can last twice this long, we recommend not rebuilding the block unless it is broken or smokin'. If you are starting with an engine that has poor compression, however, you have your work cut out for you. It is very tempting to do some porting to your engine during a rebuild, especially if you own an earlier rotary. This will certainly cut into your budget and will limit your ability to compete on an amateur level, but unlike a piston engine, rotaries respond extremely well to a little porting. Since we are addressing dual-duty cars in this section, you will need to decide whether you want to lean toward increased power on the street, or more expensive and non-streetworthy modifications that will make you more competitive on the track.

And a final word about horsepower. Often, a gain of 20 horsepower above 7,000 rpm means that you could experience a loss of torque below 4,000 rpm. A further consideration is reliability. The further you modify an engine, the less reliable it becomes. These two important points must be kept in mind for anyone who uses his or her car for daily transportation. We have a shift light installed on one of our cars that we also occasionally autocross and hillclimb. We can't remember the last time that shift light actually went off on the street, and we have it set for 6,000 rpm. Don't render your car

useless for the road by performing some mods that you will rarely get to experience in normal (or even fast) street driving. For dual-duty cars, the word is moderation.

The Low-Buck Hop-Up (under $1,500)

If you want to save as much money as possible, there are a few universal principles that any RX-7 owner can follow to make his or her car run faster and handle better. Here is rule #1: lighter is faster. Even the most picky SCCA classes allow you to remove your spare tire, jack, tool kit, and lug wrench. Second- and third-gen cars come with those stupid "mini" spare donuts that everyone hates. But all you 1G owners should think about how much weight you could save by removing your spare (likely a heavy rim with a steel belted radial mounted on it). You could chance it and go without, but you could also go to a boneyard and find one of those mini spare donuts. Weight savings will be close to 25 pounds! That's cheap horsepower. For the most part, depending on where the weight comes from, weight savings also translate into better handling.

Finally, we all love Mazda Motors for everything it has done to build these wonderful machines. And we also pine for those Japanese-only RX-7s that were never brought into this country. So proudly wear your Mazda jackets and T-shirts, buy models of your car for your desk, etc. But Efini emblems, Japanese-spec tail lights, shaved door handles, high-power stereos, and shiny metal door sill plates don't make your car go faster or handle better.

First Generation

Your goal: to improve both handling and straight-line performance with a budget of $1,500. Without access to used performance parts, this

Lowering weight is the easiest and cheapest way to help make your car go faster and handle better. The 1G drivers can switch their full spare for the lighter, modern "mini doughnut." Or you could retain your full spare, but remove all the unnecessary items in the rear hatch (as Mark Halama has done) and replace heavier components with aluminum.

can be a difficult assignment. Assuming you purchase all of the parts new, there are two things that should be given first priority. Low-cost performance springs can usually be found for around $200/set. The springs will lower the car slightly, and decrease body roll at the same time. The compromise, however, will be a harsher ride on the street. Performance struts will also bring back that stiffer, responsive feel that your car once had when it was new, while providing a fully adjustable ride that can be relaxed for the street.

Performance springs and struts will stiffen the chassis and limit the amount your 1G or 2G twists under hard cornering. *Courtesy of Eibach*

Struts will eat up another $400–$500 of your budget. To finish stiffening the chassis, a strut tower brace is a relatively inexpensive ($150–$250) and useful mod that will cut down on the high degree of chassis flex experienced in the 1G cars.

With a little less than $750 remaining, as we reviewed in chapter 7, you would find no better way to increase power with an early 12A or 13B than to improve your engine's ability to release exhaust gases. A header is one of the best bang-for-the-buck items you can buy for a rotary engine, and it costs between $150–$200. There are free-flowing catalytic converters on the market—however, they are cost prohibitive for this budget. On the other hand, a cat-back exhaust system can be had for between $250–$550 and will provide a better release for gases than the stock unit. Pre-1981 cars (without cats) will have an advantage here since for around $50 less, you can replace the entire system.

Weekend drag racers should consider a slightly different combination, as the emphasis is on speed over handling. The exhaust modifications above should remain a top priority, but you may want to put the suspension mods on the back burner in favor of getting more power. The best way to accomplish this is to achieve a balance between the intake and exhaust systems. Focusing on getting more air and fuel through the intake will take full advantage of your engine's increased ability to release exhaust gases. A Holley carb and manifold would be a logical choice. A Weber sidedraft conversion will put you over your budget and is not a good choice for the street. Mikunis and Delorttos offer a better compromise in streetability, but are very hard to find as they are no longer manufactured, would likely have to be rebuilt, and in

the end may end up costing more. The Holley is an excellent choice for both power and reliability.

If you have access to used parts (junkyards, Internet), you can get much more bang for the buck.

Since drivers often choose to progress in both class and modifications as their amateur motorsports careers advance, you will see used springs, sway bars, carbs, etc., for sale on the Internet. Larger rear

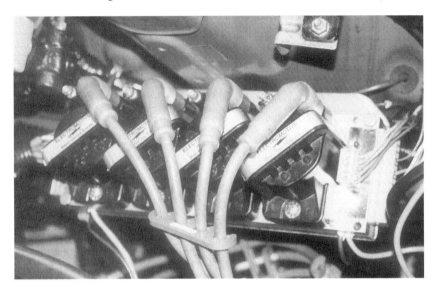

The ignition systems on both 2G and 3G cars are adequate to handle almost every level of modification you can add to your car. For some reason, however, most people who begin their projects buy an aftermarket ignition as one of their first upgrades. This is a mistake, and is probably driven by hype from the manufacturers and magazines. Yes, they look cool, but you don't really need it until you are considering a moderate or serious level of performance improvements. The 1G cars, on the other hand, could benefit from this technology a little earlier in their hop-up timetable than the 1986-plus RX-7s.

Aftermarket ignition systems can help make your engine compartment look cooler, but most fuel injected RX-7s don't really need one unless an entire array of performance improvements are planned, as is pictured here. On the other hand, first generation RX-7s with carburetors could benefit from this newer technology since they are more efficient at igniting the air and fuel mixture than the early 1980s factory RX-7 ignition systems are.

sway bars can also be found in junkyards on 2G cars, and can replace the smaller stock 1G bar.

And speaking of junkyards, replacing your tired 12A with a 13B will give you a real jolt of horsepower (35 to be exact). For all you 1G non-GSL-SE drivers who haven't yet converted, a 13B transplant is something that most weekend mechanics should be able to successfully complete with just a little help from their friends. And the expense may surprise you. While writing this book, we found a factory-rebuilt four-port 13B lying around (still wrapped in plastic) just waiting for a good home. We found one in our 1976 Cosmo, which had blown front rotor apex seals (seems that front one is always the one to go). The cost: $500, including the factory four-barrel carb. If you choose to swipe a six-port engine out of a 1984–1985 GSL-SE, grab the rear end as well. That will give you disc brakes and a limited-slip differential, which is a must for serious autocrossing. Owners of 1984–1985 GSL-SEs should also seriously consider what follows to improve the performance of their fuel-injection system.

Second Generation

Depending on how you spend your money, you may want to consider getting the fuel injectors cleaned and/or balanced and blueprinted (see chapters 8 and 9). This can really benefit cars with high mileage. Marren Motorsports and RC Engineering both offer this service. Sometimes you may need to replace an injector or two, especially if you have an early 2G. This cost can vary from around $125 to $400, depending on how inefficient your injectors are or how many you need to replace. Keep in mind that as of the year 2000, 2G RX-7s are between 7 and 14 years old. Owners of

For both second- and third-generation RX-7s (and 1984–1985 GSL-SEs), you can't get much more bang for the buck than by adding an air velocity intake system to help your car breathe better. Installing heat shielding to isolate the unit so that it breathes only cool outside air doesn't cost much money, but it will consume a great deal of your time.

If racing is your game, you will need to keep your engine cooler during sustained periods of high-rpm running. A larger-capacity aluminum radiator is available for 2G cars from SpeedSource. These radiators maintain cooler engine temps under extreme racing conditions.

1984–1985 GSL-SEs definitely need to do this to restore performance, especially low-end torque.

Even though 1G and 2G cars are very different, most of the suspension mods indicated for the 1G car will work well for the 2G as well. And all of the exhaust mods mentioned will also be a priority for 2G owners. This will finish off the budget for this level of performance improvements.

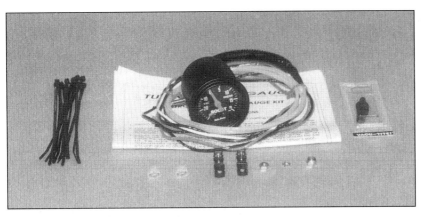

On the short list of items to keep your 3G alive and well are items that give you feedback as to how your car's systems are functioning. Often you could have a problem and not know it, especially if you have bought your 3G used and never had the opportunity to drive one that is working at 100 percent. The turbo system is particularly prone to problems, but the problem is usually nothing major. With miles of wires and vacuum tubes, and dozens of relays, sensors, and solenoids, if you can find and replace the malfunctioning part, your performance will improve. *Excellent Performance/Pettit Racing*

Third Generation

The 3G RX-7 came right from the factory ready to do battle on the weekend autocross or drag racing track. And as much as you may want to pick up the phone or click on your mouse and order some trick parts, we beg you to stop and think for a minute first. You can take all the chances you want on the track, but we ask you to be a little conservative first. Let's face facts: the coolest car Mazda ever built does suffer from reliability problems. First and foremost, you should spend your money on anything that improves reliability. Especially if you intend on doing performance driving of any kind, the following should be priority. They are in no particular order, and as stated earlier, do not include labor.

1. Front sway bar mount reinforcements. This is a cheap but effective modification that will only set you back $75–$200.
2. Install a turbo timer to avoid prematurely shutting down your engine before your turbos have cooled. Cost: $80–$150.
3. Install an accurate boost gauge to help troubleshoot your turbo system. Your car may already be suffering from a turbo-related problem and you don't know it. This is especially true if you are not the original owner and don't know how well these babies can run when the turbo system is working properly ($50–$120).
4. If you don't own an R1/R2, then treat yourself to a strut tower brace. This will cut down on front-end flex, and add some extra stiffness to the front, which is right where you need it most ($150–$200).
5. Install a performance intake. As we reported in chapter 6, this is probably the best bang-for-the-buck modification you can do other than removing weight ($175–$500).
6. In many known instances, the stock plastic air separator tank (AST) cracks at the seams, seeping coolant. Even worse, it has been known to explode. The latter was only known to have happened under extreme cases, however,

such as at a track event. But in any case, if your RX-7 is driven hard, you may want to consider replacing the plastic AST with an aftermarket aluminum version. These are available through certain RX-7 specialty shops such as Pettit Racing and Mostly Mazda (M2 Performance). There are also individuals within the RX-7 community who make these at a fraction of the cost (get on the Net). They may not look as nice, but will perform just as well. Aftermarket aluminum AST: $125.

7. Consider an improvement to the stock exhaust system. This could include adding a simple downpipe (perfect for this budget level: $150–$225) and/or a midpipe ($100–$175). An entire cat-back exhaust system should wait for the next level of mods.
8. Replace the stock intercooler hoses and piping with aluminum replacement parts ($175–$250) and/or replace all factory vacuum and pressure lines with high-temp, kink-resistant silicon hose ($250–$400).
9. Install platinum 9 spark plugs all around, or 10.5s for leading plugs if racing: $7 each for 9s, $12 each for 10.5s.

If you take the average of all you find above, you will be over your budget by more than $300, but if you look for bargains, and come in closer to the low end of these figures, you will be right at the $1,500 hop-up level, without labor.

Moderate Hop-Up (under $3,000)

If this first round of performance improvements doesn't quite get you to where you want to be, it's time to get the checkbook out and hit the Internet to find the best deals on parts and/or

For street cars (left) as well as full-blown race cars (right), adding a lightweight racing seat can save up to 25 pounds or more. These seats are obviously not as comfortable as the factory seats, but they have a high "cool" factor for use around town.

services. But before you buy anything, take a good look at your options for free horsepower and handling.

Where else could you save weight? How about those factory seats? Again, third-gen owners already have cars that have been engineered to be as light as possible right from the factory, so unless you buy racing seats for $250–$600 each, or more, you will likely not save anything here. Racing seats are rather uncomfortable for daily driving, and harder to get in and out of. But you may want to live with it to save 50–70 or more pounds. Racing seats weigh as little as 10 pounds each! This wouldn't be the way we would spend our first $1,500 unless we were planning to build a pure race car.

If you want to go a little further regarding weight, with serious compromise to driving comfort, here are some other things to throw overboard: entire air conditioning (A/C) system, all pieces of the air bag system, the stereo and all components (you can listen to the engine), and cruise control. Replace entire ABS system in favor of larger and lighter rotors and calipers. If you are going full race, then by all means eliminate all emissions compo-

nents and replace the steering wheel. To be legal for SCCA road racing, you have to disable the air bag system anyway. Now would also be the time to relocate your battery behind the rear passenger seat. See the cornerweighting discussion in chapter 3 before deciding on an exact location. A final universal choice for this more serious level of modification is to install camber plates or a camber-adjusting device (chapter 3). They will cost between $200–$300.

First Generation

If you want to have a true dual-duty, weekend-warrior machine,

For any dual-duty car, the absolute best way to improve your times at the track is to buy an extra set of alloys and race tires. Even for novice autocrossers, the gain will be as much as 2 seconds per run, and for track event drivers, it can save much more time.

the next best way to reach this goal is to invest in wheels and tires. In order to take full advantage of all of the modifications performed so far, spending between $900 and $1,200 is a must-do. Whether you are a weekend autocrosser, do time trials, or hang out at the drag strip, your times will improve substantially if you have the capability to put on a set of race wheels and tires for your weekend fun. Absolutely nothing in racing feels better than getting the traction you need, when you need it. In autocrossing, it is worth an average of 2 seconds per lap on a 1-minute course over your stock setup. The time drop is not so dramatic in drag racing, but 1/4-mile times will instantly respond to better grip off the line and when upshifting. It is important not to skimp on the wheels, since a good set can last a lifetime of autocrossing. Shortly after buying cheap steel wheels you will wish you had opted for the Revolution, Monocoque, Panasport, or Lite Speed rims. Finally, soloists should spend any leftover funds on camber plates or any other front-end camber correction device. We have raced several 1Gs over the years, and the stock camber settings have been all over the board. See chapter 3 for specifics.

Road racers and Solo I drivers will need to upgrade brakes to either a bigger system, or at least to high-performance pads. Again,

these pads are not recommended for autocrossing.

Second Generation

A good set of wheels and sticky tires will be just as valuable for the 1986–1992 RX-7s as for the 1G cars. Prices will be slightly higher since the

15-inch wheel size is more expensive than the 13-inch recommended for 1G cars. Expect to spend between $1,000 and $1,300. Just as for 1G cars, camber plates are a must-do for 2G cars that want to go autocrossing. Drag racers can, of course, pass on this option. The 2G drivers, including those driving the 1984–1985 GSL-SE, may need to save some money for upgrades to the EFI system.

Third Generation

Things are more expensive for 3G owners than for owners of the earlier cars, so now you will be forced to make a choice between more power or better handling. That choice should be made based on what it is you want to do with your car. If you want to do some drag racing or autocross, then the choice is a clear one. You need to follow the same strategy as 1G and 2G drivers: wheels and tires. That will eat up this entire budget.

If you are not planning to be a regular at Solo II or drag gatherings, keep your stock wheels and spend your money elsewhere. One suggestion includes investing in a cat-back exhaust system, which will set you back $250–$700. Replacing the turbo Y-pipe and attaching air duct with Japanese-spec Efini pieces (plastic air duct becomes aluminum) will cost another $250. Upgrade to a higher-flow fuel pump ($250), and install a J&S knock sensing computer, with display ($500–$800). That will just about do it.

Serious Project (over $5,000)

Believe it or not, even at this level it is extremely important to set a budget and a priority list for what mods you plan to do. Of course, as always, this should be based on what it is you want to do with your car

Marc Cefalo's RX-7 2G IT race car has camber plates and a shock tower bar. Note the way it is mounted to the tower.

Camber plates are a relatively small expense with a high gain in handling for the track. For dual-duty cars, you can mark the "race" and "street" locations on the plates so that your car will behave on the street without eating up your stock tires. But when you get to the track, and you are jacking up your front end to change over to your race wheels/tires, you can make a simple adjustment to the "race" setting for your camber.

For turbocharged cars with air conditioning, a very inexpensive modification (although one that's a little time consuming) is a pressure switch that senses the presence of boost, and then cuts the electrical flow to the air-conditioning compressor. Momentarily cutting this extra drain on the engine will produce a measurable gain in both torque and horsepower. *David Lane*

(autocross, drag, track time, dual duty, street only). Engine porting is reserved for this section since it can be expensive and would eat up the entire budget at the other two levels.

First Generation

You know what many of the top racers and performance shops say: How fast do you want to spend? Speed costs money, and if you are this serious, you had better take advantage of all the free things you can do to get power. With a hot air balloon, the more you throw overboard, the higher you can go. The same is true for a race car. Of course, check with the sanctioning body for the class in which you want to compete to see how much, if any, you may remove. When it comes to 1G RX-7s, $5,000 is often enough to build yourself a nationally competitive autocross car.

The first step in a serious hop-up project begins with the engine. Review

chapter 8's discussion of porting, select the job that is right for you, and invest the money. With all you have already

done in the previous sections, a good port job will complete the project and allow you to take maximum advantage of all your other upgrades. Expect to pay an additional $2,500 on a good, reliable, and professional job.

Turbo and supercharging systems are also available for 1G cars, and can be highly effective when it comes to enhanced street performance. They are also emission-legal alternatives to gaining power without porting.

Second Generation

The same goes for 2G cars. Engine porting to match the level of performance you need for what you want to do with your car will be well worth the investment. Turbo cars, however, have other options in addition to the porting, or instead of it (depending on your budget). The most popular modifications involve upgrading to an aftermarket turbo, ECU system, Electromotive ignition and/or fuel-management system, mega intercooler, or a supercharging system. All have been covered previously and are a matter of personal choice.

Lightweight and oversize pulleys can reduce both drag and rotating mass, allowing more horsepower to find its way to the wheels. *Racing Beat*

Often, a smaller competition steering wheel will provide quicker and more controlled steering. Note the lap timer mounted over the top of the instrument panel.

Third Generation

Some budgets for 3G modifications have reached $50,000, and it is common for these enthusiasts to spend $10,000 or more on performance upgrades. But we are going to be a little practical first.

Upgrading your stock ignition system to a Jacobs Rotary Pack is not a bad move, and at this level, is considered a cheap mod ($350–$400). Next, replacing the stock intercooler with a more effective aftermarket model will add much more power but set you back another $750–$1,800 depending on which model you choose. While you are at it, a performance radiator will help keep your car even cooler, and as you know, cool is good ($575–$800).

Probably the most popular mod for this level of hop-up is the installation of a performance ECU (see chapter 10). A modified stock ECU will set you back between $400 and $650. A piggyback unit is more pricey at $1,200–$1,800, and a stand-alone ECU will be closer to $3,000. And for the most part, you get what you pay for. If you go that far, then you may as well either increase your injector size ($400–$500), or add 1/2 additional injector(s) along with the appropriate controller ($300–$800).

Single-stage turbo mods are also a hot ticket item for the guy with money to burn. The price will vary, and it won't be cheap. Done properly by a professional tuner, this could cost $5,000–$10,000. But why stop there? At this level, the weak point in your engine is the fact that it only has two rotors. Expect to pay $15,000-plus for a triple rotor conversion.

Conclusions

Improving your car's performance while sticking to a budget can often be a difficult thing. There are many decisions you have to make based on the priorities you have set. Once you choose how you plan to use your car (street, dual duty, or full race), these decisions become easier. Don't give in to pressure from friends who may influence you to buy parts that are either over your budget, or that you simply don't need for your application. They may simply be trying to obtain validation to justify the fact that they just wasted their money on some new "cool" part that serves no function. And don't give in to easy credit. If a particular part is over the budget you set, instead of picking up your credit card, pick up your mouse and search the Internet for used performance parts. If you have read this book and still have performance questions, feel free to visit the Speednation webpage and ask us (www.speednation.com) or try www.mazdaperformance.com. We will try to answer your questions and keep you from wasting valuable resources on parts that either don't work, or that you don't really need.

CHAPTER FOURTEEN

A Brief Guide to Racing Your RX-7

Few modern cars will be able to join the proud heritage of American and British racing legends such as MG, Triumph, Lotus, Corvette, and Mustang. If any Japanese car is deserving of joining this club, it is the RX-7. The reason is clearly evident to any RX-7 fan. The car was designed right from the start to be a competent sports car. Throughout three generations, the RX-7's appeal was pure two-seater performance at a reasonable cost. The extremes that RX-7 engineers took to make the 3G car a lean, mean machine demonstrate the commitment that Mazda made to pure, uncompromised performance. It is only fitting that these cars take their rightful place in the racing hall of fame.

Due to the popularity of the RX-7 in IT racing, the SCCA created a "Spec" RX-7 class in 1998. Initial turnout was much higher than expected for the first year of a new class. The following year, Spec RX-7 was one of the bigger classes at an IT race. In 2000, the class continued to grow and is often the largest group of participants at an IT event. The term "spec" means that only certain, minor modifications are permitted—much less than for ITA. The good news is that it is one of the least-expensive classes in IT regional road racing. *Michelle Chute*

On any given weekend, thousands of RX-7s are competing all over the world in various forms of motorsports. Many of the fastest import drag cars are RX-7s. SCCA IT classes are dominated by loyal rotary racers who typically outnumber their Honda competition on the track. And even in the entry-level Solo II classes, RX-7s remain extremely competitive in all classes. And rotary engines are being transplanted in record numbers into everything from Formula cars to Spitfires, making it the most popular engine choice used in the Modified Hybrid classes. Therefore, it is only right that RX-7 owners are made aware of opportunities to add to their car's racing heritage. If you only try amateur racing once, or get hooked for life, here are the most popular options open to any licensed driver throughout most of the United States. Some require little or no preparation, while others demand a much higher degree of personal, financial, and mechanical commitment.

Solo II Autocross

Autocross is a very popular form of amateur racing in which ordinary people like you and me can participate. The only special equipment you will need is a vehicle (even pickup trucks qualify), a helmet (which usually can be borrowed at the event), a seatbelt (no way around this one), a driver's license, and a brain (at times, optional).

Solo II competition usually involves a group of people (usually part of a club) that gets together on Sundays (sometimes Saturdays as well) to race their cars around parking lots following a course laid out with orange pylons. The cost is about 15 to 20 bucks on the average. For that money you get about four laps around the course. Timing devices keep track of how long it takes you to complete your run. The quickest times win. Sounds a little contrived and restrained? Contrived—maybe. Restrained? By no means. Fun? Absolutely!

Many autocross addicts strongly believe that it is the most fun you can have with your clothes on. And it's so easy to get involved. First, you need the guts to go out and possibly make a fool out of yourself until you develop some fundamental racing skills

Autocross, or SCCA Solo II, is something that you can go do right now. Put down the book, and find out where your nearest SCCA or Independent Sports Car club is holding an autocross this weekend. Then just go. All you will need to do is to remove loose objects from your car's interior, and put about 40 pounds of air in your front tires, and that's it. You can borrow a helmet once you get there if you don't have one. We guarantee, you will be glad you went. And it is likely you will get addicted.

(that doesn't take very long). Second, you need to get a schedule of events in your area. If you don't know where to turn, e-mail or write us and we'll tell you. Most local SCCA regions also have Web sites. Third, you just need to go out there and do it! Don't wait until you have your car perfectly set up, or until you finish building that project that's been in your garage for the past 10 years. Chances are, if you have never been autocrossing, but are preparing your car for racing someday, you will likely make some mistakes that you will regret later. Just go with the car you are driving to work right now. You will likely learn that some of the modifications you have been planning would not be a good idea after all. Once you go racing a few times, you'll understand what we mean.

Take the fuzzy dice down from your rearview mirror, clean out the interior so that there is nothing on the floor or seats that can fly around, leave your hubcaps and floor mats at home, and stop by the gas station along the way to get some extra air in your front tires. 1G cars should start with 35-psi, while 2G and 3G cars may require as much as 40–45-psi. A good starting point for rear tire pressures is around 30 psi. When you get to the event, ask someone at registration to hook you up with a veteran racer who is running the same generation RX-7 as you are, and that person will give you further advice on what pressures to use.

And don't worry about having to run against a new Corvette with your 1979 carbureted 12A. The SCCA has an excellent grouping of classes that, for the most part, offer a fair and level playing field. There are four main levels of vehicle preparation.

The Stock class allows beefier shocks, struts, ignition wires, coils, race tires, and not much else. If you

SCCA's ProSolo is an especially fun outing, and is the only form of Solo II that is actually fun to watch. In ProSolo, there are two mirror-image courses. Two cars face off against each other at a drag racing light. The course typically runs up to the other end of the pavement, and winds its way back toward the starting line. The first car back wins.

just bought a cool set of rims, a fancy driver's seat, or a slick Momo steering wheel, you will likely be bumped into street prepared. This class allows suspension mods (including lowering), any size wheel, and many of the topics outlined in this book except for porting. Perform any internal engine modification and you are instantly in Prepared. This class allows almost everything, except some motor swaps, or the addition of a turbo where there was none previously. That will land you in the Modified class.

RX-7s are natural autocrossers. There hasn't been a year since 1979 that an RX-7 hasn't been in the running for a national title in either the Stock, Street Prepared, or Prepared classes. And rotary-powered hybrids typically dominate the modified classes.

RX-7s waiting in the "grid" for their turn to tackle the ProSolo course.

It takes a half-dozen or so races to get a good sense of what class you want to run in, and which modifications you should make. That's why you shouldn't do anything until you go to a few events. For example, don't go out and buy new street tires and assume that you will have better traction. Actually, the balder the tire, the better. That's because new tires have full tread— tread that will flex as you go around a sharp turn, causing you to lose traction. And we recommend that novices restrain from washing or waxing their cars before going to an event. No one will be impressed. In fact, you may be expected to drive that much better if your car looks too much like a race car.

Most veteran autocrossers are most impressed by guys or gals (another good thing about autocross-ing) who show up driving beat-up, crappy-looking, or tame vehicles (like stock Chevettes or Pintos), then proceed to beat the living hell out of them. You will become instantly popular if your car looks a little ratty, but you attack the course aggressively. For more information on Solo II or any of these racing venues, contact either your local SCCA chapter or the national office at www.scca.org (or 303-694-7222) for a list of clubs near you.

(Solo I) Hill-climbing, Track Events, and Driver Schools

If you're looking for a sport that combines some of the best aspects of autocross, rally, and road racing, then hill-climbing may be for you. Defined as a category I Solo event, hill-climbing takes you off the track and puts you on the side of a mountain. Actually, it's very much like autocrossing, except that the pylons are made of stone and wood (boulders and trees), and if you go "off course," the consequences are likely to be more serious. So instead of joking with your autocross friends in the parking lot about the mistake you made on your last run, a similar mistake in hill-climbing may result in discussing your blood type and trying to determine how many fingers the paramedic is holding up in front of your face on your way to the nearest hospital.

Solo I programs also schedule events on road racetracks across the country. Passing your competitors is sometimes allowed but with strict limitations. You get a great deal more track time when a Solo I is held on a

I'm proud to count myself among this group of racers, and have nothing but fondness for the sport and the people who participate in this Solo I event. Hillclimbers are nuts! You would have to be a little crazy to race your car up a hill at speeds sometimes in excess of 135 miles per hour, on roads designed to carry traffic going 25 miles per hour. Did I also mention that this was even more fun than Solo II? Pictured is Marc Cefalo's 1G GT-3 car.

racecourse. Often, pylons are set up to restrict extremely high speeds (this is also true for time trials).

In England, hill-climbing has been extremely popular for decades, but for some reason here in the United States, it has not yet

caught on. Besides the obvious rush, it's a great test of driving ability and car preparation. The scenery is usually breathtaking, and the people at the events are very friendly and supportive, especially to beginners. Its low profile in this

country makes the sport ripe for making your mark.

Since Solo I is not as popular as other forms of motorsports, a talented novice could be successful (depending on the class) in just his or her first season. Very often, you can find yourself

Ron Moreck's 13B Rotary turbo special in action. As fast as Ron is going here, you wonder if the background looks blurry from inside the cockpit, too.

competing in major events against cars that have not been prepared to the limit of the rules. And depending on your experience, certain courses or hills favor particular styles of driving. Experienced autocrossers can have a distinct advantage on hills that offer many second-gear twists and turns, while road racers tend to dominate on the high-speed hills, where precision braking and heel/toe downshifting is required.

If you already participate in SCCA road racing, simply show up at an event with your SCCA license, car, and log book. Your car will already meet the Solo I safety regulations. That's all there is to it. Events sanctioned by the SCCA require National SCCA membership. If you are not an SCCA member, you can usually join right at the event (bring your Visa card). Entry fees range between $50 and $100. But if you are an autocrosser, you have some work to do. You and your car will likely have to meet some strict safety requirements, such as a driver's suit, roll cage, etc.

Improved Touring

IT (Improved Touring) racing is a great next step for Solo I folks who are sick and tired of picking tree branches out of their radiators. Instead, they can trade paint with their friends, and take an occasional trip into a nice collection of used tires. Not that you don't end up in the trees

sometimes, but it is not as common an occurrence as in hill-climbing.

To get involved in IT racing, you will also need to become a member of the SCCA. They just don't let anyone go out on the track and compete. You have to go to SCCA-approved driver schools, apply for a novice license, and then you can earn your road racing license.

SCCA's regional road racing class is referred to as IT (Improved Touring). Many sensible mods are allowed, but no engine porting, and you are restricted as far as aftermarket carburetion and wheel size. *Colin Mason*

The only difference in mandatory safety equipment other than what is required in Solo I is that you must have an SCCA-approved full cage installed in your car. Entry fees are also slightly higher, but you get a great deal more track time. IT racers tend to feel that the rest of us are wasting our time on racing weekends, because their track time is measured in hours, not in minutes. Autocrossers, on the other hand, feel that IT racers are wasting their time during the week, as their repair and preparation time is usually measured in days as opposed to hours.

IT racing is definitely the best bang for the buck, but it is a major time and money commitment. Parts break and wear out more frequently, and they must be repaired and replaced during the week. But IT racers have something to be proud of. They don't just race around a parking lot. They do real racing in every sense of the word. It requires a great deal of skill, much more than in autocrossing or Solo I. And although Solo racing is more precise (the clock is unforgiving), most people would rather lose a race to the clock than to the tire wall.

SCCA Road Racing

The main difference between IT racing and SCCA road racing is that Improved Touring is done mostly on a regional level, whereas road racing is more of a national spectacle. There are several divisional road racing series that serve to help competitors qualify for the national event, held in the fall. Over the years, however, there have also been several national IT racing championships, including the AARC

All Solo I, IT, and road racing cars must have certain safety equipment. A fire extinguisher is required for all classes, as is a roll cage. For highly modified cars, such as the GT classes, a fuel cell is also required.

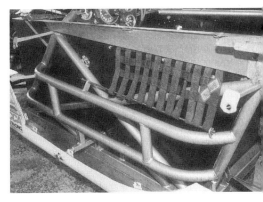

Roll cages are required for all forms of, and most classes in Solo I. An SCCA legal roll bar will suffice (at least for now) in a certain few Solo I classes. *Photo at right Courtesy of Autopower*

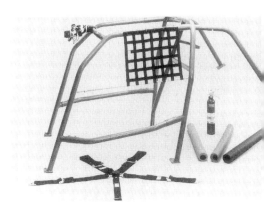

Roger Mandeville competed in the Camel GTU series back in the early 1980s. These 1G cars were highly modified, race-only vehicles. *Courtesy of Mazda*

(American Road Race of Champions) held at tracks like Road Atlanta.

Road racers have been meeting yearly at the Mid-Ohio Sports Car Course for their national race, called the Runoffs. Road racing classes are slightly different than IT, and there are usually much bigger bucks involved. Showroom stock classes A, B, and C require the least amount of start-up cash, compared to the GT classes, which consist of tube frame monsters costing as much as $100,000 to build. We have little to say about this aspect of motorsports, since it is far from being an entry level of competition. The Runoffs, however, are a lot of fun to watch,

and RX-7s remain competitive in the GT classes.

Driver Schools

A good way to get prepared for high-speed racing is to attend a driver school. If you want to go road racing, then you will need to make sure the driver school is certified by the SCCA.

There are also many schools that are marque specific, but they will often let you join in even if you don't have a Porsche or BMW (two of the most popular club schools). You have to bring your own equipment, however.

Of course, there are the professional schools, but registration fees can be rather steep. They will usual-

ly provide a vehicle and everything else you need to get some serious track time. And some individual racetracks conduct driver schools of their own, such as Mid-Ohio or Road Atlanta. Their instructors really know the track, and offer both classroom and hands-on instruction. BYOC or use one of their factory-sponsored school cars.

Last, but not least, many tracks around the country can be rented for the day. You and a group of your friends (preferably with some racing experience) can ante up the $500-plus to rent the track for a weekday. Roll cages are usually not required, and neither are driver's suits.

Drag Racing

The light turns green, and you step on the gas. What could be simpler? Drag racers are growing tired of this type of attitude, which usually comes from the guy wearing a "No Fear" hat—you know, the guy who thinks he's a race car driver despite the fact that he has never competed legally in a single racing event. Another common opinion is that drag racing is more about car preparation and engine building than it is about driving. Tell that to the guy in the RX-7 who is doing the quarter-mile in less than 9 seconds.

But car preparation is still very important because if you don't plan well, you will be disappointed even if you show up with a tricked-out third gen. If you are really serious, there are a few simple things you can do, most of which are common sense. First, reduce your weight as much as you can. That means air-conditioning, stereo, passenger seat, etc. With drag racing there is a consistent, direct, and predictable correlation between removing weight and dropping 1/4-mile times (i.e., remove 50 pounds, drop 1/10 of a second). Anything that is left (like your battery) should be moved back so that your drive wheels can get better traction. That includes you! We always move our seat back as far as it will go while still allowing us to depress the clutch. If your front shocks are too stiff, there will not be maximum weight transfer to the rear, and the rear suspension must be set to avoid squatting when you leave the line or shift into the next highest gear.

If you are getting beaten by a driver running the same car as yours, and you can't understand why, here's a simple test to perform. Go to the end of the 1/4-mile strip and listen for when he/she shifts for the last time. Then count the seconds from that final shift until he crosses the finish line. Then do the same for one of your runs. It is likely that he is crossing the line at higher rpms than you. There could be three reasons for this: 1) he has different gearing, 2) he has smaller-diameter wheels than you do, or 3) he is shifting at different points than you are. The solution may be to just shift when he does, or get smaller wheels so that your torque is maxed at the point when you cross the finish.

The best way to find out when to shift is to pay for an hour of dyno time. Just do one run, and then look at the torque curve. At some point, you may find that it is not beneficial to rev the engine above a certain rpm. Do this a few times to determine your optimal torque shift points, and then install a shift light to prompt you while you are on course. This exercise will get you 2–5 tenths of a second at the track.

With the recent boom in hopping-up Japanese cars, the drag racing scene has completely changed and is now more popular than ever. Back in the old days, the only time you would see an import car on a drag strip was at a VW Bug convention. But now, the "Import Boys" outnumber the "Muscle Car Guys" at many strips. In fact, drag racing has become a bona fide social event. There are countless local clubs out there for guys and gals who love to work on and modify their import cars. These clubs often meet weekly to help a buddy transplant a GSR engine into a Civic, figure out why the primary turbo isn't engaging properly on a third gen, or to just hang out and play video racing games. It's a great way to spend the evening.

It's easy to get started with drag racing. Just show up at the local track for a test and tune session, usually held on a weeknight. Or you can hop on the Internet. Many of the import car clubs have webpages, and can provide information about local drag strips and club meeting times.

Slower cars don't require special equipment (helmets, racing harnesses, fire system, etc.), but if you start turning sub-13-second times you may be required to install safety equipment, wear a Snell rated helmet and/or a driver's suit.

Try organizing a group of your own friends to go drag racing one day, then autocrossing the next. Use combined times to declare bragging rights. Remember, the point is to maximize fun per dollar. As far as fun goes, it's hard to beat this combination. But be warned, drag racing and autocrossing can be highly addictive, so exercise caution to insure maintaining stability in your marriage. Then again, you can bring along your spouse. Coed racing is more popular now than ever. You also see a lot of father/son as well as father/daughter racing teams. Use the excuse that it could bring your family closer together. It just might. Good luck in the new millennium, and try to save the racing for the track, not the street.

RX-7 Tuning Shops

Without these RX-7 specialty tuning shops, there would be no performance book because there would be very few performance parts available. These are the guys that race the cars and think of ways to make them go faster and handle better. They win races, and we benefit from it. On behalf of all RX-7 fans, we thank you all. *Excellent Performance/Pettit Racing*

Most products discussed in the previous chapters will simply bolt on to your RX-7. Some may take more time than others, but most weekend mechanics will achieve success with installation. There are some things, however, that should be left to a professional. In this, as well as my previous book, *The Honda and Acura Performance Handbook*, I purposely do not include specific drivetrain rebuilding techniques. Everyone should refer to a workshop manual for his or her car, even when performing a simple maintenance task. Engine rebuilding procedures are clearly outlined in a good manual, so there is no need to duplicate that here. And even if you want to take on a porting project, you will likely have to buy or borrow tools to do the job properly. Does anyone have a socket big enough to get the flywheel bolt off the back of the engine? I had to take my blown engine, along with my new engine, to a Mazda shop just so the mechanic could take the flywheel bolt and flywheel off the old engine, and install them on the new engine. We all need to recognize our own limitations, or we could end up ruining an expensive part. When in

doubt, ask. When you don't have a clue, go for help.

Many 1G and 2G non-turbo owners will be able to learn how to do some major modifications to their cars by first doing their homework, and second, watching some-

one else do the task first. The 2G turbo and 3G owners are faced with a much more complex machine that even most factory Mazda mechanics don't completely understand. In fact, it is widely believed that one of the main reasons the 3G RX-7 didn't make it in the United States is because Mazda dealerships could not properly service the car. Besides being one of the most recalled automobiles in history, the 3G is extremely complicated to work on. You can't spit into the engine compartment without hitting some sort of sensor or solenoid. And let's face it, most mechanics aren't rocket scientists. That may be a good thing, since a friend of mine *is* one, and even he can't make heads or tails out of the 3G engine compartment.

So what do you do when faced with a nagging system malfunction, or want to do some moderate-level performance improvements to your car? Well, chances are the dealership won't be able to fix your nagging problem, either. And they won't touch a project like replacing the twin turbo system with a single-stage sport turbo unit. For projects like these, you have to turn to the experts. We thought it would be helpful to list some of the great RX-7 shops from around the country, so that you had someone to turn to when faced with either a problem, or a complex performance project.

These tuning shops have excellent reputations for doing meticulous work, but as with every tuner, there are occasional mistakes. That's because the owners of these performance shops don't necessarily do the work themselves. If that were the case, the quality would likely be

100 percent. We've found that most of the RX-7 and Rotary aftermarket performance parts companies are extremely reliable, more so than companies that deal with other marques (Honda, Porsche, VW). These shops are listed in no particular order.

Name:	Peter Farrell Supercars
Location:	9141 Centreville Rd. Manassas, Virginia 20110 (703) 368-7959 www.pfsupercars.com
Specialty:	2G, 3G, three-rotor conversions
Interests:	fast street cars, drag racing

Peter Farrell should know what he's doing. His was the first shop in the country to obtain a 3G car. It came over directly from Japan in a big crate. His mission: play with it, try to break it, tweak it, race it, and provide feedback. Farrell did all those things, and in the process quickly became the first 3G expert in the country. To this day, most people trust him and only him when it comes to triple rotor conversions, ECU hop-ups, and turbo/intercooler upgrades. If there is a drawback to the Farrell shop, it is that the labor and parts don't usually come cheap. But, as they say, you get what you pay for.

Peter Farrell (on right) explaining to his customer, Gordon Monsen, the specifics of all the new performance goodies he just finished installing on Gordon's 3G RX-7.

Pettit Racing is changing its name to Excellent Performance. These people have been in the RX-7 hop-up business as long as I can remember. Cameron Worth is the brains behind the shop. He is also a very successful RX-7 racer and skilled mechanic/engineer.
Excellent Performance

Name:	Excellent Performance/Pettit Racing
Location:	1578 NW 23 Avenue Fort Lauderdale, Florida 33311 (954) 739-0100 www.pettitracing.com
Specialty:	3G
Interests:	fast street cars, road racing

Back in the early days of Pettit, when Cameron Worth and Sylvain Trembly were partners, you couldn't find a place with more expertise. Now, since Trembly left in the mid-1990s, Florida has two places for the RX-7 nut to choose from. Although experts with all RX-7s, Excellent/Pettit has settled in as *the* place in the Southeast for 3G owners who want a little more get up and go. They also have perfor-

mance parts for, and work on, every generation RX-7. And Cameron can drive! He took me for a lap around Moroso Motorsport Park in his race car, and I thought I wasn't going to come back in one piece.

Name: SpeedSource, Inc.
Location: 590 Goolsby Blvd.
            Deerfield,
            Florida 33442
            (954) 481-8331
Specialty: 2G
Interests: fast street cars,
            road racing

Sylvain Trembly founded SpeedSource when he left Pettit in the mid-1990s. Since then, his focus has been on the 1986–1992 models. Trembly not only fixes 'em, he races 'em. It is widely believed that Trembly has the world's fastest 2G legal road race car. The things that this shop can do with a wrench are hard to believe. Attention to detail is the strength of SpeedSource.

Name: Racing Beat
Location: 4789 East Wesley
            Drive
            Anaheim, CA
            92807
            (714) 779-8677
            www.racingbeat.com
Specialty: all rotary-powered
            cars
Interests: racing and Street
            performance

Cameron Worth makes a pit stop in an endurance road race. From the look of his RX-7's front end, he probably had to push his way through a group of slower Corvettes. *Excellent Performance*

Racing Beat has a rich history in rotary performance and technology. It first received notoriety when Don Sherman co-drove a 210-horsepower-plus RX-2 IMSA car with *Car and Driver*'s Patrick Bedard in 1973. From there, credit RB with several speed records, including 1977 when they competed in the NHRA, racing an RX-3. Three of the big ones were the 184-mile-per-hour run in 1978 at the Bonneville Salt Flats driving a 1G RX-7. RB would return to Bonneville several more times to capture records with a 2G car (238 miles per hour), then later in 1995 with a 3G (242 miles per hour). Other accomplishments include developing a single rotor engine for NASA (Rotaries in Space), plus engines for the Jim Russell Mazda Pro Series and Mickey Thompson's off-road series.

Racing Beat has long been a force in Mazda tuning. Now it has a great catalog of parts online at www.racingbeat.com. Pictured here is the team that won the Bonneville Challenge and set the record of 242 miles per hour—the fastest RX-7 ever. *Racing Beat*

A closer look at the RX-7 that set the record at Bonneville. *Racing Beat*

Finally, they have been featured in most major car magazines with projects like the rotary pickup truck in 1990 (*Hot Rod Magazine*) and the RX-7 roadster in 1987 (*Car and Driver* cover story).

The point is that Racing Beat knows Mazda performance. They have whatever you may need for your RX-7, as well as for other rotary-powered cars.

Name: Mazdatrix
Location: 2730 Gundry Avenue
             Signal Hill, CA 90806
             (562) 426-7960
             www.mazdatrix.com
Specialty: all rotary-powered cars
Interests: road and drag racing

Need an exhaust gasket for a 1976 Mazda Cosmo? Have you tried a Mazda dealer lately? We did. The response: "We weren't even in business when that car was built. It's not even listed on our computer." And that's a fact. We were allowed behind the parts desk to search the computer. Same with the intake gasket. Only the six-port gasket was on the books. Even a popular import parts store gave us the same story. But one call to Mazdatrix and the parts were on our doorstep the next day! They have 20 different exhaust manifold gaskets listed, plus anything else you could ever imagine wanting for your RX-7. Not only that, but the Mazdatrix catalog is somewhat of a performance

handbook itself, relaying much of the same philosophy as can be found in chapter 2 of this book.

Dave Lemon has built a major mail-order parts business, and RX-7 lovers are very grateful. But believe it or not, he wasn't always a "rotary kind of guy." One day in the late 1970s, after spending a substantial amount of money to build an IMSA-level performance piston engine for his race car, fate started him on his journey to one day become "Mr. Rotary." After just a few practice laps, his new race engine blew, and was now an expensive paperweight attached to his race car. So as he sat in the pits at Sears Point, he began to notice that some of his competitors

Dave Lemon, founder of Mazdatrix, is seen here in an early racing effort when he first switched from British cars over to reality. Once he got the taste for the power and reliability of a rotary engine, he never looked back. Dave now runs one of the biggest Mazda parts companies on the planet. If you need racing parts, or just trim pieces to help you with your restoration, Mazdatrix is your one-stop shopping center. *Courtesy of Mazda*

were abusing their cars lap after lap with no apparent reliability problems. It was then that he began to fully appreciate the beauty of the rotary power plant. These engines cost one-third the money to build, and could last the whole season without a major rebuild. And one other thing: they were fast. Fortunately for us, he never looked back. Soon he

was racing RX-3s. Several years later, after many successful racing seasons, he gave up his service business and started Mazdatrix in 1987.

Now, with some cool project cars under his belt, Lemon is finding a new audience, thanks to the import performance movement. His latest effort is a three-rotor, tube frame, NOS-charged drag car.

Name: Tri-Point
          Engineering/Pro Parts
Location: 21417 Ingomar St.
          Canoga Park, CA
          91304
          (818) 348-5385
          www.tripointengineering.com
Specialty: 1G, 2G, 3G
Interests: fast street cars, racing

The Heintz boys build serious, no-nonsense 1G race cars. Stressing function over form, they can help you despite your budget, but the more you have, the faster you can go. So how fast do you want to spend?

Mark Shuler and Craig Nagler own one of the biggest RX-7 shops in the country. They carry performance parts for all of our favorite cars. Their expertise is evidenced by their phenomenal success in SCCA Solo II racing, and they also prepare cars for road racing.

Name: Heintz Bros.
            Automotive
Location: 1475 Old Mountain
            Road
            Statesville, NC 28677
            (704) 872-8081
Specialty: 1G
Interests: racing, fast street cars

These guys put their money where their mouths are. Involved in almost every kind of racing, including Solo I Hillclimbs, they can build you a competitive motor.

Name: K.D. Rotary
Location: 862 Fenwick St.
            Allentown,
            PA 18103
            (610) 433-2033
Specialty: 1G, 2G, 3G
Interests: fast street cars

Dave Barninger doesn't have the biggest shop, nor does he have the most tools, but he certainly knows his stuff. Often folks will go to Dave after having a bad experience somewhere else. Barninger is one of those guys who just knows how to do it.

K.D. Rotary's Dave Barninger is one of those RX-7 engineering artists. He can fix stuff even after somebody else screws it up, including you. His shop isn't much to look at, but looks can be deceiving.

SpeedSource was founded by Sylvain Trembly after he parted ways with Cameron Worth. SpeedSource is a great resource for 2G high-performance parts.

Resources

Performance Parts and Services

Mazda Competition Parts
(800) 435-2508

NOPI (Number One Parts Inc.)
    sponsor of the NOPI Nationals
    in September
486 Main Street
Forest Park, GA 30050
(800) 277-6674
www.nopi.com

Magazines

Grassroots Motorsports Magazine
425 Parque Drive
Ormond Beach, FL 32174
(904) 673-4148
www.grmotorsports.com

Sport Compact Car Magazine
P.O. Box 56045
Boulder, Co 80322
(800) 767-7006
www.sportcompactcarweb.com

Turbo Magazine
9887 Hamilton Avenue
Huntington Beach, CA 92646
(800) 94-TURBO
www.turbomagazine.com

Wheels and Tires

TSW Wheels
(800) 658-0765
www.tswnet.com
Taylor Wheels
(515) 276-0992
www.taylorcorporation.com

BBS Wheels
(800) 422-7972
e-mail: marketing@bbs-usa.com

Tire Rack
771 W. Chippewa Avenue
South Bend, IN 46614
(888) 981-3952
www.tirerack.com

John Berget Tire (used and new race
    tires)
(414) 740-0180

Mid-Atlantic Motorsports (race tires)
(248) 852-5006

Clutch Components

Centerforce Performance Clutch
2266 Crosswind Drive
Prescott, AZ 86301
(800) 899-6439
www.centerforce.com

Safety Equipment

Racer Wholesale (helmets, suits, plus
    lots of racing stuff)
(800) 886-RACE (7223)
Safe-Quip (racing seat belts and
    harnesses)
(800) 247-4260

Kirk Racing Products (roll cages and
    bars)
(205) 823-6025
e-mail: info@kirkracing.com

Autopower Industries (roll cages and
    bars)
3424 Pickett Street
San Diego, CA 92110
(619) 297-3300

Solotime (graphics, safety equipment,
K&N filters)
(316) 683-3803
solotime@southwind.net

Ignition Systems

MSD Ignition
1490 Henry Brennan Drive
El Paso, TX 79936
(915) 857-5200
www.msdignition.com

Electromotive
9131 Centreville Road
Manassas, VA 20110
(703) 331-0100
www.electromotive-inc.com

Jacobs Electronics
500 North Baird Street
Midland, TX 79701
(800) 627-8800
www.jacobselectronics.com

HKS USA, Inc.
2355 Mira Mar Avenue
Long Beach, CA 90815
(562) 494-8068
www.hksusa.com

Injection and Carburetion
TWM Induction (intake manifolds,
    throttle bodies, ITG filters, adj.
    fuel pressure regulators)
(805) 967-9478
www.twminduction.com

Marren Motorsports
412 Roosevelt Drive
Derby, CT 06418
(203) 732-4565
www.injector.com

RC Engineering
1728 Border Avenue
Torrance, CA 90501
(310) 320-2277
www.rceng.com

K&N Engineering
    (air filters and intakes)
P.O. Box 1329
Riverside, CA 92502
(800) 858-3333

Overseas Distributing (Weber carbs,
    Koni shocks)
(604) 879-6288

Suspension Components
Tokico
1330 Storm Parkway
Torrance, CA 90501

Carrera (shocks, struts, and springs)
(770) 451-8811
www.carrerashocks.com

Koni North America
1961A International Way
Hebron, KY 41048
(800) 994-KONI
www.koni.com

Exhaust Systems
Kerker Performance (manufacturers
    of Supertrapp)
(216) 265-8400

GReddy Performance
9 Vanderbilt Avenue
Irvine, CA 92718
(800) GREDDY2

Thermal Research and Development
    (stainless steel exhaust systems)
    (818) 998-4865

Engines, New and Used Parts
Mazmart
4917 New Peach Road
Atlanta, GA 30341
(800) 221-5156

Mazda Auto Dismantling
3501 Recycle Road
Rancho Cordova Road, CA 95742
(800) 699-2664
www.mazda-dism.com

Miscellaneous
Auto Meter Products, Inc.
413 West Elm Street
Sycamore, IL 60178
(815) 895-8141

Carbotech Engineering (brake pads
    and shoes, cryogenically
    hardened rotors)
(954) 493-9669

Places to Go and Things to Do
Sports Car Club of America (SCCA)
(303) 694-7222
www.scca.org

The Mid-Ohio School (driver school
    and home of the Runoffs)
(614) 793-4615
www.midohio.com

Mazda Performance (tech tips and fun
    RX-7 stuff)
www.mazdaperformance.com

Fun Stuff
Speednation
Discontinued and hard to find first-,
    second-, and third-generation
    plastic model kits and out of
    print RX-7 books.
www.speednation.com
(724) 926-3735

Index

Air pumps, 71
Anti-roll Bars, 39
Brakes, 46-51
Brake pads, 48
Camber, 35, 41
Camber plates, 41, 42
Carburetors, installing, 105, 110
Catalytic converters, 71
Chassis and suspension, 34-45
Chute, Norm, 6
Clutches, 126, 127
Corner weighting, 44
Curtiss-Wright, 11
Dynamometer testing, 30, 31
Electronic fuel injection, installing,
    107–109
Engine cooling, 90
Engine transplantation, 84, 85
Engines
    12A - 1146cc, 75, 76, 85, 86,
        133, 141
    13B - 1308cc, 75–77, 85–89
    13B turbo 113, 133, 144
    13B Turbo II - 1308cc, 77
    13B Twin Turbo - 1308cc, 78, 79
    20B (triple rotor) - 1962cc, 80,
        86, 88
    L10A, 10A - 982cc, 74
    L10B - 1146cc, 74
Exhaust manifold, 68
Exhaust systems, 66-72
Farrell, Peter, 6, 8, 25, 39, 61, 68,
    79, 86–88, 100–102, 112, 118
Flywheels, 127
Froede, Dr. Walter, 10, 11
Fuel-injection conversions, 65
Fuel-injection systems, 98-110
Header performance, 67
Heat management, 69
Heat shielding, 63
Ignition and timing, 92
Intake systems, 61-64, 69
Lemon, Dave, 6, 19

Limited-slip differential, 124
Lipperini Jr., Dan, 6
Mazda, 12–14, 17, 18, 20, 21, 23,
    53, 54, 74, 79, 98, 100
Mazda models
    110S Cosmo Sport, 15
    1800, 12
    616, 12
    Cabriolet, 22
    Cosmo, 13, 17, 18
    Cosmo Sport, 74, 79, 80, 85, 86
    Familia, 12, 15
    GLX, 47
    GSL-SE, 6, 19–21, 29, 47, 62,
        85, 98, 99, 101, 107,
        125, 133, 136
    GT-X, 19
    GTU, 21, 22, 29, 37, 39, 47,
        61, 79, 92
    GXL, 21, 22, 39
    Infini IV, 22
    Miser, 13
    P747, 20
    R100, 12, 13, 15
    R360, 14
    RX-2, 12, 13, 15, 17, 19
    RX-3, 13, 16–19
    RX-3SP, 13, 62
    RX-4, 13, 16–20, 76, 85
    RX-5, 19, 76
    RX-7 1G, 21, 23, 28, 29, 32,
        38, 40, 47, 57, 59, 60, 71,
        85, 93, 102, 104, 108, 120,
        125, 126, 129–133, 135–137,
        141, 146
    RX-7 2G, 21, 23, 29, 32, 38,
        40, 41, 47, 57, 59, 60, 63,
        72, 77, 85, 86, 93, 98, 99,
        102, 104, 107, 113, 116,
        119, 120, 125, 126, 131,
        132, 136, 137, 141
    RX-7 3G, 22–25, 27– 29, 32,
        33, 38, 42–44, 53, 58– 60,

        63, 64, 66, 71, 79, 86–88,
        91, 92, 95, 98, 99, 102,
        104, 107, 112, 116, 117,
        119, 125, 126, 130,
        132–134, 136, 138, 139, 141
    X605, 18
Mazdatrix, 6
Mederer, Jim, 6
Nitrous oxide,
    (See Supercharging, nitrous)
NSU, 10–12, 74
OPEC 1973 oil crisis, 11
Polyurethane suspension bushings, 40
Porting, 81–84
Racing slicks, 58
Racing tips, 139-147
Rotary engine chronology, 74
Rotary engine timing, 96
Rotors, 48
RX-7 history, 10-25
Shocks and struts, 36
Springs, 37
Street tuning, 129-138
Suddard, Tim, 83
Supercharging theory, 119
Supercharging, nitrous, 112-123
Tire Pressure, 60
Toe, 35, 42
Toyo Kogyo company 12, 14, 74
Transmission swaps, 126
Transmissions, 124-128
Trembly, Sylvain, 6
Tuning and modification, 7
Turbocharging theory, 113
Wankel rotary engine, 5, 6, 10–12,
    14, 68, 73
Wankel, Felix, 10–12
Wheel alignment, 35, 41
Wheels and tires, 52-60
Wires and coils, 94
Worth, Cameron, 6, 25